It's Gone! . . . No, Wait a Minute . . .

IT'S GONE! . . . NO, WAIT A MINUTE . . .

Talking My Way into the Big Leagues at 40

Ken Levine

VILLARD BOOKS • NEW YORK • 1993

Published in the United States by Villard Books, a division of Random House, Inc., New York, and simultaneously in Canada by Random House of Canada Limited, Toronto.

Library of Congress Cataloging-in-Publication Data

Levine, Ken
It's gone . . . no, wait a minute: talking my way into the big leagues at 40 / by Ken Levine.
p. cm.
ISBN 0-679-42093-2
1. Levine, Ken. 2. Sportscasters—United States—Biography. 3. Baltimore Orioles (Baseball team) I. Title.
GV742.42.L48A3 1993
070.4'49796'092—dc20
[B] 92-50553

9 8 7 6 5 4 3 2
First Edition

For Debby

Acknowledgments

Occasionally, my writing partner and I have been lucky enough to be nominated for screenwriting awards. There are two major sources of anxiety: "Will we win?" and "If we do, will we remember to thank everyone?" (Usually, the answer to the first question is "No.") One of the pleasures of writing a book is that I have two weeks to write my acknowledgments and a whole page on which to write them. I apologize in advance to the people I *still* forgot.

Let's start at the top:

I am grateful to my parents, Clifford and Marilyn Levine, who have patiently smiled through several of my careers.

To my son, Matthew, and my daughter, Diana, I owe gratitude and apologies for all of the school plays, Little League games, and Hebrew-school ceremonies I've missed in the pursuit of my dream. They've hung tough throughout, and I'm proud of them both.

Debby asked me not to thank her again, as she finds all this stuff embarrassing.

David Isaacs has been my partner for twenty years. He's my son's godfather, and would like to be the owner of the Yankees. I am deeply grateful for his unselfishness in supporting me in this endeavor. This man is a tremendously talented writer (making me look good), my best friend, and yes, has been in my home.

I need to thank Bob Broder, Norman Kurland, and Elliot Webb, who have helped protect my and David's career while I gallivanted around the country. Thanks, Elliot, for saying, "Don't be a neurotic Jew. Just go. Have a good time," when this was first proposed.

Thanks must go to Les & Glen Charles, and Jim Burrows of *Cheers*, as well as Peter Casey & David Lee, and David Angell of *Wings,* who have been so flexible and gracious about my writing and consulting assignments.

Gracious is an apt description of Al Conin, one of my mentors. From the beginning of my pursuit of an announcing career, Al has generously shared his knowledge and experience with me. His expert analysis, thoughtfulness, and kindness are deeply appreciated.

To Steve Leon, my first broadcasting partner: Thanks. I never could've done it without you.

I am grateful to the Orioles and Jeff Beauchamp of WBAL radio for inviting me to "the Show" (and providing me with great seats for it).

Jon Miller and Chuck Thompson are two of the premier sportscasters in the business. I was fortunate to spend my rookie season with them. Dr. Paul Eicholtz is a super engineer and a genuinely nice person. Thanks, Doc!

Bob Miller, the Orioles' assistant director of publicity, supplied accurate data, promotional items for my kids, and friendship.

Frank Robinson and Johnny Oates made the dreaded "manager show" a pleasure.

My literary agent, Jay Acton, took on this project before I was finished typing. Thank you for your faith in me.

Peter Gethers is an editor's editor. He gently helped me tame this monster.

Also, thanks to Sherry Falk, who handled each diskette perfectly, and enabled me to complete this while on the road.

On to the present:

Dave Niehaus and Kevin Cremin have made my sophomore season great.

Let's see . . . is there anything else? Oh, yes . . .

I'd like to thank the Academy.

It's Gone! . . . No, Wait a Minute . . .

Prologue

I'd never sell it. Not in a million years. Even though I've been a screenwriter for eighteen years (along with my partner, David Isaacs), with credits that include *M*A*S*H* and *Cheers* and the motion picture *Volunteers* (well, *M*A*S*H* and *Cheers* are impressive), there's still not a movie studio in Hollywood or even India that wouldn't throw me out on my ear if I came in with this idea.

Are you ready? And remember, these are the people who brought Danny DeVito and Arnold Schwarzenegger together as twins.

A writer approaching middle age decides to follow a lifelong dream and in only five years becomes a major league baseball announcer.

Next! What else do ya got? What about that idea you came in with last year? Y'know, the one about the white version of *The Wiz*. Anything's more believable than:

A writer approaching middle age decides to follow a lifelong dream and in only five years becomes a major league baseball announcer.

Well, the reality is, it *is* reality. I spent the 1991 season as one of the play-by-play voices of the Baltimore Orioles. I spent Saturday afternoons in historic Fenway Park, the Fourth of July in Yankee Stadium, and warm summer nights in the Skydome. I hobnobbed with fellas named Sparky and Stump, and called long home runs by Fielder and Canseco. I traveled on charters, never touched a stick of luggage, and tried but never succeeded in spending fifty-six dollars a day on meals. Most nights my voice was heard on a thirty-three-station radio network that boomed up and down the East Coast from Florida to Canada. Other nights it was heard around the world.

Quite simply, I lived a fantasy—a boyhood dream. I have no

idea why, out of the zillion and a half equally deserving or more deserving people out there who have dreams and desires that they would kill for to fulfill, I was the lucky one selected to live out mine. Maybe in a past life I let Gandhi use my place for the weekend. In any event, and for whatever cosmic reason I was chosen, I made one vow at the start of this little sojourn —to appreciate and relish each and every day. That's why this journal. I was determined not to take a thing for granted, not to miss a single detail.

In 1986 the New York Mets won the World Series. They won it in grand style. Miracle comebacks, storybook finish, yada yada. Whata great day for the Big Apple. Six months later every player on that team had come out with a book chronicling the season. Gary Carter, Lenny Dykstra, Doc Gooden, Keith Hernandez, you name it. Everyone except reserve catcher John Gibbons. At the time I wondered: What would've happened if the Mets finished fifth? All these players keeping all these supposed journals—would anyone have read them if their club was eliminated at the All-Star break? My heart suddenly went out to all the Montreal Expos and Seattle Mariners diligently keeping *their* journals.

When I set out to write my book, I discovered two things: (1) the Baltimore Orioles were not going to win the 1991 World Series, and (2) much to my surprise, I was glad. The experience was so much richer, funnier, and more rewarding as a result, and certainly more representative of what life is really like in the world of big-league baseball. Sonuvagun, people *might* want to read it. This is a book about hanging around the batting cage, and restaurants on the road, and practical jokes on the plane. It's also about striking out José Canseco, only to have him hit a two-run bomb the next time up. It's about patchwork lineups, managers getting fired, helmet weekends, coping with family separation, groin injuries, bus breakdowns, taking my son on a road trip to Oakland, and doubleheaders with both games going into extra innings. A pennant race would only have gotten in the way.

Added advantage to life with a noncontender: Due to the vagaries of publishing, the events in this book will be at least two years old by the time you read this. If suspense was my intent, it would've been the biggest miscalculation since New Coke. Instead, what is presented here is a diary—with no attempt to alter the impressions after the fact. What you see is what I saw. And despite no *Rocky*-like slam-bang finish, it was a helluva ride! As I've said many times on the broadcast (actually borrowing an ad line from a sleazy fifties movie): "Join me. It'll be exciting. You'll pay for the whole seat, but you'll only use the edge!"

1958. I was eight years old and already one of the worst outfielders in America, certainly in Reseda, California. Most kids dream of someday becoming big-league ballplayers, and many are able to reach their teens before they realize they don't have the God-given talent to make it. Well, for me—gangly, bespectacled, uncoordinated—I had to wait only till I was six. Some youngsters are invariably chosen last for pickup softball games. I was usually still waiting to be selected when one of the team captains would turn to the other and say, "Okay, we got everybody. Let's play."

By eight I was wondering: How else can I crack the majors? Would I want to be a manager? No. They're old. An umpire? Nah. They have to wear that bulky equipment just like catchers, and they always have those big sweat moons under their arms. Besides, people hate 'em. If I don't mind people hating me, I might just as well still be a player. So what's left? Grounds keeper? Forget it. That's a real *job*. Scoreboard operator? You have to know somebody to get that gig.

This was a real dilemma.

And then one evening, after finishing a game in which I hit Paul Clem in the head with a relay throw—allowing Donnie Bruckner to score the winning run from the Buick (we played on the street and didn't have bases. We used cars instead. Sliding was not recommended. Anyway, the Buick was first base, as I remember)—I returned home to find my dad sitting at our yellow kitchen booth with his ear glued to a transistor radio.

"What're you listening to, Dad?"

"The Dodger game" was his reply. The Dodgers had just moved to L.A. from Brooklyn.

I poured myself a glass of milk and joined him. Within minutes I was completely enthralled. Someone had doubled and someone else singled, so the manager brought in a new pitcher, but the other manager brought in a new hitter, and the crowd was real loud, and this new batter kept fouling off pitches one after the other and then stepping out of the box and adjusting his helmet or whacking his cleats with the end of the bat, and it was time to take my shower . . . but there was no way I was leaving the radio, and finally the batter took a mighty rip and . . . struck out. Or singled. I don't remember which, but I do remember this: It was simply thrilling, a major rush, the ultimate bedtime story. And I knew right then and there that if I couldn't be that guy at the plate, I wanted to be that guy on the radio. I wanted to be . . . uh . . .

"Who's that talking, Dad?"

"He's the Dodgers' announcer, Vin . . . something."

. . . I wanted to be Vin Something.

I had found the perfect job. For not only would I be in the major leagues and get to go to every game for free and fly to exotic locales like Cincinnati and Pittsburgh, but as an announcer I would, in a vicarious way, get to *play* every game. And not just one position. I'd be everybody—the pitcher leaning in for his sign, the batter ripping the ball down the left field line, the outfielder playing the carom perfectly, and the runner from second streaking home with the winning run just ahead of the throw. No doubt about it—this was for me!

That transistor radio and Vin Scully—"Something" wasn't his last name, it turned out—became my constant summer companions. Under Scully's nightly tutelage I learned the finer points of the game, was introduced to its unique rhythms and strategies, and grew to love and appreciate the rich history and tradition of baseball that sets it apart from all other sports.

And Scully instilled in me something else, something even more important—through his masterful use of images and expert storytelling, he sparked my imagination in a way that no schoolteacher or book had ever done. Not only would I eventually become a major league baseball announcer as a result of Vin Scully's inspiration, I would become a writer as well.

Flash forward ten years and I'm in college at UCLA. By now my interests have expanded to other forms of radio (DJ work and production) and playwriting. My list of idols grows to include Woody Allen and George S. Kaufman, along with Vin Scully. I do some play-by-play on the local campus station (KLA 83, with its powerful signal that reaches the third and fourth floors of Hedrick Hall and nowhere else), and become a sports intern at KMPC Los Angeles (home of the Angels, Rams, and UCLA Bruins). But upon graduation I find it's a lot easier getting a job as a disc jockey than a sportscaster.

Three years later—after stops in Bakersfield, San Bernardino, Detroit, San Francisco, San Diego, and Los Angeles (as, among other catchy aliases, "Truck-Ken" Stevens or "Beaver" Cleaver)—I determine that the beat has gone on long enough. Four hours a night, six nights a week of *Kung Fu Fighting* by Carl Douglas will do that to a person, even a person of twenty-three.

Two significant events happened in 1973. First: I saw Woody Allen's *Sleeper* and a bolt of lightning hit me. Here was a guy with complete creative freedom, writing a movie that was being seen and appreciated by millions, for a salary probably in the millions, while I was killing myself doing the all-night show in San Bernardino, trying to be funny over every record intro for the fifteen 7-Eleven night managers who were listening to me (and eight of them were probably tied up in the back). All this for $650 a month. What is wrong with this picture????

Significant event number two: I met David Isaacs. We were both in the same Army Reserve Unit. (My draft number was 4. He was much luckier. His was 7.) At the time, David was working for ABC Television, schlepping film cans in its mailroom department. Intuitively, he knew that the glamour and luster of that position would someday wear off. He too had seen *Sleeper*, he too had a desire to write, *and he was funny*. We decided to team up.

I knew nothing about screenwriting, but David was somewhat of an expert. He had taken a writing course at the University of Miami and had received a C-minus. We began writing *Mary Tyler Moore Show* speculative scripts in our spare time, hoping to break in. (We focused on television, figuring we should try to master a thirty-five-page script before tackling a 120-page feature epic.)

A year later the rock station I worked for in San Diego decided to change formats and fire us all—a week before Christmas (the station's promotion at the time was, "Christmas the way it was meant to be"). I was at a crossroads. I could either return to Los Angeles and try to break into television, or pursue my original dream and strive to be a baseball announcer. I chose writing because at the time, quite frankly, I just did not want to move anymore. My entire life savings had been squandered on apartment-cleaning deposits.

It is a decision I certainly do not regret. Over the past eighteen years I have received tremendous personal, artistic, and financial satisfaction from being a writer . . . not to mention an Emmy and two Writers Guild awards. Also, during that period I met and fell in love with the former Deborah Cohen of Brooklyn, New York. We were married in 1979. Matthew came along in 1982, Diana followed in 1986. To quote Randy Newman: "My life is *gooood.*" But there have been tough periods, questioning periods, and numerous occasions when I would take in a game at Dodger Stadium, gaze up at Vin Scully in the booth and wonder, What if? *What if?*

One tough period in particular came in 1986. David and I had just completed creating, executive-producing, and writing a year-long wisdom-tooth extraction for CBS called *Mary*—Mary Tyler Moore's comeback vehicle (to be more precise: comeback vehicle number four). By the time the show was mercifully canceled and we bid Ms. Moore good luck on her next comeback whirl—*Annie McGuire,* which was an even more colossal disaster than ours—we found ourselves in a quandary. Just what did we want to do with the rest of our lives? I don't think it would surprise you to learn we were then in our mid-thirties—right on the cusp of the mid-life-crisis danger zone.

After months of soul searching and one lunch with our agent, we determined that writing can still be fun if the focus is on the process, not the trappings, and also that there's a lot more to life than "what's on the page." It was time to explore other interests, satisfy other needs. For David that meant travel and literature (*adult* pursuits). For me it meant the upper deck at Dodger Stadium.

At about that time a network executive at NBC, whom I had dealt with on a number of projects, mentioned to me that he was considering a change of careers. Steve Leon had recently attended a sportscasting fantasy camp and was flirting with the notion of becoming a sportscaster. I asked if he needed a soulmate.

Together we decided to throw caution and ego to the wind

and venture to the upper deck of Dodger Stadium with a tape recorder. (We selected the upper deck because there were quite a few empty sections.) Feeling like complete idiots at first, we started to call 'em as we saw 'em. How were we? Well . . . we had a real great time. And when you think about it, isn't that what's really important??? (We were so bad that an usher came down and offered to arrange a ride home for us. That's how plastered he thought we were. This was in the third inning.)

When I said I had a great time, that's not entirely true. I had a *sensational* time! More fun than I'd had in years. The same with Steve.

We were back the next night and the one after that. By midsummer we were regulars, and by September we were each bringing tape recorders, sitting in different sections so we could individually get in more innings. We had been bitten, and bitten hard.

Our growth was startling. I can say without fear of hyperbole that by the end of the season we had progressed to the point of terrible. And in only three months!

The following year we were up there again; now at both Dodger and Anaheim stadiums. As our work grew, so did our chutzpah. No longer would we sit in the top row, miles away from the nearest spectator. We ventured down to the first row, where we could get unobstructed views. I began buying two tickets—one for me and the other for my equipment, which had now grown to include a headset mike, a crowd mike, and a portable mixer. (Yes, you're right. I was truly nuts.) Nightly regulars began recognizing us and gravitating around our "booths." Our "broadcasts" were becoming quite the rage of general admission.

All the while, Debby was very tolerant of my strange behavior. It could be because she is just a warm, loving person, or, being a clinical social worker, maybe she just recognized that this was mid-life-crisis country, and after seeing how several of my other friends had responded to this hurdle (one began driving stock cars and the other got a tattoo), she thought my actions were at least benign and not life-threatening (except during the Mets series).

Following the '87 season I decided to make the big plunge. I wanted to see what it was *really* like being an announcer. That meant the minors. Could I get a team to go for this? More important, could I get my wife to go for this? Incredibly, yes. Understanding what this meant to me (and secretly hoping that 142 games would finally get this nonsense out of my system), Debby agreed to go along for a summer adventure. I gave her a list of all the minor league cities and told her to select the ones she wouldn't mind living in. I was not about to subject my family to Columbus, Georgia, or Blythe, California. Out of 114 towns, Debby selected twenty—primarily in the Northwest, Northeast, and Florida. My partner David was all for it as well. A five-month vacation did not sit badly with him. I sent off the audition tapes and went about my life. Of the twenty, I received four offers—Eugene, Oregon; Bend, Oregon; Vero Beach, Florida; and Syracuse, New York. Syracuse was Triple A, the other three were A-level. I went for the big time.

As it turned out, 1988 was the perfect year to be the voice of the Syracuse Chiefs. The Writers Guild went on strike for six months that summer. I did not miss a thing. In fact, at $1,200 a month and fourteen dollars a day meal money, I was the highest-paid writer in America. (Steve, by the way, also landed a Triple-A job—with the Tucson Toros.)

For six months I submerged myself in the world of minor league baseball. The five A.M. wake-up calls, the endless bus rides, lugging around sixty pounds of radio equipment, back-to-back-to-back doubleheaders, no days off, the cheesy bandbox stadiums—the complete tour.

And I loved every minute of it. I wanted more.

Debby was less enamored of "the 'Cuse." She did not find its heat, humidity, and polluted lakes conducive to an idyllic bucolic summer.

The next two seasons I was able to move over to the Mets' Triple-A affiliate in Tidewater, Virginia. Tidewater is really the Virginia Beach area, so it is much more of a resort—San Diego with oppressive humidity. The family liked it a *whole* lot better.

Just before the '90 season I had met Jon Miller, the voice of the Baltimore Orioles and ESPN's top baseball mouthpiece. Hearing his games frequently in Tidewater, I became a big admirer of his work. Super voice, great game call, and rarest of rare commodities—a sense of humor. We chatted for a while and he asked, out of idle curiosity, for a sample of my work. I furnished a recent tape and we parted.

Two weeks after the season, I was in a *Cheers* rewrite session when my secretary popped her head into the room to tell me a Jon Miller was on the phone. He informed me that his partner on the radio, Joe Angel, had just left to take a job with the Yankees—thus the Orioles had an opening. They needed someone to do play-by-play for three or four innings a game as well as pre- and postgame show interviews and reading the disclaimer that warns listeners that if they tape all or any portion of the broadcast and use it without the express written consent of the Baltimore Orioles, they'll be killed. Jon had finally gotten around to listening to my tape and liked it very much. I was flabbergasted—not about the opening, but just that someone of the stature of Jon Miller would like my work. Anyway, he told me if I was interested, to call Jeff Beauchamp at WBAL Radio in Baltimore. I thanked him profusely and hung up the phone, dazed. He couldn't be serious! After discussing it with Debby, I decided to give Mr. Beauchamp a call. I knew I didn't have a chance, but as a courtesy to Jon, I felt it was the right thing to do.

Mr. B took my call (always a good sign), said that Jon had mentioned I might be calling, and requested an hour's worth of unedited, uninterrupted play-by-play. I sent it off the next day, expecting that to be the end of the story. Three weeks later he called. Out of ninety-four applicants, I was one of five finalists. Unbelievable.

Debby and I were flown out to Baltimore right after Thanksgiving. Still, we believed this was not going to happen. No way. We'd take our free weekend getaway and thank WBAL very much. I interviewed Friday night, Debby and I spent Saturday cruising around exotic Baltimore, and Sunday we headed back home.

The final decision was to be made in two weeks. So what? I wasn't gonna get it.

The two weeks came and went. I heard nothing. But that was what I expected, so I was certainly not concerned. They probably just hired someone else and I'd hear about it after the deal was set, and just being a finalist was a great honor, and . . . *how come I didn't get the job????!!!!*

Suddenly, I wanted it. Wanted it bad. I was right there in the finals. I could taste it. What happened? Who got it? What did they like about his tape they didn't like about *mine?* I can send another one, y'know. I have dozens of 'em. Would you like to hear this Tidewater-Rochester game in which there's a big windstorm and a toupee blows onto the field? No one had the guts to claim it. Don't make a decision before you hear this tape. I can FedEx it to you. Or I could walk it out to you.

I was a wreck.

Three weeks went by. Still no word.

I don't have to tell you.

On December 19 I got the call. Jeff Beauchamp. After conducting a three-month search and listening to nearly a hundred tapes, they'd made their decision. Would I be interested in joining the broadcast team of the Baltimore Orioles?

Try finding a movie studio that would buy that cockamamie story.

I was requested to report to spring training in Sarasota, Florida, on Saturday, March 2, 1991.

1

Saturday, March 2, 1991, Los Angeles

Thank God for airport congestion! The wait just to check in baggage took forty-five minutes. Security check, don't ask. Concern over terrorism still being a by-product of the Gulf conflict, skycaps and convenience are a thing of the past. Normally, a morning like this at the airport would drive me beyond nuts. I'm writing this on a Toshiba 1200XE laptop computer instead of the 1000 model because it's faster . . . by at least three nanoseconds. This gives you an idea of my patience level. This morning, however, I welcomed the crowds and confusion at the Delta terminal at LAX because it softened considerably what has proven to be the single hardest aspect of going off to announce baseball games . . . namely, "the going."

Saying good-bye to my wife and children is excruciating. We've structured the season so that there's no period of separation longer than four weeks, but even two days is extremely tough. Matthew is eight, Diana is four, and they'll never be those ages again. I'm squandering very precious time here indulging in my own pursuits. That's the selfish part. There's also the guilt part. I wondered out loud to my writing partner, David, if my being away might cause irreparable damage to the kids and their development. Good ol' Dave was able to ease my conscience with this: "Look what irreparable damage you'd be doing to them by staying."

In the past these airport farewell scenes were long, drawn-out affairs usually reducing all to tears. Today, due to the commotion, it was brief, although the effect was the same. After hugging and kissing them good-bye, I headed for the boarding gate, thinking to myself: I am about to live out my lifetime dream, my ultimate fantasy. Whatever happens in the next seven months, this is sure to be one of the most memorable and exciting years of my life. . . . Do I really want to do this???

Sunday–Wednesday, March 3–6, Sarasota, Florida

My other partner, Jon Miller, and I are renting a two-bedroom condo on the beach at Longboat Key for the month. It's spectacular. A view of the ocean *and* cable. We have a running gag that we can't tell our wives how nice it is because they'll hate us (as if they don't already). "Oh, honey, it's like being back in the army. C-rations would be an improvement, the weather is terrible . . . etcetera."

They're not buying it.

In point of fact, the weather has been less than ideal. Fierce thunderstorms and cold, blustery winds have been the order of the day. By midweek it improved, and the outlook for the weekend is sunny with temps in the low eighties. Almost real Florida weather.

Our condo is a good fifteen miles from the Orioles' training facilities in Twin Lakes. That translates to forty minutes' driving time on the surface streets and two-lane highways. You just get on 41 South, keep going until you pass seven Mister Donut shops, then turn left and follow a huge dump truck about three miles down the road.

The Orioles now train in the facility originally built by the Kansas City Royals as their baseball academy. (You might remember, that was the Royals' grand experiment to cultivate and nurture young talent with the hopes of discovering hundreds of gems. Aside from Frank White, it mainly produced debts.)

For over thirty years the Orioles trained in Miami under wretched conditions. They had a dilapidated old ballpark, Bobby Medera Stadium, and nothing else. No practice diamonds, no batting cages, no workout rooms, no trainers' rooms, no men's rooms.

And the neighborhood was the worst. Players got in their running drills by fleeing muggers. Pitcher Bob Milacki once commented that the holes in the stadium's tarp were bullet holes. He wasn't joking.

So this year they decided to pull up stakes and move . . .

which was certainly commendable, except for one thing—there was nowhere to move to. A proposed new permanent facility in Naples, Florida, recently fell through, and the club is scrambling to put together an arrangement for next year or the year after. But in the meantime the Baltimore Orioles are the Baltimore Boll Weevils ("Ain't got no home"). The plan is to train here in Sarasota and play all grapefruit league games on the road. That means long bus rides, that means split squads, that means fewer workouts. The team cannot possibly benefit from this program. The only hope is that it won't, in the long run, undermine their chances in '91.

For the first few days I just hung around the workout sessions, familiarizing myself with the team. Try meeting sixty new people at a party where everyone wears the same outfit. I introduced myself to several of the players two or three times. Thank God, Dwight Evans is with us this year. Him I recognize from his seventeen years with the Red Sox. Unfortunately, he was the one player who wasn't there, a flu victim. (The Orioles, by the way, wrapped adhesive tape around their arms with the number 24 on them as an armband tribute to their fallen hero. This was also a response to Roger Clemens, who, out of respect for Dewey, is wearing his old number 24 during spring training.)

The normal training ritual is for stretching exercises at ten followed by splintered groups of batting practice, pitching, and fielding practice. A lot is made of the phrase the "Oriole Way" of baseball, which means stressing the fundamentals above all else, execution with intelligence and precision, never beating yourself. Three or four games a year might be decided by whether the correct cutoff man is hit, and with most pennant races going right down to the wire, those three games could make the difference between going on to the World Series or being Toronto. Manager Frank Robinson's drills are lengthy and rigorous. Jewish "summer sleep-away camp" was nothing like this.

It used to be that ballplayers would roll into camp out of shape and overweight. The six weeks would be needed to transform these bloated whales back into athletes. No more. There is too much money involved, and the competition is too stiff, for the players to risk losing their positions due to poor conditioning. These days most players are on eleven-month training schedules (taking October off to watch the new NBC fall lineup). And the old theory that in the spring "pitchers are ahead of the hitters"?—not really true anymore. With indoor batting cages now available, many hitters take hundreds of cuts a week during the winter. The only one in camp who could really stand to lose five pounds and get his fat ass in the exercise room is me.

The big news in camp this year is that forty-five-year-old Hall-of-Famer Jim Palmer is trying to make a comeback. It would be a first. No Hall-of-Famer (in baseball) has ever reentered the major leagues after his induction. One of the reasons why a player is not eligible for Cooperstown until five years after retirement is to guard against this very thing. Palmer had been a color commentator on ESPN and a play-by-play voice on WMAR-TV, the Orioles' local television affiliate. His contract was up with ESPN at the conclusion of last season, and they wanted to renew for three years for essentially less money. Palmer, for some reason, found the terms unacceptable. There are those who believe his only motive for the comeback is financial—considering what even marginal ballplayers make today—but I believe he's sincere in his desire to return for the love of the game. There are a lot easier ways for Jim Palmer to make money. He's still the spokesbody for Jockey underwear, and is always in demand for card shows and personal appearances. Think about it. This guy can get handsomely paid just for *showing up* places. Compare that to punishing your body and perhaps embarrassing yourself in front of millions of people. Plain and simple, Jim Palmer wants to play.

He has a winter home in Key Biscayne, and spent the offseason working with the University of Miami's assistant coach, Lazaro "Laser" Collazo. At twenty-six, Collazo is Palmer's "mentor." When the sessions began, Collazo didn't like Palmer's mechanics. "You'll never make it to the Hall of Fame pitching like that," he observed, to which Palmer replied, "Hey, pal, I'm *in* the Hall of Fame." He progressed quickly and decided to seriously pursue his return to the majors. Unfortunately, no team was really interested. Finally, the Orioles, the organization for which he served his entire career, invited him to camp as a nonroster player. The retired jersey number 22 was taken off the shelf. The front office insists this is not a pity look or a publicity stunt. Since this is the final year of Memorial Stadium before the O's move into their new state-of-the-art downtown ballpark, and since they figure to contend this year, they won't need to cart out Jim Palmer to draw record crowds. They were impressed with what they saw; they also value the experience and guidance to the Orioles' young staff that a Palmer could provide.

Does he have a chance to make the team? At this point I'd have to say it's a reeeeeaaaaaaallll long shot. Not only does he have to prove that he can get his pitches over with absolute pinpoint control, he has to hope that the many young prospects in camp this spring *all* crap out. If it's a choice between Palmer and a pitcher the age of his number, Jim's back in the booth.

Palmer pitched two innings of an intrasquad game and the reviews were mixed. He gave up a windblown home run to catching prospect Chris Hoiles, but did manage to get a few guys out. On Monday he is scheduled to pitch against the Red Sox in Bradenton, which will be his first real test. Frank Robinson claims he's got to see him pitch three outings before he'll make any decision regarding his future, but Palmer told me that if the starts don't go well, he himself might make the decision. Should he not make the team, WMAR-TV is still holding open his job, so he really has nothing to lose. What the hell? When all else fails, there's always broadcasting.

Jon Miller has been quite an amusing roommate. He can't walk down the echoed stairwell in our condo without impersonating one of the various P.A. announcers in the game. He'll be in the middle of a conversation and just break into: "Nowww baaatting, nummbber twelllve, Dusssty Bakerrrr, lefft ffielld." When the Tropicana Hotel in Las Vegas gets wise and decides to stage its gala "Folies Bergère/Public Address Announcers of Baseball Revue," Jon will finally get the recognition he deserves.

This first week has been a ball—loitering around the training complex during the day (watching ballplayers in their natural habitat) and having dinner at night with Jon at a sensational seafood joint called Moore's. Gluttons that we are, we've been back for Moore's stone crabs three days in a row. It gets a little embarrassing when the owner of the restaurant says to us, "There's other places on the island, you know."

Tomorrow is my first game. Ken Coleman, who for thirty-four years had been the voice of the Boston Red Sox and Cleveland Browns, is semiretired and vacationing a few blocks from here. He and Jon were partners in Boston in the early eighties. Ken came over tonight and offered this advice: If you want to join the fraternity of major league announcers, you have to do the following thing—be nervous on your first broadcast. In deference to Ken, who is greatly respected among his peers, I think I will heed his advice.

Thursday, March 7, Sarasota

When Jeff Beauchamp, the general manager of WBAL, called me last December to offer me the job, my first reaction was shock, followed by elation, then relief, ending with a twenty-four-hour period of blue-blind panic. The reality of what it meant to be the "voice of the Orioles" began to set in—the family separation, the relocation, the effect on my "real" career, and the possibility that I could be the biggest bomb since *Howard the Duck*.

Eventually, cognitive dissonance took over and I remembered that this was the dream of a lifetime, an opportunity that might never present itself again, and I was able to once more walk the streets of New York without the aid of a brown paper bag (although for safety purposes, I recommend it). Elation returned. But worrisome still was the thought that if I experienced this much of an anxiety attack upon merely accepting the job, how would I fare the first day I actually had to go on the air? I could be Ralph Kramden as the "Chef of the Future," going on live TV to advertise the handy-dandy kitchen convenience, managing to utter only "Hummmmina, hummmina, hummmina." It's a concern that has haunted me for two months.

Well, today is the day.

I woke up at seven and, surprisingly, was not as nervous as I thought I'd be. In other words, I was able to keep liquids down. In the minors it was a different story. My first game as a "pro" was in Syracuse in '88, and although more people could probably hear me in the upper deck of Dodger Stadium than on the "Mighty" WXRA, I was still a tad uptight. King Arthur could not have pulled Excalibur out of my ass. What got me through that maiden voyage was a little pep talk by the general manager of the club. He took me aside before the broadcast, draped his arm around my shoulder, and said in a comforting, fatherly manner, "Kenny, now I know this is your first day and you're probably worried that you're gonna screw up and make an idiot of yourself. Well, if it happens, it happens. The great thing about baseball is that there's always tomorrow. Just make sure you get in the commercials, especially Rent-a-Wreck. They're payin' the freight." Little wonder I went on to have a great day.

Jon and I took separate cars to the ballpark. Game time was 1:35. I left at eight-thirty. Jon left at eleven.

We were playing today at Ed Smith Stadium in Sarasota, a new complex. (Ed Smith is a local civic leader who spearheaded the campaign for the new stadium. "If you build it, they will name it after you.") As minor league parks go, it seemed pretty good. The press box was behind home plate, with an unobstructed view. That's not always the case in the "bushes," you know.

I climbed the three flights of stairs to the booth and found our engineer, Dr. Paul Eicholtz, already there, setting up the equipment. After my three years of minor league ball, this was the ultimate luxury—to have an engineer. No more lugging around sixty pounds' worth of mixers, microphones, Comrex units, etc. No more setting up and striking equipment and praying that nothing breaks down since I have absolutely no ability to fix mechanical things whatsoever. (The day I own a Black & Decker anything is the day they cart me off to the drooling academy.)

Quick aside, minors: Equipment breakdowns, which were about as common as equipment functioning properly, were often welcome occurrences. Most teams carry only one announcer who does every inning of every game. A breakdown meant a break. There was one spieler in Louisville several years back who would, on occasion, if he was hung over, just turn off the equipment, call the station and tell them he was experiencing technical difficulties, then sleep it off for a couple of innings.

Dr. Paul is a terrific engineer. A dead ringer for Walter Matthau without the jowls, he's gracious, supportive, and utterly thorough. And unlike me, he knows the difference between "fast forward" and "rewind."

Taking my seat behind that mike for the first time was a long-awaited thrill. Words can't express how I felt. No security guards were going to arrest me.

The "Mighty O's" finally rolled in, so I grabbed my cassette recorder and trudged downstairs to interview manager Frank Robinson for our daily three-minute "Frank Robinson Report" pregame feature. That will be one of my responsibilities, and quite honestly, I'm not looking forward to it. I hear that Frank can be tough at times; gruff, confrontational, uncooperative, "asshole-ative." But I also hear that he's mellowed considerably over the years and that if you stand up to him, he'll respect you for it and back off. Either that or he'll cut out your heart and mail it to your mother.

So far, Frank has been terrific. Early in January I went to Baltimore for two days of orientations and interviews and dined with him, along with Jon and several team and radio station officials. He held court and was candid, funny, and very charming. No trace of "asshole-ative" behavior. I haven't spent too much time with him here in Florida because he has been scooting around in his little General Patton golf cart, presiding over workouts, and because . . . hell, I'll admit it, I'm still a little intimidated by the guy. The interview today went without a hitch. One down, 177 to go.

At 1:07:30 I hit the air for the first time. "Hi, everybody, this is Ken Levine with Jon Miller. Welcome to Sarasota, Florida, and another season of Baltimore Orioles baseball. Today it's the Orioles versus the White Sox, and we'll find out about this year's Orioles team when I chat with manager Frank Robinson right after this." I was flawless.

You'd never know I rehearsed it for two weeks.

So much for not being nervous. Although I don't think it was *too* detectable on the air, I was terrified. I knew the audience was listening with very high expectations. How could they not, after being bombarded for two months with interviews and features about me? (Even before I got the job, the *Baltimore Sun* ran a front-page story in the sports section along with a ghoulish caricature of me surrounded by Homer Simpson, Hawkeye Pierce, Sam Malone and Norm and Cliff, with the caption, "Look who else might be joining the Orioles broadcast booth next season." Yikes! All I was expected to do was provide the best of *M*A*S*H* and *Cheers* and *The Simpsons* for three hours every night . . . along with expert play-by-play and commentary.) And I also knew that first impressions are crucial. By all rights you should give an announcer several weeks or months before you determine whether you like him, but most people, admittedly myself included, give a guy two, maybe three, pitches. Try to sound natural and relaxed and funny under those conditions. My only hope was that the game would be an easy, routine affair; ground ball to short, fly ball to left, etc.

Yeah, and Arena Football will become America's Pastime.

Jon did the first two innings. He was outstanding, and I resented him terribly for it. When he introduced me in the third, I told the listeners to expect an unassisted triple play, a bench-clearing brawl, or some bizarre play that hasn't occurred since 1911. After all, this was my first inning. The first batter up, Randy Milligan, promptly hit a ground ball to third. Robin Ventura gobbled it up and threw low to first, into the runner. As first baseman Frank Thomas leaned in to take the throw, which had skipped six feet in front of him, Milligan tripped on Thomas and went hurtling down the first-base line. Out came the trainers. Sprained ankle. Ten-minute delay.

Hummmmina, hummmmina, hummmmina.

The next inning Chuck Thompson, the longtime voice of the Orioles and Colts, stopped in to say hello. We have without a doubt the weirdest announcer rotation in major league baseball. Jon will do eighty-one games on the radio, splitting time between ESPN, local TV, and airport terminals the rest of the time. Chuck Thompson will broadcast the remaining eighty-one. I'll do three innings when Jon's with me, four when it's Chuck. There's absolutely no pattern to the Miller-Thompson rotation. One week Jon will be on Monday, Tuesday, and Friday, the next he'll be on every day except Sunday, and the following week he won't be on at all. The listeners will have no idea from day to day who their friendly announcers will be. For me the task is to develop a good chemistry with each partner despite the fact that their styles are very different and there's no continuity. Oh well, that's the task for the future. My goal today is to just survive this broadcast.

Chuck chatted with me during an inning in which we scored

four runs on five hits with all hell breaking loose. "Yes, Chuck, I am looking forward to getting to Baltimore and meeting the —whoa, there's a drive up the alley for extra bases. Two runs are gonna score—meeting the fans, who I hear are the greatest in the world." That inning went fine. In fact, all was fine . . .

. . . until the ninth.

The game was dragging on, and Jon, whose daughter had been staying with us this week, had to deliver her to the airport by five. It was now four-thirty, and we were just going to the ninth, so Jon tossed it to me and took off. While I was alone in the booth, another rally began brewing. The Orioles got another run and had runners at first and third when the batter bounced the ball to second. The infielder threw him out, but I announced that Jeff McKnight scored from third. Then I saw that the White Sox were leaving the field. That had been the third out. The run did not score. Ooooops. So, as deftly as I could, I covered my tracks and launched into my cue for a commercial break . . . except I now gave the wrong score. It was a nightmare. By the time I signed off the broadcast about a half hour later, I was ready to book the first flight back to L.A.

Jeff Beauchamp, the GM of WBAL, called to say he was very pleased. To him I sounded poised, professional, and even better than expected. (My God, what was he expecting, then?) He may have just been blowing sunshine up my skirt, but this *is* Florida, the Sunshine State. His call was very welcome.

That night Jon and I went to dinner with Ken Coleman. I had two drinks more than I usually do. In other words, I had two drinks.

Friday–Sunday, March 8–10, Sarasota/Port Charlotte/ Fort Lauderdale

Our second game was in Port Charlotte against a team I knew nothing about, the Texas Rangers. I was familiar with their major league roster, but had not seen their thousands of minor leaguers. Still, I did a better broadcast. I was a little more comfortable. But then, in the seventh inning, Oriole third baseman Craig Worthington doubled in two runs, although anyone listening to my description only heard about one of them. I hope these mistakes are a result of nerves and not the fact that I'm a giant, horrendous, pathetic fuck-up.

After the game Jon and I drove from the west to the east coast of Florida—across Alligator Alley—to Fort Lauderdale. The trip was very pleasant and it gave us a three-hour chance to get to know each other a little better. There has to be a movie of Jon's first year in Baltimore. He arrived from Boston, recently divorced, with custody of his two young daughters. It's hard enough being a single parent, but when you're on the road every other week, it's really a nightmare. Jon went through a series of nannies until he found a gem. Along the way was the Orthodox Jewish woman who would not answer the phone on Friday nights. Jon sure would've been spared a lot of anxiety had she told him that *before* he called home one Friday evening. Also, there was the nice lady who was convinced that "somebody else" lived in the house with them, despite all of the laws of the universe that suggested otherwise.

Saturday's game against the Yankees was better still. Only one mistake: I goofed up a double play. At least I'm consistent. My warm-up show interview, however, was dynamite. My guest was former Red Sox reliever Sam Malone. Several weeks ago in L.A., I asked Ted Danson if he'd mind recording a three-minute interview with me. He said he'd be happy to. (Ted Danson is an honest-to-goodness nice guy. If Kitty Kelley wrote his unauthorized biography, she'd have nothing to write after two pages.) My partner David and I then scripted the piece and recorded it just before I left. Jeff Beauchamp felt that today would be a good day to air it since this was our first weekend contest and we would be getting our first large audience. Among the highlights: I asked what Sam was doing now. He told me he ran a popular bar in Boston, perhaps I had heard of it—Cheers. No, I replied, this was my first year in the league. I asked if he was married. He laughed and said no, but he had been close to it once, actually five times, with the same girl. If we had a two- or three-hour rain delay, he'd be able to tell me about it. He then announced that he has an active social life. I wondered what he missed most about baseball, and he said the even *more* active social life. We talked about Coach. He recalled fondly that Coach could swallow an entire plug of tobacco and go a whole hour before passing out. We reminisced about Sam giving up the longest home run ever hit in

Memorial Stadium. There is a plaque where it landed in the parking lot, and Sam wondered casually if it was a plate in the ground or a standing monument that could accidentally be run over by a car. When he learned it was in the ground, he shrugged it off, knowing that we would be out of that park in a year anyway. Finally, I wrapped up the interview, with Sam interrupting me constantly, wanting to know what gift he'd receive: tires, maybe even a CD player for his 'vette.

From what I hear, the interview was very well received back in Crabtown.

Sunday's game was my best yet. No major mistakes. (Somehow my standards have dropped over the past week.) I had my first two home run calls, and I handled both very well. Don Mattingly crushed one for the Yankees, and Chris Hoiles hit one for the Orioles in the tenth. As part of our postgame show we replay highlights from the just completed game, and listening back, I did not cringe.

The one question I seem to be asked all the time is, What is my home run call? Many great announcers have developed distinctive home run calls that have served as their signature down through the years. Mel Allen has "Going, going, gone!" Harry Caray uses "It might be, it could be, it *is* a home run!" Dave Niehaus of Seattle has coined "It will fly away!" And so on. An individual home run call allows an announcer to put his own stamp on the game at the moment of greatest impact. Listeners look forward to the call because they look forward to the event, and a good one can really enhance the action while showing the announcer off in the best possible light. The only problem is, it's hard to invent a classic, original home run call. The good ones, it appears, have been taken. Jon, more often than not, will use, "You can tell it good-bye!" which is a variation of the call he heard former Giants' announcer Russ Hodges use while growing up in the Bay Area. I still do not have a trademark home run call. The best ones, of course, originated spontaneously, and that requires years of experience. I do not have years of experience. Also, a home run call should not be so intricate that it traps you into sounding like a complete idiot. A couple of cases in point: At one time I flirted with "Ladies and gentlemen, Elvis has left the building!" That was fine until the day I was forced to say, "Ladies and gentlemen, Elvis . . . is off the top of the wall!" Even worse was the time a certain American League announcer, whose call is "Touch 'em all [name of player]," blanked on who had just hit the homer. This was what he blurted out on a fifty-plus radio network: "There's a long drive to left, and you can touch 'em all . . . baseball man!"

The closest I have to a home run call is one I hope will not become a fixture. When you're working the minor leagues, it's often hard to see. Most stadiums have poor lighting, and practically every stadium has double- or triple-deck billboards ringing its outfield fences. (At Silver Stadium in Rochester there are also ads on the foul poles, the dugouts, the light standards, and everywhere else except the pitching rubber. It's only a matter of time before the players wear sandwich boards.) The point is that on more than one occasion my home run call has been "Belted to deep right field! It's gone! . . . No, wait a minute . . . " In Rochester I once blew a call three different ways. The bases were loaded, a guy sent a bolt to deep left, and the outfielder raced back to the wall. I was looking at downtown Tokyo with all the ads. The outfielder leaped up and I said he had made the catch. My partner shook his head no and twirled his finger around. That's the umpire's sign for a home run. So I then called it a grand slam. He shook his head no again. What he was trying to signal with the twirling finger was that the runners were moving—the ball was off the top of the wall and still in play. So I had to correct myself a third time and call it a double. For several years that stood as the worst call in the International League—topped finally in 1990, which follows momentarily. In any event, my sincerest wish this season is that whatever I decide to call a home run, it *is*, in fact, a home run.

Omaha, 1990. An Omaha Royal, Nick Capra, is hit by a pitch. As he trots down to first, this hapless visiting announcer buries his head in his stat book, as he is prone to do. How many times that batter's been hit, the team record, the league record, etc. Suddenly, he looks up at the field and makes this call: "So Nick Capra's on first, one away, and . . . ladies and gentlemen, there's a crazed madman running across the infield! . . . No, wait, that's the Omaha trainer."

Jon and I had some fun with the grounds crew during the game. A Yankee pitcher complained of the mound condition, so the two grounds crew men snapped into action . . . in slow motion. Jon said they must've been in the middle of a poker hand, and I defended them, saying that theirs was the most stressful profession next to air traffic controllers. Good clean fun on the radio at others' expense.

Monday, March 11, Bradenton, Florida

Today is the day Jim Palmer returns to the mound. He's the scheduled starter against the Red Sox. There was some question as to whether he would answer the bell. He did not join us for the weekend in Lauderdale, and there were rumors that he had Achilles tendon problems. I said on the air yesterday that if he didn't pitch, there would be a lot of national TV and print coverage of José Mesa, the emergency replacement in case Palmer couldn't start. But Palmer was apparently okay and took center stage as planned.

McKechnie Field in Bradenton is the spring home of the Pirates. They're away today, so the Orioles get to be the hosts. The Pirates are planning to leave this facility next year, and there's little wonder why. McKechnie Field is a dump. It's not old, it's ancient. Rickety wooden bleachers, a brick backstop, subpar restroom facilities, and perhaps the worst press box I've ever been in. Had we broadcast our first game of the year here instead of our fifth, I might've killed myself. The problem is simple: You can't see. Not only are you right behind the backstop net, which crisscrosses your view, but the idiot who designed this torture chamber put in horizontal slat windows. There are six metal beams that block your vision. It was truly like calling a game from behind the Burlington logo.

As you could imagine, there was a media circus at the ballpark. All the major networks and local stations had camera crews, reporters were everywhere, even Dick Vitale was present for some reason—he must be on hand for *all* forms of "March Madness," I suppose.

Jon called the play-by-play for the first two innings (Palmer's innings) and, as usual, was magnificent. Palmer, however, was anything but. He was shelled. From the first batter—Wade Boggs—on, the Sox were teeing off. Yes, it was only his first outing, and a lot of pitchers get rocked in the spring, but it looks to me as though the emperor is very scantily dressed (Jockey shorts and nothing more).

By the time I went on the air in the third inning, Palmer was hitting the showers (assuming they had hot water at McKechnie). I did a commentary on how, as a writer, I would not have scripted his comeback performance in this fashion, and Jon chimed in with how he felt Hollywood would handle the story. Palmer would go back to the hotel, dejected, and meet Kim Basinger. They would fall in love, he would be inspired, etc. Picking up on Jon's lead, I added story developments as well, and between us we concocted a pretty fair scenario. It's way too early to tell whether our broadcasts will be well received, but they *will* be different.

After the game, we learned that Palmer suffered a slight hamstring pull while warming up, and that may have accounted for his poor performance.

Funny moments today: A foul ball in the fifth inning looped over the stands out onto the street, where it hit a spectator in the foot—Dick Vitale. Watch out for those loose balls, baby! Funny moment number two: Home Team Sports is the cable outlet that televises Oriole games. They were out here today because of Palmer. From what we understand, they had transmission problems and didn't get on the air until the third inning . . . just after Palmer had been lifted. Mark my words: Television will never catch on.

Tuesday, March 12, Sarasota

Jim Palmer's comeback is over. He retired today one day after being unable to retire any of the Red Sox. This was supposed to be a day off, but I called our PR director, Rick Vaughn, at about one o'clock just to see if anything was up. There was. Palmer had just come out of a closed-door meeting with Frank Robinson, and "poof," he was a broadcaster again. Frank asked him if he was sure of his decision. "No," he said, "but my leg is." The hamstring strain was the final blow. So ends a storybook saga . . . and the prospect that two of us will be writing books about this season with the Orioles.

You have to give him credit for trying, and equal credit for gracefully stepping aside. There's nothing sadder than an old ballplayer still just hanging on, even though everyone in the world knows it's over.

I gave the people at WBAL, our flagship radio station in

Baltimore, the scoop, and they got it on the air immediately. I made a lot of friends in the news department today. (I think I'll make a lot more when I read their speculative *Cheers* scripts, which, I have an uneasy feeling, are about to pour in.)

Wednesday–Friday, March 13–15, Sarasota

This is the part of spring training everybody imagines—lying around the beach and pool, eating stone crabs and checking out ball games. It's really heaven. Well, heaven with an asterisk. I wish my family were here too. Especially Deb. She's the one who needs the vacation.

Jon's wife, Janine, flew down Wednesday from Baltimore with their three-year-old son, Alex. They'll be staying for a week. Janine is terrific: bright, attractive, cheerful. Jon and Janine grew up together in Northern California. In fact, at one time Janine was Jon's babysitter (and she wouldn't, like her older sister, let him stay up late and watch movies). They remained friends but married other people. Those relationships didn't work out, and in true Hollywood movie fashion, they reunited and married each other. I'd say that's a pretty crazy story, but I'm the one who met my wife at a Club Med in Mexico.

On Friday, Jon and I took the two-hour drive down the coast to Fort Myers for our game with the Twins. It's amazing to me how our team can win any spring games at all. This schedule of no home dates is nuts. Every day the team must bus anywhere from forty-five minutes to four hours to play. While every other team is in the batting cages or on practice mounds, the Orioles are on U.S. 75. David Janssen traveled less when he was the Fugitive. Plus, Frank leaves a few of the regulars back in an effort to conserve some of their energy for the real season. As a result, he doesn't get a chance to see his actual team. Dwight Evans, who is still nursing back and knee problems, got into a game for the first time on Wednesday. Randy Milligan's ankle has not yet healed, so he hasn't been with us, and Glenn Davis suffered a muscle spasm in his neck (official medical term: "kink") on Tuesday, so he's on the shelf till further notice. What effect will this nomadic schedule have on the ball club? Ask me in May.

At some point, however, the musicians are going to have to play together.

The Twins' complex at Fort Myers is spectacular. Their new ballpark is small but state-of-the-art. I only hope Cleveland is as nice.

We got back home at seven-thirty and immediately were met by a camera crew from *A Current Affair.* A month ago *A Current Affair* got wind of my story and thought it would make a great feature. They called the WBAL brass, who were thrilled. Personally, I'm not a big fan of *A Current Affair.* To me it's a sleaze tabloid with annoying graphics—not nearly the quality of *Geraldo.* But since 'BAL was so excited, I agreed to let the *Current Affair* folks do the feature. First they wanted to interview me in my office at Paramount to show me at work in both of my careers, but since Paramount produces the rival TV tabloid *Hard Copy,* the *Affair* people weren't permitted on the lot. Plan B was to interview me at home, but my wife, with good reason, didn't want them within five miles of our house. Their next suggestion was to film me on Opening Day, but I'll have enough pressure without a camera crew and blinding lights, so nix to that. What we settled on was that they would film me tomorrow from Port Charlotte and interview me tonight. The arrangement was that Jon and I would get home, the *Current Affair* folks would *call* at about seven-thirty, and they'd come by about nine. Well, they were there at 7:31. Before I could even wash up or change into my WBAL shirt (I'm a good little company shill, aren't I?) hundreds of pounds of equipment were being hauled into the condo. I was interviewed for an hour, then they asked if we could stage some shots. They wanted to "capture" me working on the computer, "creating genius." What a joke! While cameras rolled, I typed like a madman. At the rate I was banging away, I would finish a script in eleven minutes. (It usually takes fifteen.) The crew circled around me and at one point stopped over my shoulder and began shooting the screen. I told them I didn't want the content to be read, and they assured me the actual letters wouldn't register. Of course I believed them. I began typing "Bring back Maury Povich" (the show's original host, who defected a year ago); "The show sucks without Maury Povich!" It was a wonderful media event that lasted until eleven.

Jon wanted to stay up late and watch a movie, but Janine wouldn't let him.

Saturday, March 16, Port Charlotte, Florida

The camera crew was back at nine A.M. Today's the day they were going to show me at work as a broadcaster, so of course that meant filming me and Jon physically leaving the condo and getting into our car. They got terrific footage of me explaining the game of baseball to my very attentive partner. When we reached the parking lot, I pretended that the car had been stolen. I have a feeling that Jessica Hahn and Fawn Hall were more cooperative subjects.

We sped down the coast to Port Charlotte to face the Rangers (ditching the mobile truck at the expressway entrance). The weather was awful; low overcast, threat of rain, and temperatures in the fifties. The *Current Affair*ers caught up to us and set up shop in the booth, promising not to be an intrusion. "You won't even know we're here," they assured us. I went down to the press lounge to get a hot dog, and they followed me into the chow line, recording my condiment selections. Everyone in the room turned to look, and their expressions were all the same: "Who the hell is *this* schmuck?" In no uncertain terms I told the crew that I eat food just like everybody else. They grumbled and went back upstairs to annoy Jon.

Jim Palmer was there, broadcasting his first TV game back to Baltimore. I could tell he was really into it. He came into our booth and borrowed one of my score sheets. He had forgotten one himself.

Jim's partner on TV is Hall-of-Famer Brooks Robinson. Not only was Brooks one of the premier third basemen in the game (sixteen Gold Gloves), he's also one of the nicest men in the game. Everyone who knows Brooksy loves him, and in two minutes it's easy to see why. He's outgoing, personable, and as down-to-earth as his slight southern drawl would suggest. Mayberry may have Andy Griffith, but Baltimore has Brooks Robinson.

The game itself was much better than the weather (which rained on and off). Big Sam Horn (at six-foot-five, 250 pounds) hit two triples . . . and they were legitimate triples. It's not like two outfielders collided and the ball lay untouched for seven minutes, allowing Sam to dive into third base just ahead of the throw. He drove in six runs, including three with his last triple, which came in the tenth inning (my inning). The crew has plenty of highlights to use for my feature. They took more than four and a half hours' worth of footage. I asked how long the final piece would be. Between four and seven minutes. In that case, I sure hope a full minute of it is Jon and me getting into my car.

I talked about the crew on the air, saying that I was a *Current Affair* subject because (1) I'm a TV writer now broadcasting major league baseball, and (2) I have a different wife stashed away in every American League city.

After the game, when the crew was packing up, I requested a VHS copy of the finished product, since I won't know when it airs and probably won't see it or be able to tape it. The woman producing the piece said she'd try but they frown on that sort of thing. Why do I have the feeling I'm going to regret this entire experience???

Sunday, March 17, Dunedin, Florida

As a refreshing change, we traveled north today to face the Toronto Blue Jays. Winding along Highway 19, we passed ELVIS' TOWING. What's harder to find, a good towing service or the King of Rock 'n' Roll? I'd been looking forward to today's game more than most because it reunites me with my first organization. I began this folly of announcing baseball in 1988 with Syracuse, which is Toronto's Triple-A affiliate. Many of the current Jays were then Chiefs. I spent a good hour in their clubhouse shaking hands and catching up on old times with my "buds." Most couldn't fathom that I had actually gotten a major league job. Gosh, it was great to see them again. Really good for the ol' confidence.

In the press lounge I met Buck Martinez, a former Toronto catcher now turned broadcaster. He recently moved to Los Angeles, where his wife is taking a shot at an acting career. I wished him luck, and he gave me her eight-by-ten glossy with résumé. If I hear of anything, let him know. I asked if I could scrawl on it "Ken, I'll always remember that magic night in the Skydome Hotel," and post it in my booth in Baltimore. Buck proved to be a good sport and didn't knock me senseless with a forearm shiva.

Frank Robinson gave me my first "test" today. I've been told he'll do that and that I'm just supposed to stand my ground. I trundled into his office to record the day's "Robinson Report," and he was chatting idly with a couple of people. I sat quietly for about ten minutes, and during a break in the conversation politely asked if we could do the interview. He exploded. "Jeez, you're pushy," he barked. "Joe Angel"—my predecessor—"was never that fuckin' pushy."

"Yeah, but he got his," I replied. "He's now with the Yankees."

Frank went on: "Just what do you gotta do that's so fuckin' important that it can't wait?"

"Eat lunch," I answered.

"Oh," he said, very satisfied with the answer, "then let's do this baby."

The weather was threatening all morning. Just before game time it began to rain on and off. The grounds crew responded by rolling out the tarp, removing it, then repeating the process several times. Jon and I covered it on the air like a CNN war-coverage broadcast.

"For the latest on the tarp situation we go live to Ken Levine."

"Thank you, Jon. We have confirmation that the tarp has indeed been cleared for roll-out, the exact coordinates of which cannot be disclosed as a matter of league security. We'll remain here as long as it's safe. . . . Jon?"

"Thank you, Ken. And now to the State Department and Wolf Blitzer."

We had a fifty-five-minute rain delay before the game finally got under way. Every other major league broadcast team gets to "toss it back to your local station for some news and great Buddy Greco music," but WBAL's philosophy is that we have a captive audience of baseball fans and we should try to keep them. Therefore we stay on the air indefinitely (or until they call the game, whichever comes last). To fill up the time, we conduct a call-in show right from the booth. A studio producer in Baltimore screens the calls, and we hear them over our headsets. Talk about Russian roulette. If the listeners start criticizing the team and we defend it too vigorously, we look like house men and kiss off our credibility. If we agree with the callers, we anger the team, manager, and coaches, and thus lose access to our main source of information. We really have to straddle a fine line. (Of course, at the time I was interviewed for the job last November and was told of this format, I said, "Oh yeah. Great. I've done call-in shows. I love doing call-in shows. I look *forward* to it." What a fucking sap!)

Most of the callers were kind. A number of them welcomed me to the broadcast. One complained that I read the starting lineups too quickly, and another chided me for not saying the word "error" succinctly enough. I got off cheap—although Jon let me know about the "error" complaint all afternoon long. It turned into a cute routine for Jon and his foil.

The game finally began, and five minutes later the rains returned. Another twenty-five minutes of *Orioles Talk.* Help!! That delay would be our last, and the game itself would be worth the wait for Ernie Whitt. Whitt was an original member of the Blue Jays in 1977 and was one of its brightest stars for the next twelve years. Last year he hooked up with Atlanta, and a wrist injury prevented him from having any kind of season with the bat. This year, at thirty-eight, he's trying to latch on to the Orioles as a third catcher. Along with another veteran, former Oriole Larry Sheets, he's vying for the last spot on the roster. The odds aren't good, but Ernie's been giving it his best, and so far he's having a great spring. Between him and Sheets, he seems to make more sense since he can provide a backup behind the plate as well as hit. Today, for the first time in his career, Ernie Whitt played against the Blue Jays. He was brought in during the seventh inning (with me behind the mike) and homered. The crowd went nuts. It was a very meaningful moment in a very meaningless game.

We drove back to Longboat Key without needing Elvis.

Monday–Friday, March 18–22, Sarasota

No weekday broadcasts scheduled, so it's "announcer's choice" as to how many games I need to attend. Monday was an open day (our only one in Florida), and Tuesday we had split squad games at Sarasota against Detroit or at Fort Lauderdale against the Yankees. I selected Sarasota, not because I'd avoid the four-hour drive, but I just like to see those Tiger road uniforms. Wednesday and Thursday the club played out of town and I played hooky (staying in Sarasota to watch the White Sox host the Cardinals and Reds).

Several positions remain open for the Orioles. Third base is a jump ball. Craig Worthington, the incumbent, had a dreadful sophomore year with the bat after enjoying a very promising rookie season. He's being challenged by prospect Leo Gomez, who's a great hitter with a lot more sock than Worthington, but defensively he's not in the same league. Thus far, neither candidate has really shined. Both are hitting fairly well, but with the glove it's a different story. Both have committed a number of errors, mostly on routine plays. This one may go right down to the wire.

Mike Devereaux and Brady Anderson are duking it out for leadoff and a regular job in the outfield. Brady was labeled a "can't miss" a few years ago when he was coming up through the Boston organization and the Orioles traded pitcher Mike Boddicker to get him. Boddicker has since flourished, winning seventeen games for the BoSox last year, while Anderson has never really put it together. At what point do you expect potential to be realized? In the case of Brady Anderson, I believe this is the year. Unfortunately, he's not hitting .200 here in the spring. Mike Devereaux was a star-in-the-wings in the Dodger camp before being dealt to the O's for pitcher Mike Morgan, and he has not proved to be the "next Willie McGee," as predicted by the Dodger hype machine. He has good speed, covers a lot of ground, has a lovely wife, and can put up some impressive offensive numbers, but he is also streaky and still undisciplined. If he's to lead off, he'll have to be more patient at the plate, draw more walks, and satisfy the number-one requirement of a leadoff man: to get on base. So far, he's looking good here in Florida.

As mentioned, Ernie Whitt and Larry Sheets are two left-handed veterans trying to stick with the club. Whitt has the edge, but Sheets is still under consideration because the team is very shorthanded in the "left-hand hitters with power" department. Currently, they have Sam Horn and that's it.

The outfield is still a question mark. Randy Milligan, a first baseman by trade, is being bumped to left field with the addition of Glenn Davis. Randy played the position early in his minor league career but is inexperienced, doesn't have a great arm, and doesn't figure to cover much ground out there (added pressure for Devereaux or Anderson in center). Randy, however, brings a very potent bat to the dance and has a terrific attitude. His feelings on being shifted to left field: "Good and bad. Good because I get to play every day, bad because it takes that much longer to run out to my position."

Steady Joe Orsulak is also in the mix. Never the star, rarely in the headlines, Joe is one of those lunch-pail guys who just goes out every day and does his job. His play in right field is very solid if not spectacular, and although he doesn't hit for tremendous power, somehow he's managed to lead the team in hitting for two of the last three years. He's also a lefty. I expect to be announcing "Smokin' Joe O's" name frequently throughout the season.

The Utility Infielders' Sweepstakes. Three jack-of-all-trades are vying for two spots—Tim Hulett, Jeff McKnight, and Juan Bell. Hulett is the more seasoned of the three. At thirty-one, he's been up and down in the big leagues since '83. In '86 he was the starting third baseman for the White Sox and crashed seventeen home runs. His average, however, usually hovers around .235, so year after year he's on the bubble. Jeff McKnight is a kid who can do everything but hit well. He plays practically every position and is a switch-hitter. The best way to describe Jeff is "handy." Juan Bell is George Bell's little brother. He's "Mr. Flash"—quick, good hands, and with a crackling whip of an arm. He's also a shortstop by trade, playing behind a guy who's played in 1,411 consecutive games and has missed only thirty-one innings in the last three years. Bell also tends to make the "rookie mistake" now and again, which is understandable since he's only twenty-three and a rookie. He's had some attitude problems in the past (it must be in the blood), notably getting into a shoving match with his teammates in Rochester last year on the night they clinched the division title. The fight apparently spilled out of the dugout onto the field. Roland Hemond, the Orioles' very affable general manager, is very high on Bell. In time he's going to be a good one. The question is: Is now the time?

So far none of the three is having a banner spring. Early prediction: Jeff McKnight will be the odd man out. Who of the three do I know the best and like the best? You got it.

Pitching is ultimately the key to any team's success. Good pitching will keep any club in any game. One need only look back to the Dodgers of the mid-sixties. Not much hitting there, but with Koufax, Drysdale, Osteen, Brewer, and Perranoski, who cared? In 1965 they won 97 games, in 1966 they won 95 . . . all by scores of 2–1.

The Orioles' pitching figures to be promising. By and large, they have a very young staff. It might need another year of seasoning, but one can hope. The ace of the crew is twenty-three-year-old right-hander Ben McDonald. At six-foot-seven, 212, he lives up to the nickname "Big Bird." A star in college at LSU, Ben was the first player selected in the June '89 Free Agent Draft. He made headlines right away by signing for bigggggg bucks. Two weeks later he was in the majors. Last season he began back down in the minors but made it back to Baltimore by mid-season, at which point he won his first five starts, including a shutout in his debut effort. Opponents batted .205 against him. He has a 95 mph fastball, a wicked curve, and an unbelievably bright future . . .

. . . as long as he stays away from alligators.

Ballplayers are notorious for getting into freak accidents. Every year you read about two or three blue-chippers who have grisly accidents tripping over lawn mowers, moving air-conditioning units, or being in the wrong place when a birdhouse falls. (This winter Carney Lansford of the Oakland A's got into a snowmobile mishap and is likely to be out for the season.) Ben McDonald, for fun, likes to wrestle alligators. The Orioles have advised him against it. (Has Ben ever seen *Peter Pan*?)

Storklike in appearance, McDonald is soft-spoken, friendly, with an accent consistent with being from Baton Rouge. Ben can hold seven baseballs in one hand. Hopefully, he can get three over for strikes.

Two years ago, when the Orioles came within an eyelash of winning the A.L. East, starters Bob Milacki and Jeff Ballard won 32 games between them. Last year they won seven. The O's finished fifth. The hopes of the team's recovery rest squarely on their shoulders.

Ballard, a good-looking kid who resembles a blond Alec Baldwin—and guys, if you're not already jealous, he has a degree in geophysics from Stanford—experienced arm trouble last year. Milacki, who has a big, round baby face and specializes in a devastating change-up, never was in sync. Both are healthy and ready for '91.

Leading the club in victories last year with thirteen was Baltimore local boy Dave Johnson. Now thirty-one, the mustachioed Johnson languished for eight years in the minors before finally getting his chance in '89 as a twenty-nine-year-old rookie. (That's the equivalent of a fifty-year-old ingenue.) Johnson is strictly a finesse pitcher who forever seems to be working with men on base. "There's always a lotta thrills out there when Johnson is pitching," his manager recently observed. But in the last two years there have also been a lot of wins.

The fourth and fifth spots in the rotation are still open. Among the candidates are José Mesa, a young flame thrower two years removed from elbow surgery; John Mitchell, a sinker-baller-nothing-special-but-reliable right-hander; Jeff Robinson (recently acquired from Detroit for catcher Mickey Tettleton), who has great stuff but is very injury-prone; and finally, wily veteran Mike Flanagan.

For all the hoopla regarding the Jim Palmer comeback, Mike Flanagan, at thirty-nine, who toiled for the Orioles from '75 to '87 and won the Cy Young Award in '79, actually has a chance to make this ball club. Last year he was released by Toronto. In August he attended Jim Palmer's induction ceremony into the Hall of Fame and bumped into Orioles' GM Roland Hemond, who told him to call if he was ever interested in giving it another try. Roland's phone rang this winter. Flanagan is a wonderful guy—great personality and (unusual for players) genuinely funny. On Toronto's retractable roof he once remarked: "I wish it had retractable fences." On teammate Mike Boddicker's fastball after Boddicker had just pitched a game in Toronto, Flanagan observed: "We had him throwing eighty-eight miles per hour on the radar gun, but with the Canadian exchange rate, it was only eighty-three."

So far Flanagan has been unhittable. He's the talk of the camp. Where are the TV crews now?

Early report card: McDonald has pitched well; so has Ballard (whose arm seems to be back to full strength). Milacki has been so-so, Mesa has been somewhat wild, and Mitchell has been nothing-special-but-reliable.

In the relief department, right-hander Gregg Olson is the closer extraordinaire. He has a great fastball and one of the best and most befuddling curves in the game. Otter, as he is known (he has the good fortune to look like one), recorded 37 saves last year, and during one stretch pitched 41 scoreless innings.

He experienced tendinitis the end of last season and his effectiveness fell off considerably. The Orioles are hoping to bring him along a little more judiciously this year.

There's a whole host of middle-relief hopefuls. You can't swing a dead cat in the clubhouse without hitting five. A personal favorite of mine is the "Hick-man," Kevin Hickey. He's thirty-five but a left-hander—teams will seek left-handers until they're in walkers. He's had a thirteen-year up-and-down career with the White Sox, Yankees, Phillies, White Sox again, Giants, and finally the Orioles. He too has a great sense of humor. Three years ago he was in Rochester and actually lived in the clubhouse at Silver Stadium. He said the conditions were lousy but it had this great big lawn out back.

Right-hander Todd Frohwirth is also a possibility. He's a sidearm specialist who signed on as a free agent after an undistinguished career in the Philly organization. Last year I saw him pitch for Scranton–Wilkes Barre and he was devastating. In fact, he finished the season tops in the league in saves. He has not been overly impressive here, but I tell anyone who asks to consider him seriously. Unfortunately for Todd, no one asks.

Big news in baseball: Bo Jackson was released by Kansas City. He suffered a hip injury playing for the L.A. Raiders in January, and the Royals think it's career-threatening. They save two million plus vigorish by cutting Bo adrift, and open the door for any other team to claim him on waivers for only one dollar (plus the little two million he'd be guaranteed). Rumor had it that the richer-than-God Yankees were going to bite, but even they backed off upon advice from medical specialists. Since no one claimed him by Friday noon, he's now a free agent and can negotiate any deal with any team who wants him. Excuse me, but it seems a no-brainer that if you spend your off-season carrying a football for the Los Angeles Raiders of the National Football League, you run a certain risk of getting hurt. Of course, I come from a religious faith that frowns on participation in any sport that requires physical contact and is popular in the South.

Other baseball news: another classic freak accident. Wade Boggs fell out of his Ford Explorer last night in Winter Haven and was run over by the driver . . . who just happened to be his wife. Apparently, she backed over his elbow, but he's okay.

How he fell out of the car while she was pulling away from a restaurant is still a mystery. Considering Boggs's escapades a couple of years ago with mistress Margot Adams, the jokes have been flying fast and furious.

Boggs seems to have a history of these bizarre occurrences. Several years ago in Toronto he hurt his ribs getting off a couch. He was putting on cowboy boots (so the story goes) and suffered the injury. There's also the incident in Florida a few years back when he was held up at knife point and claimed he got out of the jam by "willing himself invisible."

Do all ballplayers fool around? No. There are quite a few faithful husbands and fathers who just happen to play major league baseball. Do *some* fool around? Oh, yeahhhhh. These athletes have money, youth, looks, prestige. Sex is not something they have to seek—it comes to them like room service. And many partake despite the risk. I recently asked a ballplayer if he ever worried about contracting AIDS, and he said no, because he never slept with sluts. His "slam pieces" (his words) were always nice girls from good families.

There is a definite code among ballplayers with regard to discretion, and since I am now a member of their inner circle, I plan to honor that code.

There is one story, though, that I just have to tell. It's been sworn to me as true, and of all the sleaze stories I've heard, this is by far the best. Several years ago a couple of players were having what seemed like an orgy in a hotel room. After about an hour the moaning and wailing died down, and the person in the next room overheard the following:

PLAYER #1: "Hey, let's switch!"
PLAYER #2: "You can't do that. That's incest."
PLAYER #1: "No, it's not incest. She's my *wife's* sister."

Saturday, March 23, Baseball City, Florida

Today Jon and I took a three-hour drive to the center of the state, to some godforsaken town called Baseball City. It's near Haines City, if that helps. Baseball City is the spring home of the Kansas City Royals, and it's adjacent to an amusement park named Baseball and Boardwalk. Not a bad idea to have a baseball theme for an amusement park and then complement it with actual games. I can see where tourists might go for that. The only trouble is, there's another amusement park only thirty miles away—Disney World. Baseball and Boardwalk went belly-up last year. The ballpark itself is terrific: very modern, stadium club, etc. Unfortunately, there's no population in the area to fill it. The Royals do okay for their one month in the spring, but their Florida State League team draws more mosquitoes than people. Jon opened the broadcast today by saying, "Live, from the middle of nowhere, this is Orioles baseball!"

Jim Palmer was here televising another game back to Baltimore. He borrowed another scorecard from me.

Randy Milligan, new to left field, made his first error. I had my problems as well. Joe Brinkman, the home plate umpire, takes forever before making ball and strike calls. Normally, an ump will signal a strike with his right hand. If he doesn't signal, then it's a ball. But since you could go to the kitchen for a sandwich and return between the time the catcher receives the ball and Brinkman makes his ruling, I assumed on any number of occasions that a ball had been called when five seconds later up would go the right arm. Brinkman is a nice man and reputed to be one of the better umpires (he's even written a book on the subject), but today he drove me scooters. I must've sounded like an idiot all afternoon.

In the minors I got to know quite a few umpires. They proved to be the best source of player information in the league. Since there are no scouting reports or publications detailing the Indianapolis Indians or the Nashville Sounds, it was always a scramble preparing for the broadcasts. Some managers and coaches were helpful; others were not. And if you had to rely on your fellow announcers, you were sometimes in big trouble. A few were on the ball, but not all. I remember once going to Toledo and seeing a curious name on the Mud Hen roster. I approached their announcer and said, "Hey, you guys got Dwayne Murphy?"

"We do?" he asked. This announcer, by the way, was also the team's traveling secretary. He had to arrange for Murphy's transportation to Toledo and his accommodations.

"Yes," I continued, "Dwayne Murphy. Why is he here? Is he on a twenty-day rehab assignment?"

"Uh . . . yeah. That's it. He's on a rehab assignment."

"For what?"

"I'm not sure, but I can find out. Murphy, you say?"

Finally, he admitted that he had never heard of the longtime Oakland outfielder Dwayne Murphy, who at the time was playing for the Hens' parent club in Detroit. (This is the same announcer whose complete game notes for the media once consisted of: "The Hens have lost 7 of 8. . . . No hitting streaks . . . no injuries.")

Umpires, however, always knew what was going on. And since they had no stake in who won or lost or who did well and who did not, they brought a certain objectivity to their evaluation of talent that no other source could provide. Plenty of times a manager would feed me the organizational line on a player ("Oh, yeah, this kid's got a great arm. He needs just a little tweaking with his mechanics, but he's gonna be a gooder"), while an umpire's assessment was much more honest ("He's a pile of shit"). In these cases the umps always made the right call.

Surprisingly, very few broadcasters ever made the effort to seek out the umpires. As a result, the men in blue would bend over backward to be helpful, appreciative of the attention.

I'll be interested to see whether the quality of officiating on the big-league level is markedly different from the high minors. I suspect it won't be. There are so few openings at the big-league level that many talented individuals are left to languish in the bushes.

However . . .

There have been a few DOOOOOOZY calls over the last few years. I saw one in Columbus in '88 where the left fielder was charging in on a ball—it bounced on the AstroTurf surface right in front of him and caromed over the wall. A ground rule double, right? Nope. The home plate umpire (330 feet from the play) ruled it a home run. Most outfielders charge and reach down for home run balls. A local Columbus TV station happened to film the play and ran it over and over during the eleven o'clock news. Oooooops. My Dodger Stadium broadcast cohort, Steve Leon, tells of the time in the PCL when an outfielder leaped at the wall and took a home run away from a hitter, only to have the umpire, who was standing nearby, signal that it was a home run. The outfielder casually walked across the green and handed the ball to the embarrassed arbiter. "It's gone! . . . No, wait a minute . . ."

No discussion of Triple-A umpires can be complete without mentioning Junior Creech and Bullets Alexander. Why? I just love those names, that's all.

Segueing back to major league umpires for a second, they are currently working without a contract, and negotiations are continuing between their union and the owners. There may be a lockout on opening day. Gee, *that* would be unusual.

Sunday, March 24, Sarasota

Today, for the first time all spring, the Orioles had a semblance of an Opening Day lineup. Devereaux, Milligan, Cal, Davis, Evans, Horn, Gomez, Hoiles, and Billy were the starting nine. The result: Twenty-one-year-old right-hander Alex Fernandez pitched 4⅓ perfect innings en route to a 9–0 White Sox win. The Orioles managed three singles, two of them by reserve players—Juan Bell and Ernie Whitt.

Monday, March 25, Sarasota

We're not broadcasting again till Friday. I had a choice of games today—the Orioles and Pirates from miserable McKechnie Field in Bradenton, or Chicago vs. Boston in Sarasota. I opted for the Sox and the Sox. It was a lousy game and I didn't miss a thing at Bradenton . . . except a triple play.

Tuesday, March 26, Sarasota

My last day on this coast of Florida. I'm already starting to get listener mail; most of it I'd have to categorize, in all modesty, as nonhate. (You can tell without opening an envelope whether the letter will be positive or negative. Supportive letters will have return addresses attached, and nonsupportive missives will be anonymous, usually addressed to "that ignoramus Levine" or words to that effect.) There are a lot of people listening, and not just to major league broadcasts, I've learned.

Last year in Tidewater we hosted a Sunday night game with

Rochester while Columbus played a day affair in Richmond. Now understand that I *hate* the Columbus Clippers—me and just about everyone else in the International League. The Clippers are the Yankees' affiliate, and yes, they have a wonderful ballpark that draws big crowds, but the organization's attitude is so smug and condescending, you want to kill 'em and then sing their stupid, insipid fight songs at their funeral. They're doing us all a real big favor by agreeing to remain in the league. Anyway, it was about seven-thirty, I was on the air, and the Clippers were busing in from Richmond. I had a commercial plug to read live for the Days Inn at Military Circle, "host to the visiting teams of the I.L." I read the spot, then made note of the Clippers heading into town. I then said, Hey, you might want to welcome the Clippers to town. Why don't you give 'em a call tomorrow morning about five? I then added, no, no, I'm just kidding. Well, sure enough, the next morning at five their manager, coaches, trainers, and several players got Tidewater wake-up calls. Do you think they were a little pissed??? That night they beat our brains in. After the game our skipper, Steve Swisher, summoned me to his office and asked that I have my audience call *his* players the next morning.

They're out there. They're always out there.

I don't know why sometimes, but they are.

Wednesday, March 27, Vero Beach, Florida

Got up early, threw my stuff in the car, and headed out for Vero Beach at eight. The Orioles are breaking camp today. They'll play the Dodgers in Vero, then head down the East Coast to train in Fort Lauderdale for the remaining week of the Florida portion of spring training. Jon is staying back and will join me Friday night for our next broadcast. The three-and-a-half-hour drive across the state was very pleasant; a lot of back roads, however. I had this fear that my car would break down and I would be surrounded by the cast of *Deliverance*. The words "squeal like a pig" kept ringing through my ears.

Dodgertown in Vero Beach is the Taj Mahal of training facilities. Nothing else compares. State-of-the-art practice facilities, a golf course, great stadium, modern clubhouse and housing, and a buffet in the press lounge that puts the others to shame!

Shortly before game time I stuck my head in the Dodger

radio booth. I had met Vin Scully on a couple of previous occasions and hoped that he might remember me.

The man who, next to my father, is my idol, did.

He could not have been more cordial. After several minutes of chatting, I noticed an amazing thing: We started discussing our respective teams and their upcoming chances, and suddenly it hit me . . . Vin Scully was treating *me* as a peer. Talk about your great moments! I had thought that broadcasting my first inning of major league ball would be my rite of passage. I was wrong. *This* was it. Comparing Mike Sharperson and Craig Worthington with Vin Scully—I can die now.

I sat in on the entire broadcast, which was like watching Michelangelo do a little touch-up work on the ceiling. The day could not have been more memorable.

Thursday, March 28, Fort Lauderdale

The team is staying at the Marriott North, an okay hotel but no beach condo on Longboat Key.

Arm trouble in paradise: Ben McDonald felt a stiffness in his elbow while warming up before today's game in West Palm Beach. He was scratched immediately and will be examined by the team's orthopedist on Saturday. Early indications are that it's nothing serious. But they always say that.

Every manager will tell you the worst part of his job is making player cuts (number two is having to do the daily interview show with me). There is no easy way to tell some kid his lifelong dream will not be realized. Nor is it a breeze to let a veteran know it's time to finally hang 'em up and get a real job. All released players claim they weren't given enough playing time. All released players feel slighted. To differing degrees they accept and even understand their rejections, but still, in their heart of hearts, they feel they belong in the Bigs. Frank has had to make a number of cuts recently, with the tougher ones to follow. Most of the hot young prospects have been reassigned, but players with a real chance—like Worthington, Gomez, Whitt, Sheets, Flanagan, Mitchell, Hickey, Hulett, McKnight, and Bell—continue to sweat out each agonizing day.

The Orioles are the only club I know in which the manager is not the one to break the bad news to the players. Roland

Hemond, the general manager, handles that grim task. In truth, it *is* the GM's responsibility—he's the one with final say-so—but most prefer to delegate that assignment to their field generals. Roland Hemond continues to impress me as the class act of baseball.

Friday, March 29, Fort Lauderdale

This is the first night of Passover, a family occasion and my favorite Jewish holiday. I observed it alone in a drafty press box in Fort Lauderdale Stadium. On the air I wished everyone a happy Passover and hoped that they all find the "*afikomen*" (ceremonial piece of matzoh). I went on to observe that this must be the first time the word *afikomen* had ever been uttered on a major league baseball broadcast.

As for the game—uggghhh! We beat the Yankees, 7–6, but it took four hours to play nine innings. Baltimore pitchers walked eleven batters and hit a man, but incredibly, not one of them scored. By this point in the spring pitchers should have full command of their pitches and should have decent control. With the season only nine days away and Ben McDonald nursing a sore elbow, things are starting to look a little glum—although my feelings could be influenced by the fact that I'm in a holiday spirit.

Saturday, March 30, Miami

Six cities are vying for the privilege of shelling out $95 million apiece for one of two National League franchises. Expansion is due to take place in 1993, and the two winning entries could be announced as early as this June. The candidates are: Buffalo, Denver, Washington, D.C., Orlando, Tampa/St. Petersburg, and Miami. Depending upon whom you talk to, each one is a lock to get in except Buffalo.

Miami is making a big push this weekend by hosting the Orioles and the Yankees at Joe Robbie Stadium (home of the Dolphins). Wayne Huizenga, the magnate behind the hugely successful Blockbuster Video chain, is the organizer of the event and the man who hopes to write the $95 million check should Miami get the nod. The stadium has been reconstructed into a baseball configuration, dugouts have been built, and all is in readiness to show the Expansion Committee that South Florida is ready and deserving of big-league ball. The only other thing needed was fan support . . . and that they received.

A crowd of 67,654 showed up. It was the largest crowd ever to see a spring training game, the largest crowd to see any game played at a non–major league site, and the largest crowd to watch the Orioles play *any* game. (The previous high, stat nuts, was 67,064 at Veterans Stadium in Philly to catch an '83 World Series game. Unlike when I'm broadcasting, I don't just make these things up.)

The atmosphere was electric. Party time big-time. The players said it felt like the World Series, only better—no pressure and no earthquakes. What a great and historic game to broadcast . . .

. . . except that we didn't.

WBAL was contractually obligated to carry the NCAA Men's Basketball Semifinals. So instead of hearing the Orioles mash the Yankees, 9–2, listeners had to suffer through Duke upsetting UNLV in the single best basketball game of the year.

Sunday, March 31, Miami

We did broadcast today's affair, and for the first time I actually felt like I was announcing a major league game. Doing these spring training games is no different from minor league broadcasts except that the microphones are better and there's a lot more pressure. Otherwise, it's tiny booths, bandbox stadiums, unfamiliar players, and small crowds. But calling a game from Joe Robbie with 60,000-plus in the house, that's "the Show." It was such a kick, I didn't even mind the fact that we had to do the game from the football press box way up the first-base line, and that all fly balls appeared headed for left once they left the bat. Somehow I managed to take my cue from the fielders and describe the game accurately. Not once did I say, "There's a fly ball to center . . . foul."

By the way, the Orioles lost—but it's spring training, so who cares?

Monday–Wednesday, April 1–3, Fort Lauderdale

Axes are falling in Florida. Off with the heads of Larry Sheets, John Mitchell, Kevin Hickey, Jeff McKnight, and Luis Mercedes. McKnight and Mercedes were sent down to Rochester. I sought out McKnight to say good-bye, but he was nowhere to be found. That's customary, it seems. Once players are cut, they don't linger, they vaporize.

Ben McDonald rested his arm and I rested my voice. No broadcasts these first three days.

Thursday, April 4, Fort Lauderdale

Frank Robinson was on *The Cosby Show* tonight. He played Frank "Payday" Potter, a former major league ballplayer. I told him he wasn't convincing in the role.

We were supposed to play a day game with the Yankees here in Lauderdale. That would've worked out great, because immediately following the game we fly back to Baltimore—"taking the ball club north," as the old bromide goes. However, the fine folks at ESPN asked if the game could be pushed back to seven-thirty to allow them to televise it. Our estimated time of arrival in Baltimore is now three-thirty A.M.

At four-thirty we checked out of the Marriott and boarded the buses for the park in a driving rainstorm. That three-thirty ETA was in grave jeopardy.

Back when George Steinbrenner used to run the Yankees, there was rarely, if ever, a rainout in his Fort Lauderdale ballpark. He took in way too much gate to surrender to the forces of nature. It was not uncommon for him to hire two helicopters to hover over the stadium with giant blowers in an attempt to dry the soggy field. George himself had been seen on occasion down on the field with his pants legs rolled up to the knees, helping the grounds crew remove the tarp.

As luck would have it, the rain stopped an hour before game time, and although more showers were expected, we somehow got in the entire game. It's not whether you win or lose, it's whether you can make the airport by midnight.

Friday, April 5, Fort Lauderdale/Baltimore/Washington, D.C.

Major league travel—here's how it works . . . in theory. You summon the bellboy to your room, and he picks up your luggage. He leaves it down in the lobby with the rest of the team's. You bus to the ballpark, broadcast the game, get back on the bus, and zip to the airport. The bus deposits you on the tarmac right next to the plane. No terminals, no metal detectors, no Hare Krishnas. You board the chartered jet, get a seat in either first class or your own row, take right off, eat en route, land, board the awaiting buses on the tarmac, whisk off to the luxury hotel, where your room key is waiting for you in an envelope in the lobby, wander up to your spacious room, and in fifteen minutes let in the bellboy, who has your luggage. It's "Lifestyles of the Spoiled and Famous."

Believe it or not, the minors are not like that. And I spent three years in Triple A, which was a trillion percent improvement over the lower minors where you routinely made fifteen-hour bus rides through picturesque states like Texas and Arkansas, then played those nights. At least we got to fly, although air travel often presented worse problems than busing. The league demanded that we always take the first available flight. That made sense, considering USAir's on-time record has been compared to that of the Second Coming. SOP was to finish a game and get back to the hotel around midnight, only to have to report down at the lobby at five A.M. for the bus to the airport. Flights were usually around six-thirty, with obligatory stopovers at USAir's hub in Pittsburgh. It was not unusual on a travel day to see half the league milling about the Pittsburgh airport from seven-thirty to eight-thirty. Barring delays, you were usually at your destination, utterly exhausted, by eleven. That left several hours for a nap before that night's game, if—and it's a big if—the hotel had rooms available. Oftentimes it did not. Once I sat in the Des Moines Holiday Inn lobby for four hours waiting for a room.

And then, of course, there's the usual commercial airline obstacles—being bumped from flights, flight cancellations, and lost luggage. In August '88 a Syracuse at Maine game had to be canceled because USAir somehow lost *all* of the Maine Phillies' equipment en route from Philadelphia to Portland,

Maine. Now it's one thing to lose Aunt Phoebe's valise, but it's another to misplace sixty large heavy-equipment and bat bags that are bright burgundy in color and say PHILLIES on them. (Some idiot had unloaded them onto the tarmac and just left them. This is why you tip skycaps.)

With all these nostalgic memories still fresh in my mind, I was, needless to say, excited at the prospects of my initial big-league charter. Well, first off, the bus pulled up at the terminal, not the tarmac. Why? No one knows. That meant a stop at the metal detector, where, of course, I had to turn on my laptop computer to prove that it wasn't a bomb or a contorted terrorist. Once we were inside the plane, things improved. We were greeted by our own stewardess, Janice, who was the picture of cheerfulness in her Orioles jersey. Frank sat in the first row next to a giant platter of fruit, cheese, and crackers. There are unofficial seating arrangements on team planes. They are as follows: manager up front, followed by announcers, then coaches, and finally the players. I'm not sure how this pattern was established. I'm hoping it's by order of importance. (Team buses have their own seating orders. Two buses are always provided, one for players, the other for manager, coaches, media, others. The skipper always sits in the front row on the right. Announcers sit next to the faulty heating vents.)

Jon and I found ourselves in first class, right behind Frank. I buckled my seat belt and expected to just take off.

Wrong.

We sat on the ground for forty-five minutes. Finally, a baggage handler entered the plane and announced that there was too much luggage to fit into the lower storage section. Everyone had five weeks' worth plus dozens of golf bags—not to mention the hundred bat bags and trunks of team equipment. To get everything on, the baggage handlers began loading the overflow in the main cabin. We finally took off an hour after schedule.

The flight itself was fun. Not only was Janice a topflight stewardess, her assistant was even better: Frank Robinson went up and down the aisle all night handing out dinners and taking drink orders. Jon says he does this all the time, and from what I gather, he is unique in that regard. I don't know whether he does it to promote team camaraderie or just to pass the time, but I continue to be impressed. Anyone can be a Hall-of-Fame ballplayer, major league manager, and actor on *The Cosby Show,* but an excellent steward?—that takes a very special individual.

We landed in Baltimore at three-fifteen and were told it would take a while for our luggage to be loaded on the truck. We could pick it up at the ballpark in the morning. By the time I got to the Cross Keys Hotel (with only a change of clothes and a toothbrush), it was after four. The day ahead promised to be extremely hectic, but as long as I could get a good night's sleep, I knew I'd be fine.

Four hours later the phone rang. A local reporter with a couple of questions: Aren't I going to feel intimidated being in the booth during my very first year with two of the finest broadcasters in the country, both of whom have the world's greatest voices? And, How do I feel about replacing an announcer who had been here for three years and was very well liked? In other words: "How does it feel being inadequate *and* Deborah Norville?" So much for sleep.

Several months ago I was contacted by an executive relocation service, offering to help me find a place to rent in Baltimore. Bonnie Levitt and I have spent days on the phone ever since. My needs are very specific: My wife, Debby, has to like the place.

Three years ago in Syracuse I made a very bad mistake. Since Debby and the kids were not joining me until after the school year was completed, I selected the house on my own. Monumental error! Now granted, I had only two homes to choose from . . . and the one I picked had some very nice features . . . and there were three bedrooms, which was a must . . .

. . . but . . .

. . . it had no central air-conditioning (I was told I wouldn't need it), there were some plumbing problems, and all the furniture was on casters. *All* the furniture. The Syracuse University professor/spinster who owned the house, for reasons known only to her, had wheels attached to every stick of furniture. The plumber told me she requested casters on the sink, but of course he couldn't oblige because of those pesky things called pipes that are attached. In any event, Debby was not a happy camper.

This year we tried to avoid a repeat by having Bonnie Levitt scout possibilities beforehand, then having Debby pick the place when she and the family are in Baltimore for the opening of the season. Great plan! And things were in full gear too. Bonnie had a couple of candidates, even sent us snapshots of one (which looked very promising). Then, two weeks ago, I got a call. Bonnie. That very promising one was going to be shown to someone else. However, if I agreed to take it, I could have it. Otherwise, I faced the real possibility of losing it, and according to Bonnie, the other town houses under consideration were not as good (except for one bachelor pad that boasted an extensive porno tape collection with the titles listed in alphabetical order). I was now in an even *worse* situation than Syracuse. I proposed a compromise. I'd sign a two-month lease on the recommended place with an option for the remaining four. If Debby didn't like it, we could still look for something else, and I could live in a Maytag box for two months if I had to. The owner agreed and a deal was struck.

Bonnie picked me up at noon to take me to my new house. First, however, there were side trips to the stadium to pick up my luggage, and to the radio station to retrieve two large boxes of stuff I had UPSed from L.A. Plus, I had to get my rental car. A local company dropped off this Pontiac Grand Am with 18,000 miles on it, but then didn't want to rent it to me because it couldn't instantly verify my insurance. And this after I assured them I hadn't been in an accident in ten years *and* was willing to take their additional coverage. What finally convinced them that I was a good driver worthy of their well-worn automobile was the sight of my Avis "Wizard" card.

Wouldn't you know it, ten minutes later, on the rain-slick streets of Baltimore, I got into an accident.

I hit Bonnie.

She stopped quickly to avoid a motorist who cut in front of her, and I kissed the back bumper of her Volvo. Her car didn't have a scratch, but the Pontiac grille and hood buckled like an accordion. What better way to thank somebody for helping you relocate to a new city than to rear-end her!

We finally arrived at the town house about four.

Well . . . it's not Syracuse.

Split-level, central air, a pool in the complex, a den off the kitchen, a fenced-in patio off the den. So far, so good. But the furnishings and the decorating, HOLY SHIT! Black walls, bright, busy yellow-and-silver wallpaper in the kitchen (Peter

Max and the sixties live!), Buddhas, lamps in the shape of naked women, hundreds of pictures of the owner's dorky-looking daughter, and (believe it or not) a black velvet painting. (The photographs conveniently omitted these niceties.) I passed up one of the world's great porn collections for this?? Bonnie assured me that any or all of these fabulous furnishings could be removed. Other than the black velvet portrait, it's all gotta go.

Next up on my agenda was making the hour-and-a-half drive to Dulles Airport to pick up Debby and the kids. They arrived at 9:45.

It's amazing how the frustrations and exhaustion of a horrific day can disappear in a blink when you hear the word "Daddy!!!"

Saturday, April 6, Washington, D.C.

We're staying at the Grand Hyatt Hotel for the weekend while the club wraps up the spring with a two-game series against Boston at RFK Stadium. Matthew and Diana love the accommodations, and for good reason—the hotel provides ROOM SERVICE. To an eight-year-old and a four-year-old, this is cool beyond belief. Eating in your bedroom when you're not sick, WOW!

I happen to have two of the world's greatest kids. Now I know all parents say that (or at least *should* say that), but in this case it's true. It's due, I'm sure, to the fact that they have the world's most extraordinary mother. I like to think I'm an okay dad, but credit where credit is due, Debby has provided a loving and stable environment that already is paying enormous dividends. Both Matty and Diana are bright, creative, and most important, extremely happy children. The kids and I both got very lucky.

I took Matty on the Metro to RFK while "the girls" went to a dollhouse exhibition at the Smithsonian. Matty likes to go to every game, which is okay by me. He tags along on the field and in the clubhouse when I do my pregame preparation, and sits with me in the booth during the game keeping score (yes, at eight he can keep score . . . accurately).

The proud papa introduced him to all the players, and you

can imagine the look on his face as he shook hands with "the actual" Cal Ripken, Jr., and Dwight Evans. "Wow, Dad, it's really *them*!" All the guys were great to Matty, and he too was a charmer. "It's nice to meet you, Mr. Orsulak." "You're a real good pitcher, Mr. Olson," etc.

Frank Robinson was especially sweet, even shadowboxing with Matty. (And this is the man who is supposed to be such an ogre.)

The weather was incredible. Clear skies and temperatures in the eighties. RFK was transformed back into its baseball configuration for the first time in twenty years, and by all rights it should've been a sensational day. It wasn't. The folks in Washington staging this series—in the hopes, of course, of snaring a major league franchise—hired some private promoter to oversee the event. What a complete and utter blunder. Inspector Clouseau could've easily done a better job. Nothing was organized. Fifteen thousand prepaid ticket orders were left at will-call, and only three windows were open. *Three.* People waited in milelong lines up till the sixth inning to get their thirty-dollar tickets. There were near-riots.

As for our facilities, they were a joke. The baseball broadcast booths had long since been transformed into luxury boxes, so the promoter sold them. Only one was left, unreserved, for radio. Too bad there were two teams broadcasting. We had to share the booth with the Red Sox announcers, separated only by a flimsy two-foot riser. We could hear their broadcast as loud as we could hear our own, and vice versa. Jon's been broadcasting for twenty years and had never seen anything like it.

At least we had some fun with the situation. Jon reached his microphone over to Bob Starr, the Sox mouthpiece, and had him call every other pitch. You never know what or whom you'll get when you tune in to the Orioles radio network.

To many hardcore baseball fans, this is the best weekend of the year because this is the weekend of the annual ROTISSERIE LEAGUE DRAFT!!! David and I have shared a club in a league for the past six years. Our eight-team league—which consists of comedy writers, agents, and lawyers—is somewhat unique in that we play games head-to-head. A schedule is drawn up, lineups are exchanged, and based strictly on offense —one point for a single, two for a double, three for a triple, four for a home run, two for a run or RBI, and one for a stolen base—games are played on a daily basis. Each day's results are phoned in to the commissioner (Alan "Fay" Eisenstock), and after noon each day a message with last night's results and current standings is available on the commissioner's phone. The weekend before the season is the big player draft, and every two weeks there is a reentry draft lunch in which teams can drop up to two players of their twenty-man roster. You're right. This is a serious sickness. Actually, it takes only about ten minutes a day to run the team, but there is the obligatory half hour in front of the TV to watch *Sportscenter* each night, and no owner in good conscience would actually wait until the morning paper arrives; he has to be up and waiting for the paperboy. (One team member had to quit the league a couple of years ago because his wife threatened divorce, but that's only one.)

David and I have never finished higher than second. But our team at least has some character. We have created an entire scenario whereby our club plays in the worst ballpark in the league—"the Pit." The other teams dread having to come in and face us, and why not? Our conditions are the poorest, the facility is beyond run-down, and our fans are the meanest. Last year's promotions: "Ball Night," where we just took down the backstop screen; "Twenty-five-cent Beer Night," for fans ten and older; and in an unfortunate foul-up of scheduling, "Beer Night" and "Bat Night" and "Delinquent Youth Gang Night" were all on the same night. The riot was a long one, delaying play for more than an hour. Some contend that things still might not have gotten out of hand had we employed security personnel or even ushers, but I say "bitch, bitch, bitch." The fact of the matter is—when we owners are paying these ballplayers the exorbitant salaries they're getting today, we've got to scrimp somewhere.

David and I have been on the phone for hours making our lists and preparing for this weekend's big draft. I really hope we do well this year, because when I got the Orioles job, I told the other league members that I'd understand if they wanted me to resign since I have the unfair advantage of actually being with a major league team, privy to a lot of inside information. They just laughed.

Sunday, April 7, Washington, D.C./Baltimore

Following the final game of the spring (and the final loss of the spring) the Orioles announced their twenty-five-man Opening Day roster. It was a good day for long shots. Mike Flanagan, Ernie Whitt, and journeyman left-hand reliever Paul Kilgus all made the squad. Journeyman right-hand reliever Roy Smith did not. Last year's Opening Day starter, Bob Milacki, failed to make the cut. The Orioles, still concerned with his inconsistency this spring, want him to get in more work. They gave him a choice of AAA Rochester or AA Hagerstown, and he selected the latter because it allows him to commute. The Orioles hope to see him back in Baltimore by May. I suspect Milacki does too.

Gomez vs. Worthington. It ended in a dead heat. The team decided to keep them both. Worthington will be first-string due to his experience, but talk about hearing the sound of footsteps. Personally, I could not be happier for Leo Gomez. He worked so hard and played so well that the Orioles couldn't keep him off the club. Score one for the good guys. Of course, the question remains: Does the team need to carry a backup third baseman? (It's not even Opening Day; I'm already second-guessing.)

This brings up an interesting point: Just how far should an announcer go in criticizing his team? A number of factors come into play. How big are your ballplayers? Can they hurt you? Are you employed by the radio station or the team? Do you have integrity? Do you have the background or experience to support your criticism? Personally, I feel an announcer needs to establish his credibility if he's to be taken seriously, and to that end there are times he has to point out what he feels are mistakes. "What he feels" is the key. As long as the broadcaster can support his position and clearly conveys to the audience that what he's reporting is in *his* judgment, I believe occasional criticism is appropriate. The audience needs to know that you're not just some team carny. Besides, oftentimes viewers see the plays themselves and come to their own conclusions. If you alibi for an obvious mistake, you look like a bigger mullethead than the player. Plus, there are so many *other* ways in which I can make a fool of myself (bloopers, miscalls, etc.), I figure why make it worse?

Second-guessing the manager is another story, however. Rarely, if ever, will I consciously do that on the air. First off, I'm not privy to all the factors that go into his decisions. Second, that's not my job. I'm here to report; he's here to bring in the wrong pitcher. What I like to do is present the options and let the audience be the second-guessers. I'll say something like, "Okay, you be the manager. X, a left-hander, is warming up, but if you bring him in, then Y, a right-hand hitter, is available to pinch-hit. What do you do?" It's a way of skirting the second-guess issue and allows the audience a chance to participate.

You may even come across an example or two of this during the course of the book.

Returning to the roster, utility man Juan Bell also made the cut. He is out of minor league options, and if the O's send him down, another team can claim him on waivers. The Orioles don't want to let him get away, so he's here despite the fact that he figures to get in very little playing time. He and Gomez are the only two rookies to make the squad.

Jon Miller is very close friends with syndicated talk show host/author/columnist/sports anchor/banquet speaker/critic/Jewish person/radio star Larry King. He joined us on the broadcast today (so add "sportscaster" to the list) and welcomed me to the area. Larry thinks I sound like Dick Cavett on the air. I thanked him and asked if it was because of my voice or the fact that every day on the warm-up show I interview Groucho. Larry looked at me blankly. I explained that it was a joke; Dick Cavett used to interview Groucho Marx practically every week. Larry then nodded and laughed and I'm sure regretted that he paid me even the smallest of compliments.

The idiot game promoters lost the tickets I had left for Debby and Diana, so they were forced to buy ducats and fry in the hot sun way out in the center-field bleachers. Everything about this weekend series was handled poorly, and I hope the people in Washington (who do deserve a major league team) don't get the shaft as a result.

Hot and tired, we drove back to Baltimore, and Debby got her first look at the town house.

She didn't love it.

She didn't hate it (she hated Syracuse), but she didn't love it. She did like the neighborhood, the pool, the stationary furniture, and many of the amenities, but if we were buying instead of renting, she probably would've said, "Not if it meant world peace!" Just to make sure there is nothing better out there, we've arranged with Bonnie Levitt to go looking on Tuesday.

Spoke to David tonight. Our rotisserie team looks pretty good. Among our gladiators: José Canseco, Bobby Bonilla, Willie McGee, Benito Santiago, Tim Wallach, and Jody Reed. Opening Day promotion at the Pit this year: "Recycled Bottle Night"—all beer will be served in bottles so that those empties not thrown at the players can be recycled. Our motto this year: "The Pit—it's a hole 'nother ball game."

My *Current Affair* story aired tonight . . . fortunately, at twelve-fifteen A.M. What a riot. Mine was one segment of *A Current Affair Extra,* their hourlong waste of airtime. I was lumped in with some guy who kills little girls in church, people whose skin has fallen off while mowing the lawn (due to pesticides), and the latest fashion in underpants. I followed the murderer.

In the piece, I was referred to as "Hollywood Glamour Boy" Ken Levine. I was one of the top writers in show business, according to them (proving how inaccurate their sources are). They said I could be doing "this," and showed some wild, pulsating disco scene, then they said I could be spending time with "this," and featured two buxom beauties in string bikinis with the camera lingering on their bouncing breasts. But no, they continued, he's doing "this," and they featured me sitting in the cheesy broadcast booth in Port Charlotte calling a spring training game before a crowd of maybe two thousand uninterested senior citizens. Several *M*A*S*H* and *Cheers* clips were then haphazardly interwoven into an inane interview segment. Jon answered a question about whether I discuss Hollywood parties with him, and as he spoke, his name was superimposed on the screen, spelled incorrectly (John Miller). The only play-by-play they captured was, "Here's the pitch . . . low, ball two," and "There's a foul ball out of play." What happened to lumbering Sam Horn's two triples? The segment ended with me saying I can never get a good table at Spago.

Since the program aired in the middle of the night, I have to wonder how many groggy viewers got up the next morning and said to their wives, "Hey, did you hear about that Baltimore Orioles' announcer who killed all those kids in church?"

2

Monday, April 8, 1991, Baltimore

OPENING DAY!!!!

It was finally here.

I awoke to find the *Baltimore Morning Sun* had done a huge article on me. Front page, the feature section, with a giant close-up that literally took up a quarter of the page. (As my partner David said, "Boy, that'll make it hard for the cornflakes to go down.") The article itself—by Randi Henderson—was very complimentary. I couldn't've written a more glowing piece myself. Even with a little knock of my voice, I was pleased. "This is no stentorian baritone Mr. Levine brings to the booth," she writes, ". . . but what he may lack in tone quality, the new announcer certainly makes up in content, trading quick gibes with Mr. Miller, weaving anecdotes around at-bats, describing precisely and accurately each play as it unfolds."

A word about my voice. It's certainly not a radio classic (i.e., stentorian baritone), but it is pleasant and crisp, and it has not kept me out of major markets like Los Angeles, San Francisco, Detroit, and San Diego. There are even a few misguided people who actually *like* my voice. But I suppose when I'm on with Jon or Chuck—who have magnificent instruments—by contrast I must sound like one of the Chipmunks. Yet there's very little fear that dogs will go berserk or garage doors will open automatically when I get on the air, so my voice must be good enough. After all, it's gotten me all the way to the big leagues.

There's a certain comfort for a writer in being behind the scenes and working in relative anonymity. Rarely am I criticized or humiliated publicly. On the other hand, it can be mighty frustrating to see others receive credit and kudos for something my partner and I have actually done and are quite proud of. I can't tell you how many times some nimrod has approached me and said, "You used to write for *M*A*S*H*? Boy, that Alan Alda is a riot. How did he come up with all those funny lines?" The answer is: HE DIDN'T!!!!!! The writers did!!! Yes, he wrote a few episodes himself, but otherwise he was an actor—a superb actor, but still, someone who performed a script that someone else had written. I suppose deep down in the recesses of my soul and ego, I felt the need to step into the limelight myself. On the one hand, I'm enjoying it, but on the other, it is still verrrry scary. I'm not used to picking up the morning paper or tuning in a local radio talk show and hearing total strangers discuss me yea or nay. (At least the radio is free. It's bad enough to read some columnist question the tenor of my voice, it's another thing to have to pay thirty-five cents for the privilege.) So far, however, no dear listener has said that I've ruined his life due to my broadcasting style, so I really can't complain.

Opening Day in Baltimore is a citywide celebration. There is a love affair for this team that goes back almost forty years. It's the only game in town now that the Colts have defected, and the people of this region live and die by their cherished Orioles.

Had it snowed on Opening Day, there would still be 50,000 people jammed into Memorial Stadium. Today, however, it was 85 degrees under crystal blue skies. Paid attendance: 50,213.

The promotional phrase for this year is A SEASON TO REMEMBER. Much will be made of the fact that this is the final season the Orioles will play at Memorial Stadium. A new downtown ballpark is under construction, due to be ready next Opening Day. Memorial Stadium has served as the Orioles' home since their arrival from St. Louis (the former Browns) in 1954. Horseshoe in design and seating over 50,000, this brick-and-concrete structure is functional and adequate but certainly nothing special. The old gal's seen better days. There is one feature of Memorial Stadium that I do truly love, however—it's in a neighborhood. The address is on Thirty-third Street. The center-field backdrop is trees that reflect the coming and going of the seasons and row houses unique to the city of Baltimore. People watch the games from their windows. The team is loved by the community because it's part of the community.

My first stop was the broadcast booth. Words cannot describe what it felt like, sitting behind that microphone high above home plate, surveying the world from my lofty perch.

The dream had actually come true.

Bonnie and her husband had arranged to give Debby and the kids a ride to the park at a decent hour. I left for the stadium four hours before game time. I figured I might need a little extra time to fill out my score sheet.

Every camera crew in town was down on the field for BP. If there was a bus plunge today in Baltimore, there would be no "film at eleven." As if there weren't enough confusion, hundreds of Secret Service men and attack dogs were patrolling the ballpark. Vice President Quayle was throwing out the first ball. (All the *good* "Operation Desert Shield" heroes had been taken.)

Jon was not my broadcasting partner today. He's calling the game for WMAR-TV, Channel 2, so Chuck Thompson was by my side. If Miller is respected and appreciated in Baltimore, Thompson is revered. In 1955 Chuck began a twenty-four-year association with the Orioles. He was also the voice of the Baltimore Colts throughout all their glory years. Over CBS-TV he called the classic 1958 NFL Overtime Title Game between the Colts and the Giants. He's announced five World Series on national radio and television, including the memorable final game of the 1960 Series when Bill Mazeroski hit the dramatic ninth-inning home run to give the Pirates the championship over the Yankees.

Chuck has a unique style that can best be described as "elegant": "For Mr. Ballard to give up a run right now would be most inopportune." "Nolan Ryan will be facing the right-handed swings of Mr. Cal Ripken." "Today we are in Texas, deep in the heart of." His voice is deep and rich, and words just seem to flow from his mouth like honey.

Off the air he is the consummate professional and the ultimate gentleman. Within two years I suspect he will be in the Hall of Fame, an honor richly deserved.

We hit the air at 1:05, and you know something—I wasn't nervous. No, really. In Sarasota I was a wreck, but here before this capacity crowd and hundreds of thousands of listeners, I was for some reason the picture of calm. There are times in your life, I suppose, when you just step into the moment and seize it, and for me this was one of those moments . . . actually, it was the first. The anxieties of the spring melted away, and what I was left with was the pure joy and exhilaration of doing the single thing I had wanted to do since that night I sat with my father listening to Vin Something.

As if my very first inning of play-by-play (the third) were not memorable enough, I had a color man—the vice president of the United States. Dan Quayle had come into the booth, and I was asked to interview him between pitches. Quite honestly, I didn't have a clue as to what to ask him. I know what I *wanted* to ask him: "When you traveled to Latin America recently, how come your wife wouldn't let you buy that figurine with the large penis? And just how large was that penis? Oriole fans want to know." Instead, we chatted about the first pitch he threw and other banalities. Finally, I said: "When you and the president are meeting late at night in one of those high-level confabs, and you're discussing the state of the economy and foreign affairs, do you ever just stop and say, 'Hey, what do you think the Orioles' chances are this year'?" He answered that the president was indeed a baseball fan. It was riveting stuff. I will say this, he was a good sport and has a voice worse than mine.

After a stint in our booth, the VP went next door to where Jon Miller and Jim Palmer were calling the game for Channel 2. Randy Milligan caught a ball in left that the veep said was a routine play, and Palmer actually corrected him, explaining how Milligan was new to the position. Protocol dictates that you can not publicly contradict the vice president of the United States unless you are the president of the United States or Jim Palmer, so his comment was within the boundaries of acceptability. (He probably could've asked the phallic figurine questions as well.)

The game went much better for me than for the Orioles. After Baltimore jumped ahead with a run in the first on a two-out single by Cal and a double to left by Davis, the White Sox scored three in the second, five in the sixth, and another in the ninth to breeze to a 9–1 win. Mo Siegel, a venerable Washington reporter, strolled into the TV booth around the ninth inning and said to Jim Palmer, "You couldn't make *this* club?"

Jeff Ballard, starting for Ben McDonald (who's on the DL with that tender elbow), was shaky early but settled down and retired thirteen straight at one stretch. If only he hadn't given up those gosh-darned six runs.

The singularly genuine bright spot of the afternoon was former Cy Young winner Mike Flanagan, pitching a perfect inning in relief. Before the game, when the players were introduced, Flanagan, the returning Oriole, received by far the largest ovation; 50,000 people on their feet cheering wildly. And then to see him have a perfect day on the hill, it was right out of Hollywood.

After the game I took the family down to the Inner Harbor for dinner. This whole section of town has been renovated and is now smashing. The city of Baltimore stands as a shining example of what can be accomplished in urban renewal with a mayor and city government committed to progress and vision.

Sitting on a bench with Debby, watching the kids laugh and play on a giant anchor suitable for climbing, for me it was the perfect close to the perfect Opening Day.

Tuesday, April 9, Baltimore

Bonnie showed us some alternative town houses. The one we have is looking better and better. We decided, at least for now, to stay put. I'm sure that when all the furnishings are removed (and burned), the place'll be just fine.

This quiet day with the family was the ideal complement to the excitement of the day before.

Wednesday, April 10, Baltimore

I had been warned about Phil Jackman. Phil Jackman is a failed local sportscaster who, after being dismissed from several stations in town, landed on his feet at the *Evening Sun* as its radio-TV sports reviewer. (Those who can't tell others they can't either.) From what everybody tells me—and that includes his *colleagues*–he's a little sniper who uses his forum to take shots at everyone and everything. The only consolation, I'm told, is that nobody takes him seriously. His "TV Repairman" weekly column is considered very much a joke in the press box. In fact, there's a certain status that comes from being one of his targets.

Well, today I got my first review. He was relatively kind but said certain things that made me wonder if he was even listening to the same broadcast.

First off, he spent half the article trashing Palmer. He then took shots at Jeff Rimer, who handles the Orioles' postgame talk show on WBAL, and at Larry King for just being there. As for me: "Not to worry what was happening over on Miller's old stomping grounds, WBAL Radio. Chuck Thompson and newcomer Ken Levine had a fine-fine day, as Chuck would say." Later, he added: "Thompson and Levine worked like a slick double-play combination, although the new kid on the block overdid his first major-league game broadcast to a fare-theewell. Be blasé, fella." Here's an example he gave of how I overdid it: "Chuck wondered about Tim Raines changing his first name to Rock. 'I picked up the nickname Rock as a kid because of my intellect,' said Levine." (Huh????)

When I got to the ballpark, everyone was razzing me on my "rave" review. "What'd you do—buy him dinner, option one of his scripts, get him a hooker?"

I have every confidence that by the end of the season Phil Jackman will hate me.

Matty came along tonight, which made the game more fun. Some of the players already know him (more than know me, so Matty should feel very honored).

Tonight we squandered a good pitching performance by José Mesa and lost to the White Sox, 2–0. The only thing I remember about the game is that the wind came straight into our booth and it was so cold that by the fifth inning I could no longer hold a pencil. Meanwhile, Matty sat in the back row with Dr. Paul next to the heater. By the fifth inning *he* was eating ice cream.

One other member of our broadcast team should be mentioned—Hank Thiel. During all home games, Hank keeps the "Esskay [hot dogs] Hand-Operated Fenway Park/Wrigley Field –Style Out-of-Town Scoreboard" (as Jon calls it). He watches the ticker tape and marks down the scores. On many busy days Hank has the toughest job in the booth.

Thursday, April 11, Baltimore/Arlington, Texas

Debby and the kids went home today. It was tougher saying good-bye now than before at LAX. I'll be in California in three weeks, but today that seems like three months. They're flying out of Dulles and I'm flying into Dallas. I'd arranged for a limo to take them to the airport, and the kids were thrilled. They have this fascination with limousines. Two hours after they had left, I received a call from the limo company saying the car had arrived on schedule. The company also apologized for not having a color TV in the back and a fully stocked bar, as my son had requested.

By the way, I'm the new spokesman for Acura West in Ellicott City. If you're lookin' for an Acura, go see Jerry Maizlish and the wacky gang at Acura West and they'll take care of you, I guarantee it. WBAL worked out a deal for me to do Acura's radio commercials in exchange for use of a car. I, of course, would've been thrilled to pitch any car (scruples are never a problem with me), but as luck would have it, I own an Acura and really do love it. Now if I can only find a town-house developer who needs a carny . . .

Our United Airlines charter to Dallas left at midnight. (The club saves money if we fly after ten.) The flight was quite bumpy, as we encountered violent thunderstorms. One of "Levine's Laws" is that turbulence will always begin just as you're being served food. I hope the dry cleaners can do something about this teriyaki stain. (Of course, it's my fault for ordering anything teriyaki on a plane flight.)

We landed an hour late and there were no buses. They were confused as to where to meet us. (Dallas, Texas, or Dallas, New Jersey?) They arrived forty-five minutes late. We got to the hotel at four. Our luggage, we were told, would arrive by five . . . if we're lucky. This major league travel is like glass, isn't it?

Friday, April 12, Arlington, Texas

I suppose we're near Dallas. That's what they tell me. But the Sheraton Centre Hotel is in the middle of nowhere, flanked only by Arlington Stadium, which is directly adjacent, and Six Flags Over Texas, a nearby amusement park. Oh yes, there are a couple of restaurants across the parking lot from the ballpark. We might as well be in Oklahoma City or the Sudan.

But the location is great because of one of those restaurants —the Atchafalaya River Café. Sensational Cajun cuisine! I recommend the grilled shrimp Thibodeaux, crawfish étouffée, redfish Pontchartrain, cochon de leaux, and of course the red beans and andouille poopeaux. It's some of the best unpronounceable food I've ever eaten.

The Orioles will not start this year 0–21. They beat the Rangers, 3–0, thanks in large part to a strong pitching performance by Baltimore native Dave Johnson.

Arlington Stadium is not very impressive. It's a converted minor league park with additional seating jammed into any open space. It's the world's largest Lego blocks project.

We were very fortunate to get the game in tonight. Thunderstorms were predicted, and all night long we could see gigantic bolts of lightning ripping through the prairie in the distance, but no rain pelted the area. On the air I referred to the light show and commented how glad I was to be watching it from a little booth filled with electronic equipment.

Saturday, April 13, Arlington

It rained all morning, but by the time I got out of the Atchafalaya River Café around two, the weather began to improve. I think the temperature got much warmer too, but that could just be the chicken tchoupitoulas.

Jeff Ballard made his second start, and the Orioles got him five quick runs in the first two innings, highlighted by Cal's single and triple and three RBIs. Ballard had trouble holding the lead but still won, 11–4. Cal Ripken, Jr., had another career night. In addition to the single and triple, he hit two home runs and finished the evening driving in seven runs, a personal best. Cal is a very reserved, private individual. He's the ultimate competitor who goes about his work in a quiet, methodical manner. Rarely will you see a display of emotion from Cal, but tonight, when I told him he had been selected our "Loyola Federal Peak Performer of the Game," I thought he was going to burst.

One advantage to covering a team on a daily basis is that the ballplayers always see you around and eventually get comfortable in your presence. You're not just one of the dreaded "media." Even Cal, who is extremely shy, now says hello and will even exchange a little small talk on occasion. Once players sense that you're not just after them for a quote or a story, they usually loosen up and become quite friendly. My latest breakthrough has been Dwight Evans. I strolled into the clubhouse today with my tape recorder, looking for a helpless victim—I mean "pregame guest"—and sat down next to Dewey. Just spotting the tape recorder, he was, I could see, a little reticent. I mentioned as an ice breaker that he and I grew up in neighboring suburbs in the San Fernando Valley. At the time, I worked after school in a record store that featured listening booths where customers could preview albums. I told him I had probably thrown him out of the listening booths on several occasions. We hit it off immediately. Within a half hour we were chatting about everything under the sun. When it was finally time to go out to the field, *he* asked *me* if I wanted to interview him. I said no. He shook my hand and smiled. I was one of the good guys.

Besides, Bobby Valentine had already agreed to today's interview.

Sunday, April 14, Arlington/Milwaukee

This was a game the Orioles should've won. Facing Nolan Ryan in the first inning, Sam Horn—who was 0 for 6 for the season, all on strikeouts—crushed the first pitch into the right-field bleachers for a three-run home run. When you're leading 3–0 against Nolan Ryan, you can't let him off the hook. The Orioles did. Final score: 15–3. Jeff Robinson couldn't get out of the third inning. Reliever J. J. Bautista was worse. He gave up eight runs and nine hits in two innings.

It's our second blowout in the first week. Meanwhile, Toronto is off to a great start in the A.L. East, and Boston is doing so-so.

When the Orioles traded Mickey Tettleton to Detroit for Jeff Robinson over the winter, the talk show mob was not pleased. Tettleton was a very popular player in Baltimore, one of the keys to the Birds' miracle '89 season. (Remember the big how-do-you-do over Fruit Loops when Tettleton revealed that's what he ate for breakfast?) Whereas the Mick has a very engaging, outgoing personality, Robinson is more in the Jack Morris mold—quiet, brooding, fiercely competitive. He's also brutally honest—even about himself—which is most refreshing. "I couldn't get my forkball over for strikes and I pitched like shit" was his explanation for today's performance. It might take the fans some time to warm up to Robinson, but I hope they do. And I hope he gets his forkball over for strikes.

Our flight to Milwaukee was one of the worst I've ever experienced. Another storm cell. It was so bumpy that even the macho ballplayers were yelling "Whoaa!!!" with every five-foot swoop.

We arrived at the Pfister Hotel at about ten. The Pfister appears to be pfirst class. It's an old regal downtown hotel that's been recently renovated. I unpacked and caught the last two innings of Jon calling the ESPN Sunday night *Game of the Week* from Oakland. He'll be catching a red-eye to Chicago, where a car will drive him here to the hotel. He should arrive around eight. Our game with the Brewers begins at one.

Monday, April 15, Milwaukee

Well, at least it's not raining. Today is the Brewers' home opener, and sunshine is expected . . . along with a high temperature of 55. Please understand that I'm from California, and to me, if you're outside in 55-degree weather for an hour, you should come down with trenchfoot. I was sooooooooooooo cold. But to the people in Milwaukee (or "cheeseheads," as they will proudly answer to), this was summer.

County Stadium. It's forty years old, it's generic, it says "baseball." A large factory with an ominous smokestack serves as the backdrop, and you really get the feeling that this is America. No glitzy luxury boxes here. Don't expect to see Dyan Cannon. This is a yard for "the folks."

Aside: I hate seeing celebrities at sporting events. Now I don't mind those celebs who really *are* fans and go to the games because they love the games (Jack Nicholson is at the Great Western Forum even when the Lakers are playing Sacramento, Bill Murray and George Wendt get out to the park whenever they're in Chicago, and Cary Grant used to be a fixture at Dodger Stadium every night, just to name a few), but the ones that grind my guts to garters are the stars who show up only for the in-groovy "events"—play-off games, Super Bowls, Laker championship series. They're there not to see the games, but to be *seen* at the games. Like Jane Fonda is suddenly a big Atlanta Braves fan. Riiiight!! (Now that that's off my chest, I feel better.)

County Stadium has something that no other ballpark in the land can match—the world's greatest bratwursts. That comes as no surprise, certainly, this is Germantown, but they're even better than expected. One bite and you can actually feel an artery clog up, but it's so good you finish it anyway. The record for most bratwursts consumed here in one day is seventeen by a gentleman from California. From what I understand, he's buried somewhere down the left-field line. The condiments for these brats consist of the usual mustard-onion-relish fare along with sauerkraut and something they call "Secret Stadium Sauce." Nobody will divulge just what is in this thick red secret sauce, but it was allegedly invented during an early experiment of the Manhattan Project.

The other distinctive feature of County Stadium is the tailgate parties. Folks here jam the parking lots long before game time and crack out the barbecues and coolers, filling the air with heavenly aromas and grease. If you love block parties with total strangers whose only common bond is the search for any excuse to celebrate and the mass consumption of life-endangering substances, you've gotta love Milwaukee. I, of course, do.

One thing I've discovered about Milwaukee—it's in a time warp. The buildings, the cars, the people—it's 1956. Tonight's postgame concert features newcomers Buddy Holly and the Crickets.

Before every series with a new team, I try to go down to the locker room and introduce myself around. The responses range from "Hey, nice to meet you. Can you say hello to my aunt in Annapolis?" to "Who the fuck cares, man?" Two of the Brewers' pitchers, Kevin Brown and Julio Machado, used to be with me in Tidewater. It was nice reuniting in the major leagues. Machado, by the way, is known as the Iguana Man because he actually eats those savory little lizards. I asked if he ever put "Secret Stadium Sauce" on them, and he said no but it sounded interesting. He and I will not be dining together. Two other Brewer players, Rick Dempsey and Robin Yount, grew up with me in Woodland Hills, California. (I threw them out of listening booths too.) Actually, I was good friends with Robin's brother Larry, and on any number of occasions I would hang out at Larry's house after school, and there would be his dorky little brother. Robin probably pays more in taxes now than I make in a year.

Today, before a crowd of 50,000, the Orioles were the home opener spoilers. Glenn Davis hit his first American League home run, and Cal contributed a two-run shot. (A Glenn Davis home run is a work of art. Two seconds after the ball leaves the bat, it leaves the park, a missile still rising as it clears the fence. No towering fly, no monstrous blast, just a trolley line from home plate into the upper deck. It's as unique as a signature.) In the eighth, with the Orioles leading 3–1, Sam Horn was due to bat with two outs and the bases loaded. Milwaukee manager Tom Treblehorn had a left-hander and a right-hander warming up. He went out to the mound just before Sam approached the plate. Sam had gone 0 for 3 with two strikeouts against starter Chris Bosio. In fact, the only hit Sam had all year was that home run yesterday against Ryan. Everyone expected Treblehorn to bring in the lefty, which would have forced Frank's hand to pinch-hit for the left-hand hitter Horn. Instead, Treblehorn summoned the right-hander, Edwin Nuñez. He *wanted* Horn to bat. Not much respect for the big guy. With the count 1–1 Horn got ahold of a fastball and hit it a mile. A grand slam. The Orioles ran away with it, 7–2. The O's are back at .500. Horn, meanwhile, has two hits and seven RBIs—talk about the most with the least.

Jon was wide awake and wired for the game despite his lack of sleep. The minute the game was over, however, he crashed and burned. How he keeps this schedule all season long I will never know.

Dr. Paul Eicholtz—our spark chaser—and I had dinner at Sally's. Pretty good steaks, but why are their Christmas decorations still up in April?

By the way, you might be wondering—Dr. Paul is a doctor of what? Answer: nothing. The "Doctor" is completely fabricated. Jon thought it gave him a little distinction and pizzazz. There are several Dr. Paul running bits in the broadcast. My favorite is that he is a CIA operative always feeding information on the road to shady characters in out-of-the-way rendezvous. We don't have a broadcast team so much as a cast of characters.

Tuesday, April 16, Milwaukee

During the season there are precious few days off. How fortunate that we have one here in Milwaukee. Jon and I walked to the mall. I then wandered into the "Adlai Stevenson for President" campaign headquarters—1956, what a year!

I remember a friend of mine once had a day off in St. Louis in the middle of a sweltering summer. He was so bored he hand-washed his rental car.

I did have a great dinner. Another friend of mine has a brother who lives in Milwaukee. Jim Neubauer and his wife, Elizabeth, took me to a great steak joint called the Five O'clock Club. Boy, I never would've found *this* place. It's in the worst section of town and from the outside looks like a redneck bar after a big brawl. A guard stands watch of the cars. Inside, it's warm, homey, and perfect except for the Christmas lights. (What is it with this town?)

Our rotisserie team is off to a start much like the Orioles'. And attendance is down at the Pit despite "No Weapons Check-in Night."

Wednesday, April 17, Milwaukee

Tonight's game with the Brewers began at six. Last night we had 50,000; this evening, 8,053.

I bought long underwear today for the first time in my life, and I am glad I did. Whoa, was it frosty!! Temps in the low forties or high thirties. My longjohn purchase turned into tonight's routine on the broadcast. I reminded the audience that I was from California and had never bought them before. Perhaps the salesman took advantage of me.

"They *are* a hundred and fifty dollars a pair, aren't they?" I asked Jon.

He said, "For you, yes." Jon then said he heard that I got the kind with the pink bunnies. I assured him that rumor was false. Jon continued, "I dunno. That's what the ballplayers say. And they wanna see. Maybe tonight on the team bus."

Our broadcast tonight was picked up by Armed Forces Radio and was beamed around the globe. You talk about a thrill—there is still something magic about radio, to think that I can talk into a microphone and be heard literally throughout the world. Imagine how much *more* impact it would have if I actually had something to say.

Dave Johnson was not sharp tonight, and the Brewers hammered out a 7–3 win. Gary Sheffield was the big star with a double and a home run. Dwight Evans drove in all three runs for the Birds.

Thursday, April 18, Milwaukee/Baltimore

The Orioles let another 3–0 lead get away, and this time lost in eleven innings, 4–3. Glenn Davis made three errors at first and he's lucky it wasn't four. His bad toss to Billy Ripken in the ninth cost Billy an error that could've easily gone the other way. To Davis's credit, he took a lot of razzing from the crowd throughout the chilly afternoon and finally acknowledged them with a doff of the cap as he entered the dugout following the ninth inning.

Since this is getaway day, naturally we went into extra innings. Mike Flanagan shut 'em down in the tenth, but in the eleventh with one out and right-handers Paul Molitor and Robin Yount due up, Frank elected to play the percentages and go with the righty Bautista. I turned to Jon during the commercial break and said, "We're just five minutes away from the postgame show." Bautista was coming off the eight runs in two innings performance against Texas. The first batter, Molitor, blasted a deep drive to left center. Joe Orsulak made the catch while slamming into the wall. Robin Yount then followed with a 400-foot home run to left center, and that was that.

As for me, I called a third-inning Robin Yount home run. Too bad it was a double. The ball hit the top of the fence and bounced straight up into the air. I thought it was headed over the wall, but it wasn't. It came back onto the field and was still in play. "It's gone! . . . No, wait a minute . . . " Jon assured me that this happens to everyone, but I can't help thinking that in the back of his mind he's saying to himself, "What the fuck was this guy thinkin'?" My greatest fear in this job is mistakes (well, *that* and being trapped in a small room with any team mascot). I know I'm going to make them, I'm relatively inexperienced, only human, etc., but the thought that I will be embarrassing myself from time to time is a terrifying one. Depending upon the night, I go from thinking I'm the oyster's ice skates to wondering if I'm a gigantic fraud. Tonight I'm leaning toward the latter.

The flight home was very quiet.

It wasn't a super day for the Chicago White Sox either, although it was supposed to be. Today was the christening of their new Comiskey Park. The Detroit Tigers thrashed them, 16–0.

Friday, April 19, Baltimore

I got to Memorial Stadium determined to just forget about the Robin Yount blown call. Jon was waiting for me with a new pair of binoculars. Hey, thanks oodles, partner.

At least *I'm* back for another day. Ben McDonald was activated today, and you'll never guess who was released to make room. I'll give you a hint: J. J. Bautista.

Every week on ESPN they air a half-hour show called *Major League Baseball Magazine* with Warner Fusselle. Three or four baseball-related features are assembled for each half hour. Well, they're doing a segment on me scheduled to air early next month, so today a camera crew was dispatched to capture me in action. (Thank God it wasn't on hand yesterday.) As luck would have it, I did one of my better games so far and had a decent Glenn Davis home run call. I also did a pretty nifty job of describing Randy Milligan taking a pitch low for a ball, should they wish to use that instead (à la *Current Affair*).

The homer by Davis couldn't've come at a better time for him. Just moments before he stepped to the plate, we received word that the Milwaukee official scorer had changed a ruling on yesterday's game and took the ninth-inning error away from Billy and charged it to Glenn, who thereby ties an American League record of four in one game.

The Orioles beat the Rangers 5–0, and the best news was that Jeff Robinson finally got his forkball over for strikes. He hurled seven shutout innings, scattering just four singles. Over 21,000 spartan people showed up in 51-degree weather to see it. If this were L.A., the paid attendance would not be as high as that temperature.

Saturday, April 20, Baltimore

The Orioles rarely play a Saturday day game. This year they're sprinkling in a few on an experimental basis. A good gathering showed despite the cold weather and promise of rain. Jon feels that's because Nolan Ryan is pitching for the Rangers, but I contend it's because this is "Tony the Tiger Cereal Bowl Day," with all kids fourteen and under receiving a cereal bowl in the shape of an Orioles' helmet, filled with a little box of Kellogg's Frosted Flakes.

Ryan was masterful. He went 7⅓ scoreless innings, allowed four hits, while striking out ten. Mesa, for his part, was almost equally effective. In seven innings he too just gave up four hits, but, unfortunately, one very cheap run. Gary Pettis singled in the fifth, stole second, went to third on a scratch base hit by Geno Petralli, and scored on a sacrifice fly by Rafael Palmeiro. And that would be the only run of the ball game. Texas 1, Baltimore 0. This was a lot harder to swallow than the 15–3 drubbing against Ryan a week ago.

A.L. East report: Toronto is coming back down to earth, and Boston, spearheaded by Roger Clemens, is beginning to make its move. The O's are now 4–6. Detroit beat the White Sox again. The "Palehose" are still winless in their shiny new digs.

I spent my rare Saturday night off at the Loew's Valley Center, or as comedian Jay Leno would call it, "the bunker at the end of the mall." Albert Brooks's *Defending Your Life* was very funny. I always enjoy watching another neurotic Jew.

Sunday, April 21, Baltimore

It rained all last night. It rained all this morning. Rain was predicted for all afternoon. Chuck and I went on the air with *Orioles Talk* and literally treaded water for an hour and a half before the game was finally called. (Jon's in Montreal tonight for ESPN.) Doing a talk show is far more draining than calling play-by-play, and much more unpredictable. Some guy called and wanted to know when this game would be made up if postponed. I told him the Rangers return to Baltimore on August 13 through 15, so a doubleheader would be scheduled for one of those dates; in all likelihood the first. He then asked if Nolan Ryan was going to pitch in one of those games. I said, "Yes, he's scheduled to start on the fourteenth." The caller then replied that that's the night he'd like to come.

Monday, April 22, Baltimore/Chicago

Our United charter touched down in Chicago at noon. There were no buses. They got confused and went to the wrong cargo area. In my four years of covering baseball I have come upon one universal truth: Bus drivers will not ask directions. They'll drive around lost and befuddled for eternity (with you in the back, of course) before they'll stop and actually ask someone where the hell they are. Two years ago in Pawtucket our bussy literally couldn't find his way out of the stadium parking lot.

When they finally did arrive (forty minutes late), we headed for town and encountered bumper-to-bumper traffic all the way in. It took longer to get to our hotel from the airport than it did to fly from Baltimore to Chicago.

All clubs stay at the Westin. It's in an ideal location, right across the street from the Hancock Tower on Michigan Avenue. The hotel itself is very large and commercial. We were the only thirty-five guests who weren't there for the Pastry Chefs' Convention or the Embalmers' Seminar.

The lobby was teeming with autograph hounds. A note about seeking autographs: Most players will be happy to give them IF YOU SHOW SOME CONSIDERATION. Let me repeat: SHOW CONSIDERATION. Don't disturb a player while he's eating in the coffee shop, or renting a car, or (and I've seen this happen) when he's standing at the urinal taking a whiz. (*That* idiot did get the player's autograph, and eventually his pant leg dried.) If the player is free, approach him and politely say something along the lines of: "Excuse me, Mr. Ripken, could I please trouble you for your autograph?" Knowing who the player is is a big help. Don't do this: "Excuse me, are you somebody? Can I have your autograph?" or "Do you play?" Never *demand* a signature—"Hey, sign this!" rarely works. Neither does: "Listen, buddy, I help pay your salary!" If a player does consent to give you his autograph, give him a pen and ONE item to sign. Don't stick fifteen baseball cards in his face. It's a sad state of affairs, but players are somewhat leery of kids asking for autographs. Oftentimes adult card dealers will draft neighborhood youngsters to get autographs. These dealers will give the kids a couple of bucks, then turn around and sell the autographs for a considerable profit. Players, understandably, don't like being ripped off. These baseball-card sharks are making large sums of money off their signatures while they receive nothing. (I recently said to Frank Robinson, "When you go out to dinner and pay for it with a credit card, do you realize that your signature on the charge slip is worth more than the cost of the charge?") Ballplayers understand that to most fans autographs aren't just salable commodities; they're mementos to be saved and cherished. I'd venture to say that many major leaguers themselves have autograph and baseball-card collections they've been keeping since they were kids. So again, if you want a player's autograph, show him some respect and consideration . . . and don't tell him I sent ya.

The Orioles had the distinction of playing the first-ever night game at the new Comiskey. As for my impressions of the new stadium: clean, modern, functional, impersonal. There's very little sense of character or ambience. In center field you gaze out at huge scoreboards, billboards, and white steel latticeworks. It looks like a roller coaster or a gigantic Erector Set. The upper deck is steep to the point of vertigo. I went up there once. Never again.

But all in all, Comiskey is extremely comfortable and an enormous improvement over the old ballpark, which is being demolished across the street.

My sign-on tonight: "For eighty years the Chicago White Sox have played at Comiskey Park. Recently, people have complained that the park is old, run-down, falling apart. Well, this is my first time here, but just looking around, I don't understand what their problem is. This place looks great to me. Brand-new."

Big Ben McDonald made his first start tonight and was anything but sharp. He squandered an early 2–0 lead (on Glenn Davis's first-inning "stream of milk" over the left-field fence) and was yanked in the fifth, trailing 6–2. After the game he said he felt fine and was just rusty. No pain, but unfortunately no sharp breaking ball either. In a sense, Ben has spotted the league a good month, so it may well take him one or two turns to fully get up to speed. He says he's not worried, so neither am I. (Of course, can you believe either one of us?)

The O's kept battling back on this clear, brisk night (temps in the raw forties), but still lost, 8–7. Cal had another big night:

two hits, including a homer and three RBIs. Considering how few runs the team is scoring these days, it's a killer to score seven and still lose. However, Frank says he's not worried, so neither am I.

Tuesday, April 23, Chicago

Tonight we lost, 10–4, and it took almost six hours to do it. We had over a two-hour rain delay in the second inning. That meant Chuck and I had over two hours of *Orioles Talk*. Uggghhh! We signed off close to one (two in the East) and already I could feel a cold brewing. Dave Johnson must've felt worse. He gave up nine runs and eight hits in four-plus innings.

One aspect of the old Comiskey that has been carried over to the new home bearing its name is the "Exploding Scoreboard." When a Sox player hits a home run, the center-field scoreboard turns into the world's largest slot machine that just paid off. Lights flash, colored disks whirl, and fireworks explode into the night. "Overstatement" is how I described it on the air. I find it amusing that the P.A. announcer tells the crowd to please exit the park orderly and quietly because this is a residential neighborhood and they wouldn't want to disturb their neighbors—and yet at twelve-thirty in the morning they blow off fireworks.

Wednesday, April 24, Chicago/Baltimore

What to do on the road? In Chicago—eat pizza at Gino's, oysters at Shaw's, steak anywhere, check out the observatory in the Hancock Building, and attend the Embalmers' Seminar.

Three cheers for Jeff Ballard! Two years ago this young man with matinee-idol looks from Stanford University won eighteen games. Last year he won two. Arm problems and lack of support were the culprits, but tonight he seemed to return to form. Jeff hurled eight-plus innings, stingily doling out six hits and one run. The Birds snapped their three-game losing streak with a 5–1 win over the ChiSox. Gregg Olson registered the save, and he looked dynamite as well. When Otter's curve is sharp, the ball looks like it was dipped in bat repellent. The ball starts up around the batter's shoulders and darts down to his ankles. I cannot fathom how anyone can hit that pitch (and tonight no one could).

We chartered back home after the game. There is no better way to shake a cold than to spend an evening out in 45-degree weather and then fly all night in a pressurized cabin. Phil Itzoe, our traveling secretary, announced on the plane that this was our final charter with United. In June we are to get OUR OWN PLANE, and in the meantime we'll be flying Continental charters. What this means, though, is that Janice, the team's stewardess for the past three years, will no longer be with us. The team got together and bought her a stunning gold bracelet that Jeff Ballard presented during the flight. Janice was very moved and could hardly speak. It was a lovely gesture by the guys and one more example of what a class bunch they are. (Chuck told me that as a matter of routine the old Pittsburgh Steelers used to stuff the stewardesses into the overhead bins for a few yucks.)

We arrived back in Baltimore at three-thirty. Dave Johnson boarded the bus with us back to Memorial Stadium, shaking his head. "I guess when you get lit up, your wife don't come to the airport to pick you up," he muttered.

Thursday, April 25, Baltimore

An off-day. I tried to sleep. I did laundry. I sneezed a lot.

Friday, April 26, Baltimore

If the Orioles didn't have bad luck they'd have no luck at all. Remember way back in spring training when Glenn Davis missed a few days with a "kink" in his neck? Today the team placed him on the fifteen-day disabled list. The spinal accessory nerve in his neck has caused a weakness to the trapezius muscle in his right shoulder, limiting his ability to throw or to hit without pain. The recommendation: surgery. The prognosis: Glenn Davis may be out for the year. Well, that's the season, folks. Stay tuned for the postgame show coming right up. It's hard to believe the Orioles want a second opinion. Arrangements are being made now to send Glenn to New York Hospital–Cornell Medical Center in Manhattan for further tests.

If you've never heard of this injury, that's because no one ever has. Here's how rare it is: Surgery to repair this type of trauma has been performed three, maybe four, times *total*. Let's just hope Glenn Davis winds up in the record books, not the textbooks.

Despite Mike Devereaux's two home runs, the Orioles lost to Milwaukee, 5–4. Flamethrower José Mesa, who pitched so well and lost against Nolan Ryan last Saturday, is now 1–3.

My cold isn't getting much better, but at least my spinal accessory nerve is working like a champ.

Saturday, April 27, Baltimore

Frank Robinson walked out to the mound in the seventh. It was not an unexpected visit. Starter Jeff Robinson had battled through six scoreless innings but in the seventh was in a jam. Milwaukee had runners at second and third with two outs and left-hander Jim Gantner coming to the plate. A right-hander, Gary Sheffield, was on deck. In the bullpen were lefty Mike Flanagan and righty Mark Williamson. There was no score. Frank had any number of options. He could lift Jeff and bring in the southpaw Flanny to face the lefty Gantner (although Treblehorn had two veteran right-hand hitters on the bench in Rick Dempsey and Willie Randolph). He could opt to walk Gantner intentionally and let either Robinson or Williamson face Sheffield. Or, he could stay with Robinson and let him go after Gantner. "Gumby" (or "Jim," as Gantner is sometimes known) was 0 for 3, having fouled out, bounced out, and flied out. However, with men in scoring position he was batting a red-hot .375.

Here's one of those examples of "You make the call."

This was Frank's:

After consulting with Jeff (who wanted to pitch to Gantner) and weighing all of the factors, Frank elected to stay with Jeff.

The result:

Gumby was jammed on the first pitch and muscled it over

the infield into no-man's-land in right center to cash in both runs. No one figured in the "fluke factor."

If you're thinking Frank should've walked him and taken his chances with Sheffield, *he* singled in two more runs in the ninth. Final: Milwaukee 5, Baltimore 2. Since they have to make decisions like this on a nightly basis, you can better understand why every manager is sooner or later fired.

The Orioles have now lost seven of nine and are in last place, five games back of Toronto. The fans need something to cheer about.

Thank God for Rick Dempsey.

From 1974 through 1986 Rick Dempsey was a catcher for Baltimore. Never much of a hitter, he did have his moments. Rick was the MVP of the 1983 World Series. He was truly a crowd favorite in Baltimore, more for his off-the-field exploits than on. During rain delays he was famous for taking headlong sprawling belly-flop dives onto the infield tarp and sliding across the field. While in the bullpen, if idle during a rally, he would stand on the bullpen roof and spell out O-R-I-O-L-E-S, much to the delight of the crowd. One day he enlisted the help of Eddie Murray and several other teammates to sing the Bob Seger hit "That Old Time Rock 'n' Roll" before a large Memorial Stadium audience. Eddie and the others played instruments while Rick provided lead vocal. Well, tonight on DiamondVision they replayed that music video, then showed Dempsey, now the backup catcher for Milwaukee, in the bullpen. He received a standing ovation. (Do you think his teammates give him shit for it? Unrelenting.)

I worked the game with Chuck, and he recalled the shenanigans of another former Oriole bullpen dweller—pitcher Moe Drabowsky. In the days that Drabowsky pitched, there were no water fountains in the bullpen, just water bottles. He would put goldfish in the opposing team's water bottle. Another time Moe called the opposing team's bullpen, posing as that team's manager. He then had them warm up one of their pitchers.

Sunday, April 28, Baltimore

So far the best game of the year, although in the third inning it appeared it was going to be the worst. "Big Bird" brought an

0–1 record and an 11.57 ERA to the mound against Milwaukee. In the third inning with the score tied 1–1, he gave up six hits in a row. Bob Milacki finished up the frame by yielding a hit of his own. In one of the freakiest innings I've ever seen (or called), the Brewers went seven for seven, and that includes all three outs. Here's how: Molitor led off with a double. Gantner sacrificed him to third (which does not count as an at-bat), Sheffield doubled Molitor home, Yount singled home Sheffield, Franklin Stubbs singled Yount to third but was thrown out by Dewey Evans trying to stretch it to a double, Darryl Hamilton singled in Yount, Greg Vaughn followed with a base knock (shorthand for a base hit, even though it contains more letters) to chase McDonald, and B. J. Surhoff hit a snowflake single off of Milacki to left. The inning finally ended when Hamilton tried to score from second on the play and was thrown out by Joe Orsulak. Three runs, seven hits, two left.

And then things turned around. With the Birds trailing 4–1 in the bottom of the third, Cal drove in two. In the fifth Cal singled in the tying run. (Do you detect a pattern?) Meanwhile, Bob Milacki (just recalled from Hagerstown) was magnificent. That initial bloop single by Surhoff would be the only hit allowed in 5⅓ innings. Bob completely silenced the Brewers' bats. In the eighth Cal led off with a scratch single (his third of the day), an out later Leo Gomez did the same, and then with two away Craig Worthington took Darren Holmes's 1–2 pitch into center to score Cal. Finally! An exciting inning to call! Olson came on in the ninth, registered the save, and you'd've thought the O's won the World Series. Sometimes a win like this can turn a team around. Let's hope.

I celebrated by having dinner with Hersch Pacino and his family at his Hersch's Orchid Inn, one of the best restaurants in Baltimore. Dynamite seafood. Hersch is a noted local figure in town with longstanding ties to the Orioles. He and Jim Palmer are best friends. (In fact, Palmer was invited to join us but had other plans—he told me he had to wash his socks. See if I loan him a scorecard again.)

One thing I'm experiencing here that I've never had before is celebrity status. Practically everywhere I go now, if I pay by credit card, the waiter or cashier will spot the name and ask if I'm the Orioles' announcer. I was in a bookstore recently (checking to make sure no one has written *this* book), and a customer recognized my voice. I'm sure if you're an actor this is commonplace, but for me it's *weird*. I'd be a liar if I didn't admit I enjoyed the compliments, but still, it's somewhat disconcerting to be singled out. When I go to restaurants now, I guess I'm going to have to leave tips.

Monday, April 29, Baltimore

I had lunch today with Jeff Beauchamp and was told that WBAL is prepared to commit to me for the '92 season. Although it is waaaaaay too early for me even to think about next year, it was tremendously gratifying to receive so great a vote of confidence. I'm currently working under a one-year contract. There are a lot of questions to be answered regarding my family and juggling two careers before I'm in a position to consider any long-term deal. The station was under no obligation until well into the fall to inform me of its future plans, so this gesture, made less than a month into the season, was completely unexpected and enormously appreciated. WBAL paid for lunch too.

The Seattle Mariners are in town. The Mariners entered the league in 1977 and have *never* had a .500 season, much less a winning one. This year they possess a good young pitching staff, some worthy prospects, and Ken Griffey, Jr. (Jeff Smulyan, the owner of the team, has joked that when Griffey, Jr.'s contract expires, he and the budding superstar will simply switch places, with Smulyan working for Griffey. The cost will be that great.)

So far '91 has been an up-and-down season for the M's. They lost their first six, then won their next eight (including a three-game sweep of Oakland), and have since lost their last five. The Orioles have to hope the Mariners' streaky pattern doesn't continue, because they bombed Baltimore, 10–1, tonight. For the third straight outing Dave Johnson got shelled in the fifth. Mariners' catcher Dave Valle, who is hitting .200 (fourteen points lower than his final average in '90), hit his first home run of the year. So did walk-on Henry Cotto. If the Mariners played the Orioles all year long, Mr. Smulyan might have to switch chairs with Dave Valle.

Tuesday, April 30, Baltimore

I toured the new downtown ballpark today. Few people look as stupid in hard hats as I do. All systems are still go for a '92 Opening Day kickoff. The upper decks are in, the concourses are coming along, and the outer facade is taking shape. The Orioles are taking great care to ensure that their stadium will be rich in character and tradition (unlike, say, any National League megasport concrete saucer built after 1962). The plan is to blend the architecture of the old-time ballparks, circa 1900, with the high-tech conveniences of today's modern facilities. The facade will be brick, consistent with its surroundings. An old warehouse will be renovated beyond right field instead of being torn down. This will justify the ballpark sporting irregular dimensions. A twenty-five-foot wall will be erected in shortened right field. There will be a large scoreboard featuring all games in progress, and a concourse area that will suggest a boardwalk, not a concession center. Oh, yeah, and a flag garden. I can't forget the flag garden. Janet-Marie Smith, the Orioles' vice-president of planning and development, is in charge of overseeing this massive project. To say she is doing a bang-up job is an understatement. You can't fathom the aggravation and sheer frustration involved in major construction unless perhaps you've tried to add a small service porch onto your house.

Since Memorial Stadium is still a great ol' park, the question arises: Why build a new ballpark for the Baltimore Orioles?

The answer: the Baltimore Colts.

The city of Baltimore is still reeling from the defection of its beloved Colts, and many believe they would not have left had the city provided the team with a new stadium complete with all the modern necessities (namely, luxury boxes).

Luxury box sidebar: What a scam! By isolating seats in certain prime-location sections or by providing mini–efficiency apartments with views of the field, (some terrible) ball clubs can charge hundreds of thousands of dollars for seats instead of twelve or fifteen. We can thank the Houston Astros for the first luxury boxes, just as we can thank them for the creation of AstroTurf.

Anyway . . .

Baltimore was not going to let what happened to the Colts happen to the O's. Edward Bennett Williams, the late owner of the Orioles, would not sign another long-term lease at Memorial Stadium. He felt the park was inadequate. The implications were thus clear—build a new stadium or risk the loss of major league baseball. To many that meant blackmail, but in truth Mr. Williams *still* could've made a much greater fortune for his family and estate by relocating the club. The "Miami Orioles" might've been the "Los Angeles Dodgers" of the eighties. Personally, I feel Williams should be commended for his commitment to the city of Baltimore.

There is still the question as to the name of the park. It has been a question for about a year now. Since Babe Ruth was born a block away, one camp is pushing for "Babe Ruth Park." Others contend that Ruth is associated with the New York Yankees, not the Baltimore Orioles, and would prefer "Camden Yards." Still others find that too nondescript. Other candidates include "Oriole Park," "Memorial Stadium," and "MemOriole Stadium." I vote for "Chavez Levine," but so far am a lone voice in the wilderness. From what I hear, the early favorite is "Oriole Park at Camden Yards." I've asked my listeners to send in letters. Maybe "Chavez Levine" will sneak in at the eleventh hour.

Dave Valle killed us again! He hit his second home run in as many nights, and the Mariners made it two in a row, 6–3. The Birds are now 6–12, having lost seven of nine. What's that I see drifting way out to sea? It's the pennant!

Ken Griffey, Jr., had the play of the night, perhaps the year, and I was on the mike at the time. In the third inning Chris Hoiles hit a blast to deep center field. Griffey raced back, made a spectacular catch and crashed into the padded wall. He hit the wall with such force that he literally knocked out one of its panels. A section of the wall toppled over. He told me afterward that the play took him back to his football days. He knew when he threw his shoulder into it that the wall was "taken out."

In my growing-ever-more-difficult search for good news comes this: A trio of specialists at Cornell Medical Center in Manhattan examined Glenn Davis, and independently all reached the same conclusion—surgery is not recommended. Rest and exercise should do the trick, and perhaps in five to six weeks Glenn could be back as a designated hitter. I'm going to go on record as saying we could use him.

Wednesday, May 1, Baltimore

Preparation is essential for doing a good broadcast. It's also one of the great aspects of the job, because as a baseball fan I would be doing most of this work anyway. Keeping up with the major leagues is hardly a chore. I usually try to read two to four papers a day—the local papers, the New York or Chicago papers, depending upon where we are, and *USA Today*. If possible, I try to pick up Tuesday's *Philadelphia Inquirer*. Jayson Stark's weekly column is a gold mine of information and trivia. Along those same lines, Peter Gammons of *The Boston Globe* is a gem. *USA Today*'s "Baseball Weekly" is helpful, as are *Baseball America* and the *Sporting News*. And for greater depth there is always *Sports Illustrated*.

I have a system whereby I prepare index cards on every player in the league. Information is culled from scouting reports, the Bill James *Baseball Book, Elias Baseball Analyst*, statistics, media guide info, and data from coaches, players, and managers. Oh yes, and hearsay. Throughout the course of the year I will update the cards to include notable performances or injuries. For example, here's my card on Oriole killer Dave Valle.

DAVE VALLE CATCHER R 6'2" 200 30 B: BAYSIDE, N.Y.

- Fearless receiver. Four collision injuries at the plate
- Needs to control his long swing. Has a pronounced hitch. Opens his front shoulder too much and as a result breaking balls away hurt him. He lunges.
- Good mistake hitter
- Slow on the basepaths
- Superb arm. Great defensive catcher
- Lefebvre thinks only Tony Peña is comparable behind the plate.
- Since M.L. debut in '84 has been on DL nine times and missed over a season (214 games)
- Signed a three-year $3.6 million contract. Defensive catchers are a rare commodity.
- 1990: Seattle .214 7 HR 33 RBIs (cracked rib last May)

I try to get out to the park at least three hours before the first pitch. That gives me plenty of time to "schmooze." The best tidbits come from sitting around the clubhouse and wandering around the batting cage. Plus, I still get a major rush stepping out onto a major league playing field. So far, my best sources have been hitting coach Tommy McCraw and pitching coach Al Jackson. And more important, they're usually *right*! On the other hand, my worst source is the trainer. Should it ever slip out that a certain player is nursing a tight hamstring, it very well might bring down the Baltimore Orioles franchise as we know it. Information like that in the wrong hands—say, an opposing coach—could lead to your children speaking Russian. Both head trainer Richie Balcells and his assistant Jaime Reed are terrific guys, and I understand that they're merely following orders, but it does make it tough when I have to go to the Watergate parking garage and seek out Deep Throat to learn that someone has a pulled groin.

Usually, an hour before game time the "game notes" will be distributed. These contain volumes of statistics along with updated player info prepared by the team's PR department (e.g., Joe Orsulak is 4 for 12, .250, and has hit in three straight). I try to allow myself at least a half hour to digest and assemble all I've accumulated for that game, and hope that the fifty percent I forget is not the fifty percent I'll need.

During the game I'll try to jot down questions I might want to ask Frank or a player, and usually the next day I'll seek the answers. (I find it's a lot easier to ask a guy why he struck out with the bases loaded on a pitch right "down the cock" the day *after* as opposed to ten minutes after, when he might stuff me into a ball bag.)

After the game, depending on the time, there's no better way to keep up with the races than by watching *Baseball Tonight* on ESPN. How did we exist without it??

Since it's my first year, this has really been a crash course for me—but also one I've enjoyed thoroughly.

Thanks to our "ace," José Mesa, the Orioles squeaked by Seattle, 2–1, to salvage the final game of this very disappointing home stand. Mesa could sue for nonsupport. In his five starts, the O's have hit a combined .176 and scored thirteen runs total. Two of his losses were shutouts (1–0 to Nolan Ryan and 3–0 to Chicago's Greg Hibbard). For a while tonight's game looked to be the worst. Mariner starter Randy "The Big

Unit'' Johnson had a no-hitter going until the sixth. But then he walked the bases loaded, walked Evans to score the tying run, and finally gave up his first hit, a little bleeder down the third-base line by Bob Melvin that got the go-ahead run home.

Melvin also saved the game, although most fans in the park didn't know it. In the seventh the M's had Ken Griffey, Jr., at third with one out. The batter hit a fly ball to Evans in medium right field and Griffey scored. But Melvin alertly noticed that Griffey had tagged up too soon. He instructed Randy Milligan, the cutoff man, to throw over to third, and sure enough Griffey was out. Whenever there's a potential sacrifice fly, it is the catcher's responsibility to check whether the runner tags too early. Bob Melvin was our Loyola Federal Peak Performer of this game.

The weather was glorious all day, but just as the Orioles took the field at 7:35, a row of angry thunderclouds rolled in overhead. We had a forty-seven-minute rain delay, the band of clouds moved on, and it was clear the rest of the night. The Orioles are starting to resemble that character in the old ''Li'l Abner'' comic strip who always walked around with a single rain cloud over his head. As I rode down in the elevator after the game with Dave Niehaus (the Mariners' announcer since their inception), he put his hand on my shoulder and said, ''Kenny, I've seen a lot of this. You may be in for a very lonnnng summer.'' Quite frankly, I don't really care. I'm still too new at this to realize how miserable I am.

There were two notable events in baseball today. Rickey Henderson stole his 939th base in Oakland, eclipsing Lou Brock for the all-time record, and Nolan Ryan pitched his seventh no-hitter, this one against the Blue Jays in Arlington. Henderson proclaimed that he's the ''greatest of all time'' (although Brock graciously was in attendance for the moment), and Ryan said he was lucky to get through the first inning. I found it revealing that Ryan was mobbed by his teammates while Henderson received one or two handshakes. I was also glad to see that on this day of days, ''the greatest of all time'' was overshadowed.

3

Thursday, May 2, Baltimore/Los Angeles

What better way to spend an off-day than to wing to Rochester, New York, play a meaningless game in subfreezing temperatures, then fly all night to Southern California with a refueling stop in Omaha? That's what the Orioles did today. Ben McDonald and I took a nine o'clock direct flight to Los Angeles instead. (Ben is starting tomorrow night, so was sent ahead to get a good night's rest.) As we waited for our luggage at baggage claim, we overheard a fellow passenger talking to his friend, who had come to pick him up. "You can't believe how bad the Orioles suck!" he told his pal. "If you ask me, they oughta fire Frank Robinson and send that big jerk Ben McDonald down to the minors where he belongs." Ben just smiled. When you take plane flights with real human beings and not charters with ballplayers, you leave yourself open.

I arrived home at one-thirty, and I suppose it serves me right. For a year Debby and I had planned to add a wooden deck to the backyard and replace most of the windows in the house. Construction began shortly after I'd left for spring training, and when I walked into my own house, it was very different, almost as if I didn't belong. Then our dog romped in to greet me, and I hardly recognized her. In two months our puppy, Dodger, had grown considerably. I had only been gone for eight weeks, yet it seemed like *The Return of Martin Guerre.* Fortunately, my family remembered me. Whoever's house this was, it was wonderful to be back in it.

Friday, May 3, Los Angeles/Anaheim

Matthew and Diana have been handling the separation very differently. When I call home each night, Matthew doesn't want to get off the phone, while Diana doesn't want to get *on* the phone. Even a "Hello, Daddy" is hard to coax from my four-year-old. She always insists she's not angry, just "busy." However, last week when I told her I would take her to her preschool park picnic today, she suddenly became my best phone mate. Matthew will hopefully look back with great fondness at the unique opportunity he had as a young boy to be a part of major league baseball, but for Diana all this means is that she doesn't have her daddy for long periods of time. I just hope I'm not missing too many picnics.

I started out for Anaheim Stadium at two-thirty. (My parents and family would follow at a more civilized hour.) For six years I have gladly endured the smog-choked Santa Ana Freeway and its rush-hour snarl because I knew there was a chance to practice announcing a big-league baseball game at the other end. This was just a typical day . . . except that instead of sitting in the upper deck or an empty booth and calling the game into a tape recorder for no one but myself, I would be in the press box broadcasting to an audience of close to half a million. Same car, same freeway, same congestion—just that one tiny difference. Of all the stops on the American League circuit, there is no greater personal triumph than to be calling a game here, in my own hometown.

No organization has been more supportive or has had a greater effect on my success than the California Angels. John Sevano, the assistant PR director, has been my guardian "California" angel. Over the years, on a space-available basis, he allowed me to use the press box and provided all the necessary game notes and statistics. As a result, the improvement in my work was startling. Not only did I begin to sound more confident and prepared, the tapes really benefited, I believe, from not containing one or two people yelling in the background, "Hey, what the fuck is this guy doin'? You think you're Vin Scully or somethin', pal?"

Al Conin, the Angel radio voice, has also been a great help. He's critiqued my tapes over the last several years and has been an excellent (if not tough) teacher. There are no books or college courses that teach baseball play-by-play. You're very much on your own. So to have the guidance and counsel from an actual, working major league broadcaster is a godsend. I've always encouraged Al to try his hand at screenwriting so I could return the favor.

The Angels were off to a great start this year, then came back down to earth in a hurry. They've lost seven of nine. They've certainly got some experience and thunder with veterans like Dave Winfield, Dave Parker, and Lance Parrish, but there's always the risk that enough hamstrings will pop to re-create the hit song "Dueling Banjos." Their big contributors this year, however, have been Wally Joyner and spray-hitter Luis Polonia (who keeps and talks to a voodoo doll).

The Orioles won 2–0, on solo home runs by Mike Devereaux and Sam Horn. More important, Ben McDonald looked like the pitcher of old. Big Ben has Roger Clemens–like potential, but thus far has been plagued with injuries. If he can stay healthy and put together a few more performances like tonight, the Orioles' fortunes could well change.

Tonight's broadcast was very off-the-wall. Roy Firestone of ESPN joined us, and like Jon, he too is a sensational impressionist. So in addition to Vin Scully and Harry Caray, Keith Jackson, Woody Allen, Howard Cosell, and Biff Barnes graced the Orioles' radio network. I even chipped in Jack Benny. It's fortunate that the broadcast was heard on the East Coast during the very wee hours of the morning.

Saturday, May 4, Los Angeles/Anaheim

Our booth was the hottest ticket in town. Matthew, my folks, Debby, and Diana all spent time eavesdropping over my shoulder. Jon headed up to Seattle for the ESPN game, so I'm partnered with Chuck for the weekend. Kind soul that he is, he didn't mind the traffic.

And how was the game? Well, starter Jeff Robinson lasted a third of an inning before being taken out. The Angels scored five in the first and never looked back. Final: Angels 6, Orioles 3.

The only Bird who is hitting consistently is Cal. After experimenting with a number of different batting stances last year, in a very disappointing season, he seems to have settled on one this year, and that one is paying dividends. He's also more patient at the plate, diving less for pitches low and away. Cal's been an MVP before. Who knows? He's sure capable.

Up in Oakland today the floundering Cleveland Indians squeaked by the three-time defending American League champion Athletics, 20–6. It just goes to prove that on any given day any team can beat any other team. Of course, that theory will be put to its most stringent test this week when the Orioles play the A's.

Our rotisserie team is already in the tank. Tim Wallach and Jody Reed are killing us.

Sunday, May 5, Los Angeles/Anaheim

With the Orioles in a tailspin, Frank tried to shake things up with a rather unusual lineup. Devereaux still led off, but then Evans batted second (where he used to hit in the early eighties with Boston), Cal occupied his usual third spot, but then came Milligan (hitting .179), Hoiles (.147), Worthington (.196), Hulett as the DH (.125 in only his ninth game), Anderson (.182), and Billy (.176). Several of the reporters wondered if Frank didn't just use a dartboard to select this order.

Desperate times call for desperate measures.

At game's start Frank looked like a genius as the O's scored three quick runs, but starter Jeff Ballard couldn't hold 'em, and the Angels scored six in the fourth. Billy Ripken committed an error in that frame, opening the door for three unearned runs, and to add injury to insult, he sprained the ring finger on his right hand on the miscue and had to come out of the game. Cal also committed an error, and that hasn't happened since the Pleistocene Era.

The O's are now 8–14, and they'd be in last place except that the Yankees are really atrocious.

Chuck and I got into a lively on-air discussion regarding the concessions here at Anaheim Stadium. I made note of the fact that they now serve sushi (raw fish) at this ballpark. Sushi is one item that must be served cold and fresh, and I wondered whether that was possible in this case. I imagined the boxes of sushi being dumped off at the ticket kiosk at eleven A.M., then the food service guys picking them up at four, after they've been baking all day in the sun. "They do serve it, however," I said. "In fact, from time to time you might hear on our crowd mike one of the vendors going up and down the aisles yelling, *'Eel here! Get yer eel! Yellowtail! You can't be at the ballpark without yellowtail!'* "

Up in Oakland the A's pitching staff had a much better day, holding the Indians to only fifteen runs. The Tribe stomped the A's, 15–6. In fairness to Oakland, four of their pitchers are on the disabled list. Rick Honeycutt, Todd Burns, Eric Show, and Gene Nelson are all on the shelf, so the A's have been forced to bring up rookies from Tacoma. Today, however, Cy Young winner Bob Welch, who won 27 games last year, was the starter, and in 4⅔ innings he gave up thirteen hits and eleven runs, eight of them earned. Perhaps LaRussa should've sat Welch for Joe Slusarski or maybe Kirk Dressendorfer???

Monday, May 6, Los Angeles/Anaheim

Channel 7, the local ABC affiliate, is doing a story on me, so it's camera-crew time in the booth again. Craig Worthington and Mike Devereaux helped me out by hitting home runs during my innings. The O's went on to sock four homers (Cal and Tim Hulett getting the other two) en route to a 7–0 pasting of the Angels. José Mesa got the win and, for the first time this year, some support. Before today the Orioles were batting a stout .176 in his five previous outings.

Tuesday–Thursday, May 7–9, Los Angeles

The team flew up to Oakland for a two-game series with the A's, followed by an off-day in Seattle. I, however, have been given a three-day pass by WBAL to remain with my family. Y'know, when I get back to Baltimore, I'm going to have to set a car button for that station.

The time was spent with Cub Scout pack meetings, car pools, dinners with Debby or the family, a lunch with Diana, and several long sessions of catch with Matty. I count these three days as among the highlights of the year so far.

The Orioles, meanwhile, got handed their heads in Oakland. They lost Tuesday night, 11–3, with Maryland native Harold Baines hitting three home runs, then dropped Wednesday's affair, 9–3. Mike Flanagan got the start on Wednesday. He was back in the bullpen on Thursday. Ben McDonald, who looked so sharp last Friday in Anaheim, was the bombee on Tuesday night.

Among my stops this week was a trip to my agent's office. David and I are planning our agenda for the upcoming TV season. It appears my agent doesn't have to worry that I'll miss an additional three weeks due to the play-offs and World Series.

By the way, the Channel 7 feature on me ran Tuesday night. It was a short piece, only about two minutes in length, with half a minute devoted to Jon doing his Vin Scully impression describing me. After the piece was over, the cameras went back to the anchors. One said, "Boy, that Ken Levine is good," to which sports anchor Jim Hill replied, "Yeah, he's good, but that Jon Miller, he's fantastic! What a great Vin Scully!" Thanks, Jim. And thanks, Jon.

Friday, May 10, Los Angeles/Seattle

After a full week at home, it was *really* tough to say good-bye and get on another airplane. How do announcers do this for twenty years? Or three?

Here's the game plan for the remainder of the season, familywise: In three weeks the Orioles will be in Boston for a long weekend. Debby and the kids will fly out to spend it with me. We'll take the kids on the Freedom Trail, show Matty historic Fenway Park, and in general just have a nice family vacation. Come the middle of June when school is out, the Levines will head east for the summer, returning in mid-August when the new school year begins. Thanks to all the frequent-flyer miles they'll be accumulating, they'll come out to Baltimore one final time in September, for the Jewish holidays. Also, we have some very good friends in New York who have a gorgeous East Side apartment that will be vacant during the summer. It will be ours to enjoy and hopefully not destroy. Since the O's play the Yankees in the Bronx right before the All-Star break, we plan to all go to New York, spend the three-day break there, then Debby and the kids will remain for another two weeks while I'm on the West Coast with the team. When I was a kid, I used to complain that the summers were real boring. Nothing ever happened. I don't think Matty and Diana will have that same complaint.

This is my first time in Seattle, and I must say the Space Needle looked every bit as impressive as it did in the classic motion picture *It Happened at the World's Fair,* starring Mr. Elvis Presley (now a successful auto tower in Dunedin, Florida).

The Kingdome was less impressive. It's a no-frills structure to be sure: a giant concrete bowl. At least now there is blue-and-gold bunting hiding large exposed pipes.

Frank looks like the dog's breakfast. He's come down with a bad case of the flu—is there such a thing as the "losing" virus? He did manage to lift his head long enough to do my interview and admit that things were going so badly he would consider using *me* as a pinch hitter.

You laugh, but he could've used me tonight. Seattle won 3–1. The O's are now last in team hitting and pitching in the American League.

Tonight was only the second time I had ever seen an indoor ball game. The first was at the Astrodome for the '86 All-Star game. There were 60,000 people under the roof that night and the noise was deafening. With 24,000 in the Kingdome it felt like baseball in a nuclear reactor. Credit where credit is due, however. The Mariners do a great job in providing interesting DiamondVision features between innings and their seventh-inning stretch is one of the best in the league. After the obligatory "Take Me Out to the Ballgame," they play "Louie, Louie," made famous by Northwest natives, the Kingsmen. The reactor really rocks.

Saturday, May 11, Seattle

My brother Corey and his wife, Jan (who live in Portland), and my parents (who don't), all came up for the weekend. We spent the day wandering through Pike Place Market, a huge open-air marketplace down by the waterfront. Notable among the many vendors was Pike Place Fish Mart, where the clerks literally throw the floppy fresh fish back and forth to each other à la circus jugglers. Also worth noting—Seattle Cutlery, which sported the following Mother's Day sign out front: DOES YOUR MOTHER HAVE GOOD KNIVES??

Jeff Robinson, my warm-up show guest, was, to say the least, candid. Recently bumped to the bullpen, he said Frank should either return him to the starting rotation or leave him in the pen, but not both. He "won't" bounce back and forth between the two (as if it were his choice).

The lead in tonight's game went back and forth like windshield wipers. Seattle led 1–0 in the first, the O's jumped out 2–1 in the third, then the M's came back 3–2 in the bottom of the third with a two-run inside-the-park home run by Henry Cotto. Dwight Evans hit his second home run of the year in the fourth (both coming off of Erik Hanson), and the game was tied going to the fifth.

Every Saturday, CBS Radio broadcasts two major league games coast-to-coast. Ours was one this week. In the fifth inning they have a feature entitled the "Hometown Inning," where they invite the local announcers of the competing teams to each call the half-inning in which their club bats. So tonight I got to broadcast the top of the fifth inning on the CBS Radio Network. I was kidding my color man on the air, Gene Elston (the longtime voice of the Houston Astros) that I have heard these hometown innings often in the past and they all seem to have one thing in common—they last no more than three minutes. For some reason, nothing ever seems to happen in the hometown innings. It's almost uncanny. I said I had bribed some of our players to at least "take a pitch." Well, wouldn't you know, Mike Devereaux did take a pitch and then homered on the next one. That lit the spark for a six-run/five-hit/two-pitcher/nine-batter inning. It was the Orioles' biggest inning of the year. I was on the air for close to half an hour. I might've set a record. Dave Niehaus of the Mariners did the bottom of the fifth and was off in three minutes.

The O's won 11–5. Devereaux, Anderson, Cal, Hulett, Milligan, Worthington, and I all had big nights.

Sunday, May 12, Seattle/Baltimore

A lovely but rushed Mother's Day breakfast, then it was off to the yard. There are some days I miss being home more than others, and this is one. Matty and Diana always prepare breakfast in bed for Debby, and their menu selection is invariably interesting. Two years ago when Matty was six, they served a bowl of cold cereal and a Tab. I'm sorry I'm going to miss this year's entrée.

There seems to be only one topic on the sports-talk shows in Baltimore these days—fire Frank. That, of course, is par for the course, but Frank didn't help his case today. The O's were leading, 4–1, in the seventh with Ben McDonald pitching a great game. He had retired thirteen Mariners in a row before yielding a two-out walk to Pete O'Brien. Alvin Davis then hit the next pitch into the seats to close the gap to 4–3. Frank brought in closer Gregg Olson to start the eighth. Last year Olson's effectiveness diminished at the end of the season due to overwork, but this year it's just the opposite. With fewer save opportunities available, Frank has hardly used Otter. He and the Orioles paid the price today. Olson was rustier than our remote equipment. He gave up a walk and three singles (two with two out) and the Mariners pulled it out, 4–3.

It was a longgggggggggg flight home. What might've been a reasonably respectable 4–5 West Coast trip ended up 3–6 instead. Roland Hemond said this was one of the few games he ever caught himself reacting like a fan, cheering and groaning on each play. "This game can be so unforgiving and heartbreaking," he went on the say, "but the winning . . . the winning is so intoxicating it makes up for everything."

I got to bed at four-thirty A.M.

Monday, May 13, Baltimore

I slept.

Tuesday, May 14, Baltimore

We won. Jeff Robinson, back in the rotation, held off Oakland, and the offense chipped in four solo home runs (one each by Cal Ripken, Joe Orsulak, Mike Devereaux, and Chris Hoiles) as the O's beat the A's, 6–1. Tony LaRussa's pitching staff has been decimated by injuries, and tonight he was forced to trot out four rookies, but with the Orioles struggling so badly, I prefer to focus on the fact that *they whipped the three-time defending American League Champions!*

Wednesday, May 15, Baltimore

A typical day, really, except that the queen of England and the president of the United States attended the game. They saw the A's win, 6–3, although Randy Milligan hit his first home run of the year and then his second.

Her Majesty Queen Elizabeth II and His Royal Highness Prince Philip are visiting the United States and wanted to view something that represented "the epitome of America." That meant either the Shopping Channel or baseball. So our little ol' ballpark on Thirty-third Street got the nod. The weather was glorious, the traffic horrendous, and the crowd merely moderate (32,591) to see this historic occasion. (The queen was not as big a draw as free wristbands.)

The entourage arrived at six-fifty via motorcade and were whisked into a private reception hosted by club owner Eli S. Jacobs (whom I have yet to meet, by the way). The VIP party, which also included Mrs. Bush, baseball commish Fay Vincent (who told me before the game that the role of the commissioner in affairs such as these is "to be seen and then leave"), Secretary of Defense Dick Cheney, Mrs. Secretary of Defense, the honorable governor of Maryland William Donald Schaefer, British Foreign Secretary Douglas Hurd, and a number of the queen's personal valets, secretaries, and foot stools. They all dined on crab cakes and hot dogs. (What, no crumpets and nachos??) Orioles' president Larry Lucchino presented Her Royal Highness with gifts—engraved bats for each of her six grandchildren (including Prince Harry).

Everyone lingered over dinner for fifteen minutes, and then the royal party moved on to the Orioles' dugout to greet the players of both teams. A path of red carpet led the way.

Quick aside: In 1978, when I was working on *M*A*S*H,* Prince Charles was in Los Angeles and wanted to visit the set. His motorcade route through the Twentieth Century–Fox studios was mapped out, and to impress the prince, the studio had every building and soundstage along his route freshly painted . . . except they didn't paint the entire buildings, *only* those sides visible by the royal guest. In other words, the front of some structures, a side or two of others. The City of Illusions lived up to its name that day.

We at *M*A*S*H* were not much better. The prince watched a scene being filmed—but there was no film in the camera. I got the chance to meet him, shake his hand, and ask him a question. I don't know what possessed me to do it, but I asked the prince of Wales: "What advice would you give young people thinking of getting into your profession?" To his credit (and my good fortune) he laughed and said something to the effect of, "You *M*A*S*H* writers are so jolly funny. Can we visit the *Charlie's Angels* set now?" End of aside.

I did not get to meet the queen. Jon and I were on the air describing the proceedings. At seven-twenty a receiving line of players was rushed through (viewed by the crowd on DiamondVision), and to the horror of the Secret Service, the president escorted Queen Elizabeth (or "Sausage," as Prince Philip calls her) up the top step into the on-deck area in full view of the masses. Personally, I feel Harold Baines would be in greater danger than the queen, but the Secret Service men held their breath just the same. The crowd roared its approval. From there the royal party repaired back to Mr. Jacobs's sky box on the mezzanine level just to the left of the press box. They sat comfortably behind bulletproof glass as a high school chorus mangled "God Save the Queen" and "The Star-Spangled Banner" over a sound system wracked by feedback.

They stayed for two whole innings, and I sort of felt bad, because they were two very boring innings. Five walks, little action. Really, Your Highness, baseball is not that dull! I wanted her to stay longer, but by 8:45 the motorcade had shuttled her away. I also was hoping to have her stop by our booth to possibly read the "Esskay Meats Out-of-Town Scoreboard," but that was not to be. See if I vote for her in the next election!

All in all it was a very exciting night. In three previous years in the minors the most important dignitary I ever saw attend a game was the Phillie Phanatic.

Thursday, May 16, Baltimore

The feature that *Baseball Magazine* did on me for ESPN aired tonight . . . at one A.M. I'll probably be mobbed when I walk out onto the street tomorrow. The piece itself was sensational. These people went that extra mile. Besides including play-by-play snippets, interviews, and film clips, they traveled to the set of *Cheers* and taped comments from Ted Danson, George Wendt, Kelsey Grammer, and John Ratzenberger regarding my little adventure. (My favorite comment was from Kelsey, who, as Dr. Frasier Crane, said, "I find Ken Levine's desertion reprehensible. It shows a complete and utter lack of maturity. Disgraceful!") The feature ran twelve minutes, and the only quarrel I have with it is that nowhere did it mention Debby and the sacrifice she's making. I discussed that at length with the interviewer, but I suppose that aspect detracts from the fantasy angle of the story. It's too bad. In many ways Debby's story is the more compelling (and certainly more heroic) of the two.

The A's sent rookie Kirk Dressendorfer (who leads the league in syllables) to the mound against the Orioles' most consistent starter, José Mesa. José was so wild that the Orioles' Bird (our goofy, bulbous mascot) was afraid to leave the dugout for fear of getting drilled with a fastball near the on-deck circle.

By the way, I have no idea why we even have a mascot. Orioles' owner Eli Jacobs thinks it's undignified for the Bird to dance on the dugout, spell out "Orioles," or perform any kind of slapstick comedy routine. So instead, all the poor schlepp can do is wander around, shake hands, and get kicked by little kids. I don't understand it. Why hire a team mascot when you can't showcase his genius?

In 1⅓ innings, Mesa gave up five runs and only one hit before being yanked. The hit was a three-run homer by Oriole nemesis Harold Baines after two had been walked. The final score: Oakland 11, Baltimore 3. Bring on the Angels!

Friday, May 17, Baltimore

It's Preakness Weekend in Baltimore, and the town is jumpin'. The 116th running of the Preakness is tomorrow here in the city, and even the Orioles are taking a backseat. Although, considering they're in last place, nine games in back of Boston, it's somewhat refreshing to pick up the sports page and *not* be greeted with THIS TEAM SUCKS!

As part of the Preakness festivities, the Orioles held an autograph party down at the Inner Harbor at noon. Guess who got to emcee it? In record-breaking heat I brought on Mike Devereaux and Brady Anderson, gave away choice prizes such as Frisbees and batting helmets, and introduced the Gangplank Ragtime Band ("And now they'll be playing a medley of hits from their latest movie soundtrack album, 'Ragtime Favorites from *Silence of the Lambs*' "). The crowd numbered maybe five hundred, and no one collapsed from the oppressive heat. The marketing department couldn't ask for more.

Getting out and meeting the fans is a real eye-opener. Most are normal, well-adjusted people, but there is also this fringe element of diehards who seem to emerge from underneath their rocks whenever they hear the call of functions such as these. These folks are not hard to spot. They're dressed entirely in Orioles' paraphernalia and usually carry prized "collections" or memorabilia. One guy had a large gourd in the shape of a bat he's been toting since the seventies. These are the people who fall under the category of *GET A LIFE.*

The Angels bring with them the hottest hitter in baseball, Wally Joyner. He's currently batting .380, with a twelve-game hitting streak. I taped today's warm-up interview with him and, among other probing questions, asked about his free agency at the end of this season and whether he would consider leaving the Angels. He answered that it was too early to tell, but he did like living in Southern California and enjoyed raising his four children there. I then wanted to say, "Continued good success, Wally," but what came out instead was, "Well, continued good sex, Wally." He thanked me and moved on.

The *Morning Sun* reported today that tonight's starter, Ben McDonald, was complaining that his elbow has flared up again. I asked Ben, and he said it was still a little sore, but that it had always been a little sore. It actually was feeling better. Frank was livid at the story because it made him seem irresponsible for starting McDonald if he indeed was hurt. This is not the kind of article you want to see appear when your job is shaky at best.

Well, Ben proved that his arm was okay as he pitched a complete game victory, 5–1. Joyner kept his hitting streak alive with an infield single, and red-hot Luis Polonia doubled (the voodoo spell is still in force), but that was about the extent of the Angel attack. Mike Devereaux went three for five and stole three bases, and Cal picked up another hit and RBI to keep him among the league leaders in both categories.

Hey, ESPN reran my feature tonight . . . at two A.M. Is it time to worry about overexposure???

Saturday, May 18, Baltimore

Hansel, ridden by Jerry Bailey, won today's Preakness. Tomorrow in the papers I fully expect to see the losing trainers blame Frank Robinson.

I had ("did") lunch today with the Angels' assistant PR director, John Sevano, and their traveling secretary, Frank Sims. We went to Sabatino's in Little Italy. If you're ever in Baltimore, go to Sabatino's and order their "bookmaker salad," filled with cheese, salami, shrimp, and covered with a creamy garlic dressing. *Molto bene!* Tell them I sent you and maybe I'll get a free lunch.

The weather has changed somewhat. Yesterday it was 90 with ninety percent humidity, today it's 60 with sixty percent humidity. How do you pack for the East Coast in May?

Wally Joyner single-handedly beat the Orioles tonight. With the score tied 2–2 in the ninth—the Angel runs coming on his homer—Joyner faced lefty Mike Flanagan in the single most dramatic confrontation of the year. Flanny, who is murder on left-hand hitters, worked the count to three-and-two. Joyner then fouled off five pitches. Finally, Wally looped a slider into right to drive in the two winning runs. Discussing it on our postgame show (where Wally received a dinner for two at Berry & Elliott's, "Fine dining high atop the Hyatt"), he said that Flanagan threw everything at him "including tables and chairs." First base was open at the time, but Flanagan, competitor that he is, never gave a thought to walking a left-hand hitter.

It's not as if the Orioles didn't have their chances to score some runs tonight. With men in scoring position they were two for sixteen. The end result was not only another Oriole loss—number 21 in 33 tries—but Mike Devereaux (one of our few hot hitters of late) had to leave in the third with a groin pull. And the thirty-nine-year-old Flanagan, who's pitched mucho innings thus far, has come down with a tender shoulder.

When a team is in a tailspin, injuries are usually a key factor. The Orioles' woes can easily be traced back to Ben McDonald's spring-training elbow problems and Glenn Davis's nerve troubles. When two of your four stars go down (Cal and Otter being the other two) and you are not a club loaded with depth, you are in trouble deep. Last year the team hung in there until a rash of injuries in late summer—Billy Ripken, leading hitter; Randy Milligan, home run leader; Dave Johnson, winningest pitcher; Mark Williamson, most active reliever; and Bob Milacki, along with Gregg Olson, Craig Worthington, and Ron Kittle—caused the Birds to have their worst August in thirty-six years. On August 3 they were in third place, only four games out of first. By September 5 they were 15½ off the pace, dead and buried. We haven't had too many nagging injuries (à la Devereaux) yet, but the way things are going these days . . .

Sunday, May 19, Baltimore/Detroit

David Segui was called up from Rochester today just to be on hand should Mike Devereaux need to go on the DL. Well, Devo didn't (although he's still too sore to play), but pitcher Dave Johnson did. He too came up with a groin injury (although it was the first I'd heard about it). Sam Horn, it seems, now has a slightly strained hamstring, and Mark Williamson's groin is giving him problems. Did I jinx this team by discussing injuries yesterday? Suddenly, *everything* is going wrong for this club.

David Segui is a solid line-drive hitter who plays a little outfield and first base. He's lacking in the power and speed departments, but the O's are hoping he'll hit for a high enough average to compensate. How high? Well, with that kind of profile, I'd say in the Wade Boggs range (i.e., batting crowns). David's dad is Diego Segui, longtime major league pitcher, which is why you might recognize the name. (Diego had a classic move, by the way, which was to stand on the mound and bounce the ball off his cup.)

The game was a disaster. The very first batter, Luis Polonia, hit a pop-up to the right of the mound. Billy dropped it for an error. Polonia tried to stretch it to two bases and was caught in a rundown, but Randy hit Polonia on the shoulder with his throw to second, and the ball caromed out into center field. Polonia was safe at second base on the two errors. And that was the high point of the inning for the Orioles. The Angels scored four times. They would win, 10–2. Jeff Ballard has given up thirteen unearned runs this year, a staggering amount.

I'm getting progressively more worried about Frank's job. Although the front office continues to support him, at least publicly, I get the feeling that's just balloon juice. Should the club wish to go the scapegoat route for this terrible team, Frank would be the guy. Very little of what's happened is his fault, of course, but it's the old story—you can't fire twenty-five players, so you fire the manager. At least for now, Frank seems unconcerned, so I hope he has a better reading of the situation than I do.

After the game we flew to Detroit. I've been feeling homesick anyway, what with the Angels being in town, but seeing their bus pull out of the lot en route to Los Angeles while I was ticketed for the only major city in America that no longer has a downtown department store really put a crimp in my evening.

Fortunately, we're not staying in Detroit per se. We're out in nearby Dearborn, the world headquarters of Ford. Unlike the city itself, which is decaying and disgusting, Dearborn is lovely—lush, green, and seemingly safe to walk outside in in the daytime. Our hotel is the Ritz-Carlton, of all places, and needless to say, it's four-star. There's a dress code to enter the gift shop—but still! These are among the most luxurious accommodations I've ever been in. I am really quite surprised. My idea of being pampered in Detroit was being mugged with a padded object.

Monday, May 20, Detroit

I strolled over to the nearby mall to see a movie today, *Mannequin II*. You're probably wondering: Why would I go to see something stupid and juvenile like that? Answer: because I'm one of the writers.

This requires an explanation. Five years ago David and I had a few weeks to kill and did a quick polish (rewrite) on the first *Mannequin* film (plot: Kim Catrell, in her most wooden performance, is a mannequin who comes to life for Andrew Mc-

Carthy). It was easy work, a pot of money, and no credit. (You'll notice that nowhere in this book do I refer to myself as an "artist.") Other writers subsequently rewrote our draft, and when the movie finally came out, we were so appalled that we walked out of the theater after half an hour. Very little of our script remained, and what did made little or no sense. To my knowledge there was not one single good review for this film anywhere in the country. The *L.A. Times* reviewer charitably said, "It was like stepping in something."

Mannequin grossed over $70 million. That number again: $70 million.

Hence *Mannequin II*. David and I were again asked to rewrite ("For luck," they said—always the ultimate compliment for a writer). We did (for a lot more lucky bucks), and went on about our lives. Last summer the film was shot, and this time we received shared credit along with three other writers. There is the potential for royalties and cassette sales down the road, but let's just say there have been other projects we've been involved with that have given us more pride.

Anyway, I went to see it. There were maybe four people in the theater. And you know something, it wasn't that bad. I was astounded. Yes, it was seriously stupid, and some of the actors were way too broad (notably, Terry Kiser, as the Nazi villain, missed the extreme subtlety of that character), but unlike the original, this was good-spirited and somewhat sweet.

Expect it to make $3.75 at the box office.

Dr. Paul and I took an early cab out to the yard. Tiger Stadium is one of the great venerable ballparks in the land, double-decked throughout in a boxy configuration. The Tigers have been playing here at Trumbull and Michigan avenues since the turn of the century. The irregular dimensions reflect a downtown ballpark. It is 325 down the right-field line, 340 down the left, and 440 to straightaway center (as Chuck says, "A half-day ride on a bicycle"). Unlike in modern stadiums, the upper decks here are supported by poles. As a result, they do not have to be recessed—thus the fans are closer to the action. In some portions of Tiger Stadium the upper decks actually hang out closer to the playing field than the decks below. (For some reason, Memorial Stadium has a recessed upper level *and* poles.)

There have been several classic World Series and All-Star

games played here, along with some memorable home runs. In the '71 Summer Classic, Hank Aaron, Johnny Bench, Frank Robinson, Harmon Killebrew, Roberto Clemente, and Reggie Jackson all had "homeric hoists," with Jackson's almost leaving the park. It's been twenty years, but people in Motown still talk about it.

Tiger Stadium has the best broadcast vantage point in all of baseball. There's no close runner-up. The booth hangs out above home plate just high enough to see the entire field and low enough that you can literally hear an argument at home plate. Jon tells the story of doing a game here his first year with Oakland—when the booth was up the line a little farther, but just as low—and Gene Tenace fouled a pitch off his foot. It was late in the year, the crowd was small, and Jon could hear Tenace cursing and grunting as he tried to walk off the bees and hornets. Jon said on the air, "Well, one thing we can say for sure—Gene is in a lot of pain," to which Tenace looked up at the booth and shouted, "That's a fucking brilliant deduction!"

The sole drawback of the booth is that you are an easy target for foul balls. They come rocketing back in a hurry. Announcers deserve combat pay for calling games in Tiger Stadium.

The people of Detroit have been blessed for over thirty years with a Hall of Fame announcer, Ernie Harwell (inducted in 1981). Last December the Tigers decided this would be his final year. Ernie called a press conference and announced his firing. The public was outraged. The Tigers are a terrible team playing in a bad part of town, and the only positive thing they can point to is Ernie Harwell. Ernie is hovering around seventy, but as with Chuck Thompson, you'd never know it. He still sounds alert, enthusiastic, and that crackling southern voice is as rich as ever. And Glenn E. "Bo" Schembechler and the Tigers want to dump him. (Does the name "Jane Pauley" mean anything to these people???) I'm sure of two things: (1) Ernie will have more offers than he'll know what to do with, and (2) You'd have to line up Brink's trucks from Detroit to Baltimore to get *me* to replace him.

Ernie Harwell is also one of the most decent human beings you'd ever want to meet. Last year he interviewed me for his warm-up show when the Tigers were at Anaheim. After the piece, he asked if I was going to be in Detroit in the near future.

I said, "No, why?" (Actually, I said, "Good God, no! Why?") Since I had been his guest on the show, he had a gift certificate for me for a pair of shoes at a local Detroit outlet. He scribbled his home number on a scrap of paper and said that if I don't get to Detroit, I'm to call him and he'll arrange to get me my shoes. (That story has made such an impression on me that when one of my warm-up show guests says he won't be in town and can't cash in his Melart Jewelry gift certificate, I get out a scrap of paper and scribble down Ernie's number for the guest.)

Goofy.

That's the term Tiger manager Sparky Anderson uses to describe his team. He has Cecil Fielder, Rob Deer, Mickey Tettleton, and now Pete Incaviglia (released by Texas at the end of spring training), four guys all capable of hitting at least thirty home runs a year and striking out 200 times. A good crop of fine young prospects are being seasoned on the farm, but for '91 the Tigers don't figure to contend but do figure to score a million runs (probably over the course of eleven games).

Left-hander Kevin Hickey ("the Hick-man") has been called up in the absence of Dave Johnson. Why we need three lefties when there are only two righties (and one of them is the closer) beats me, but if nothing else, Hickey brings a real spirit and sense of humor to the dance, and the clubhouse could use all the lift it can get. On my warm-up show tonight he described his career as a "toxic waste dump."

Hickey got his first action of the season right away. He came on to relieve starter Bob Milacki . . . in the first inning. Milacki walked four batters, then gave up a grand slam to Pete Incaviglia. For good measure he walked the following batter. Hickey surrendered another run in the second, and by the time I came on to do my innings, the O's were down, 6–0. This is happening lately with alarming regularity. Our starting rotation is in shambles. Frank cannot for the life of him understand why these pitchers are not challenging hitters, going right after them. They're nibbling, trying to be too fine, and as a result are always behind in the count.

Oh those bases on balls!

To their credit, the Orioles fought back, getting five runs during my two innings, but in the fifth Mark Williamson gave up five more runs. Tigers 11, Last Place Team in the Division 5.

Our broadcast was picked up tonight by Armed Forces Radio

and heard around the world. I suspect there were more people listening in Oslo than in Baltimore by the seventh inning.

Tuesday, May 21, Detroit

Spent the day with Dan Hoard, my broadcast partner in Syracuse in '88. He's still the Voice of the Chiefs, playing this week in nearby Toledo. He drove up and we had lunch at a pseudo-Benihana-style Japanese steak house, where the food wasn't as good and the chefs didn't dare juggle knives for fear of horrible accidents. Sooner or later Dan will crack the big leagues, although he deserves to be there right now. It's a numbers game, with openings few and far between. Hopefully, there will be a spot for Dan without Vin Scully, Jack Buck, or Harry Caray having to be fired.

Trivia note: In the *Simpsons* episode that David and I wrote called "Dancin' Homer" (Homer becomes a bush-league mascot who gets his cup of "instant" coffee in "the Show"), I do the voice of the minor league announcer . . . named Dan Hoard.

Nowhere is the disparity between the majors and the minors more apparent than here in Michigan and Ohio, where Toledo sits only seventy miles from Detroit. Last year while toiling for Tidewater, we were in Toledo for a night game while the Tigers were hosting the Angels in the afternoon, so I drove up for the day. Big mistake. I was so depressed that night calling the Toledo game. Whereas Tiger Stadium is teeming with energy and tradition, Ned Skeldon Stadium in Toledo is a dimly lit dive on the outskirts of town. No one comes out there to see the Mud Hens play (and lose, as they frequently do), and if someone did, one trip to their pathetic (and apathetic) confines would probably dissuade him from ever doing it again. After sitting with 25,000 fans in the sunshine at Tiger Stadium, I spent the evening with less than 1,000 at Ned Skeldon. Their mascot, a scraggly Mud Hen with a limp felt bat, was up in the press box in the fifth inning, head removed, pounding down a beer. "I can't go out there again," he moaned between swigs. Another can of Lite-courage and he made the death march back into the stands to be ignored, ridiculed, and spat upon. Whoever was scheduled to be the scoreboard/message board operator that night had gotten drunk in a bar the night before and fell, suffering a concussion, so a substitute was hired. With the Tides leading handily in the later innings, the message-board keeper, in an effort to combat the ennui, started taking liberties with the batters' names. On the screen, for all to see, was "Dick Hurts," "Jack Meoff," and "Mike Hunt."

Only seventy miles from Detroit.

Don Zimmer was fired by the Cubs today. No successor has been named to the man who guided the Cubs to a divisional title two years ago.

Is Frank next? He doesn't seem to think so, but he told me, "Don't give anybody any ideas."

The injuries continue to mount. Craig Worthington pulled a hamstring and was placed on the fifteen-day DL. Jeff McKnight, who was just sent down yesterday when the Hickster came aboard, was called back up today. (What's especially lucky for McKnight is that he misses a trip this week to Toledo). Brady Anderson has a sore knee, Mike Flanagan a tender shoulder, Randy Milligan is still bothered by the ankle he twisted in spring training, Joe Orsulak has a sore hand, and groin injuries have sidelined Dave Johnson, Mike Devereaux, Mark Williamson, and Dewey Evans. It's unbelievable. Since when are groin injuries contagious? (While reading a Hechingers Home Project Center spot on the air tonight I feigned a groin injury myself.) Seventeen players sought out the trainer for some form of pregame treatment.

The Orioles won, however. Tim Hulett hit a dramatic two-run homer in the ninth to lift the "Walking Wounded" to a 5–4 victory.

Wednesday, May 22, Detroit/Baltimore

Tom Gage, the excellent beat writer for the *Detroit News*, opened his column today like this:

> Ring. Ring.
>
> Hi, this is Sparky [Anderson]. I'm not home right now but you can't give up five runs every night and expect to win. Leave your message at the beep.

That has been the Tigers' problem all year long (they have just lost nine of ten), but it's nothing compared to the Orioles'. Frank's message should be, "You can't give up *nine* runs every night and expect to win." Detroit prevailed, 9–5. Starter Ben McDonald, after a perfect first inning, fell apart in the second, yielding six runs, four hits, and three walks. Cecil Fielder led off with a home run (the first of two he would hit for the night). Again, I came on for the third, trailing 6–0. The club is now 13–24 and I see no end in sight. Back in '88, when the Orioles lost 21 in a row, they were *so* bad they received national recognition and support. This team doesn't even have *that* going for them.

Another manager was fired today. John Wathan of Kansas City was shown the door. The Royals are at the bottom of the A.L. West, but still have a much better record than ours.

Jon Miller was a guest on the David Letterman show tonight. I didn't see it because I was in the air flying back home, but I hope Dave didn't ask him to show any "Stupid Orioles Tricks."

Thursday, May 23, Baltimore

An off-day. I slept late (after having arrived home at three-thirty) and turned on the radio to learn that the Orioles had announced a major press conference for four-fifteen.

Uh-oh. I know what that means.

I got dressed, read the *Morning Sun* (Peter Schmuck's lead was that Frank's job was safe for the foreseeable future), and headed to the stadium. Sure enough, Frank Robinson was "reassigned to the front office," while first-base coach Johnny Oates was named manager. Frank was saddled with a weak, injury-riddled club and unfortunately had to take the fall. This is the same man who was the American League Manager of the Year a scant two years ago. Now he's a bum? I don't think so.

In terms of his "reassignment" to the front office, that's still a murky area. When Frank signed his contract, all parties agreed that should he be relieved of his on-field duties, he would become the assistant general manager. Well, the Orioles have an assistant general manager, Doug Melvin, who is one of the sharpest people in the entire organization. He's not going anywhere. Roland Hemond remains the general manager, overseeing all player-related activities. So what's left for Mr. R? Frank has made it very clear that he doesn't want a figurehead position, and at the moment no specific responsibilities have been spelled out. There will be a meeting next Tuesday to discuss these matters. Stay tuned.

The media was incensed. Expressions like "scapegoat," "passing the blame," and "cowardly decision" flowed freely at the press conference. Team president Larry Lucchino took the brunt of the hits.

Personally, I don't know how much difference a new manager is going to make (the expression most often heard: "This is just rearranging the deck chairs on the *Titanic*"), but I am very happy for Johnny Oates. He's a good person, an excellent baseball man, and has certainly paid his dues. John and his family have moved over fifty times in his baseball career. During one five-year period, his daughter went to thirteen schools. That's a lot of sacrifice for no guarantees. John's wife and two of his children were there. It was a great moment for all of them.

Some of the questions these reporters asked were a riot. Johnny had been at a barbershop getting a haircut when he called home to check in and got the message that Roland wanted to see him. "What was the name of the barbershop?" one of the reporters asked.

I got hoodwinked by Jeff Rimer to go on his WBAL talk show to discuss today's change of command. I found it interesting, and said so on the air, that for weeks his callers wanted but one thing: Frank Robinson's dismissal. And now that they've gotten their wish, all the callers are crying, "Poor Frank," "He didn't deserve this," "Robinson's not the problem," etc. I speculated that by the time we were off the air in an hour, we would get our first "Fire Johnny Oates" call.

Bob Miller, the assistant PR director of the Orioles, is fast becoming a very close, trusted friend. Originally from Detroit (where he worked for the Tigers for several years), Bob is single, in his thirties, and has many of the same interests I have. There are some people who for some reason are just on your wavelength, and Bob Miller is one on mine. Since neither of us have family in Baltimore, we've been hanging out together quite a bit lately. Tonight we went out to dinner and hoisted tankards to Frank Robinson. "Here's to Frank and the next club that has the good sense to hire and fire him!"

Friday, May 24, Baltimore

The papers were merciless. Mike Litwin, in the *Morning Sun,* went after the Orioles' front office with Scud missiles. He accused the current regime of ruining a once-proud organization and claimed the real culprits for the failure of the club were Larry Lucchino, Roland Hemond, and Eli S. Jacobs. Referring to Mr. Jacobs, he said that the owner's only concerns are how many people show up at the park and whether Dick Cheney will join him in his sky box. It was a blistering piece.

I bumped into Frank at the stadium around noon today. He is still fuming but has not lost his sense of humor. I evoked a big grin when I said, "Boy, what some people won't do to get out of having to talk to *me* for five minutes a day." He'll meet with the brass on Tuesday. We exchanged home numbers in Los Angeles and shook hands. During the off-season we'll "do" lunch.

The New York Yankees are in town for a three-game series. They're only one game ahead of us, so this weekend will not be the "battle of the titans." Devo and Dewey are still groaning and groining, so they're not available. Ben McDonald has been placed on the fifteen-day DL again—same old same old. The tender elbow has not improved. Roy Smith has been called up from Rochester.

Smith, a husky, soft-spoken kid from Mount Vernon, New York, is what you'd call a journeyman. He's had an undistinguished career bouncing back and forth from the minors to the majors, primarily in the Twins' organization. There have been flashes of greatness . . . well, flashes of "goodness," and he's managed to put together a few decent stretches, but ultimately his big lazy change-up betrays him and he's back in the bushes. Smith is a finesse pitcher, which is why he's always on the bubble. He must rely on pinpoint control, because with no blazing fastball, he's not going to fool anybody or get away with anything. There's also the constant concern of "footsteps" for a Roy Smith. If a youngster with blue heat is even close to being ready, guess who's closest to the door. But Smith made it back again and is in uniform and available for tonight's game.

The Yanks spoiled Oates's managerial debut with a 7–1 win. Here's the kind of night it was: Cal Ripken, Jr., who committed only three errors all of last year (in 162 games), made two tonight. New York scored three runs in the seventh after the final out should've been recorded. With runners at first and third, two gone, Barfield struck out on a wild pitch and made it to first. A run scored, and the inning stayed alive. The following batter doubled in two more. (I called this game "Frank's Revenge.")

The highlight for me was being invited to sit in for an inning on WPIX, the Yankees' TV outlet. I shared the mike with Bobby Mercer and the legend, Phil Rizzuto, "the Scooter." HOLY COW, WAS THAT FUN! Rizzuto is one of the true characters of the game. There are many "Scooter stories" floating around, but I hesitate to mention any, because their validity cannot be assured. However, there are two that I've heard often enough and from enough different people that I will at least assume they might be true.

The first involves Bill White, now president of the National League and once Rizzuto's broadcasting partner. White was out of the booth for an inning, and when he returned, he asked to see Rizzuto's scorecard to fill himself in on what he had missed. Several WW's were scrawled into players' boxes on Rizzuto's card. White inquired as to what WW meant and was told "Wasn't Watching."

When Pope John Paul I died after serving for only a month, the bulletin announcing his death came during a postgame show. The Scooter reportedly came back on the air, shook his head, and said, "Wow, news like that can spoil even a Yankee win."

He's famous for leaving games early to avoid traffic, doing little or no preparation, and calling ballplayers "Huckleberries." Still, I'd rather listen to the Scooter than just about any other commentator on TV today. There once was a time when baseball was a game of personalities and colorful figures; a Damon Runyon–like world with bambinos, bums, and gashouse gangs. Regrettably, very little of that remains. Players are distinguished by their salaries and statistics; teams are measured by their cable contracts. The game itself is not even played exclusively on grass now. Throwbacks like Rizzuto remind us why the sport is unique and special.

Saturday, May 25, Baltimore

The Orioles led, 3–0, going into the seventh, then dipped into that "bullpen of death." The Yankees pulled it out, 6–5. Johnny Oates is now 0–2.

Sunday, May 26, Baltimore

Make that 0–3. José Mesa pitched great, and the O's had a 1–0 lead going into the ninth, but Gregg Olson gave up a home run to Mel Hall, and rookie Pat Kelly doubled in the winning run in the eleventh. It's bad enough to be swept, but by the Yankees???? As that noted philosopher Chester A. Riley used to say: "What a revoltin' development dis is!"

A word about Pat Kelly: Gobble up his rookie cards. He is going to be a standout. Both with the bat and the glove, he was most impressive. Even though the Yankees shelled out over $3 million for Steve Sax this year (a decision questioned by one or two people in the world of baseball), they want to make a place for the twenty-four-year-old rookie right now. Word is the Yankees are shopping Sax in the worst way. Chances are they'll have to eat a large chunk of that three mil to find any takers.

Michael Hill, the TV reviewer for the *Evening Sun,* invited me to join his family for a barbecue. What a treat to eat a home-cooked meal. My schedule prevents me from meeting a lot of people and socializing at decent hours (i.e., evenings), so I'm left pretty much to my own devices here in Baltimore. It's a very lonely existence. My children are growing up three thousand miles away while I spend my days rattling around an empty apartment with black wallpaper, watching repeats of *Baseball Tonight*.

4

Monday, May 27, Baltimore/Los Angeles

Memorial Day.

Debby and the kids are on a Cub Scout campout at Mount Whitney, California. The pack leader (an expert outdoorsman) is driving and supervising. At 5:09 this morning I was awakened by the phone. It was the pack leader. Debby broke her ankle. She's being attended to in a tiny hospital at a place called Lone Pine. The kids are still sleeping back in the tent. Apparently, Deb got up in the middle of the night and needed to use the bathroom. En route to the site, she tripped and felt the ankle snap. On her hands and knees she crawled well over a hundred yards to the pack leader's tent. The prognosis on the ankle was not good. She was given a temporary splint and told to get to a real hospital. She immediately packed and headed for L.A.

Meanwhile, I called Jeff Beauchamp and told him of my need to get to Los Angeles. As always, he could not have been more accommodating. Fill-in arrangements would be made, and I was free to go. (Jim West, the morning sports reporter for WBAL, would be my substitute. Fifteen years ago he had done some baseball in Chicago with Jack Brickhouse.) Eight hours later I was on the other side of the country.

In the interim, Debby had gone to Cedars-Sinai Hospital, where an orthopedic specialist we knew took one look at the ankle and rushed her into surgery. The operation, lasting over three hours, was a success. The surgeon said it was like putting puzzle pieces back together. The ankle had been shattered. We would know tomorrow the game plan for recovery.

Four years ago, when I first went off to do baseball, I told the kids that even though I wasn't there every day, if there was ever an emergency, I would rush home. They were very relieved and happy to see their daddy walk in the front door. For the most part, the kids have been champs through this ordeal. Matty was very attentive to Debby during the ride back to L.A., while Diana was very quiet, choosing oftentimes not to look at her mother. But both stayed calm; neither cried. Debby did her best to mask her intense pain, and the pack leader's kids kept our brood suitably occupied.

Once I was certain Matty and Diana were fine, I sped off to the hospital. (The pack leader's family provided babysitting and brownies.) Debby was in pretty good spirits. Her left leg is heavily wrapped up to the knee. Debby has that rare ability to see and appreciate the humor of any situation. In the midst of this very scary operation, she got a big kick out of the anesthetist. He was a large black man who, as he prepared to put her under, said cheerfully, "Enjoy yo' drugs."

For now we'll take it one day at a time. Debby was given some medication to help her sleep, and after putting Matty and Diana to bed, I too collapsed like a dead one.

Baseball update: The Orioles lost to Cleveland, 3–2. Oates still hasn't won a game, and the team has now dropped five in a row. At the moment I couldn't care less.

Tuesday, May 28, Los Angeles

Debby had a pretty good night and remains in high spirits. She'll get her permanent cast tomorrow, begin physical therapy to learn how to use the crutches, and is expected to be released from the hospital on Friday. I'll remain here until she's home, rejoining the team Friday night in Boston. Debby will be in a cast that will extend over her knee for ten days. She'll be reexamined and another knee-length cast will be put on. She'll wear that for roughly three weeks, and then, if all goes well, she'll be fitted for a smaller walking cast that will end below the knee. She'll just need a cane to get around on that. As a result, the family obviously won't be able to come to Boston this weekend, and as for Baltimore, the middle of June is now looking like the first part of July. Of course, all of these plans are contingent upon her recovery. For the first week after going home, she is to stay off the foot as much as possible.

There are a lot of rental movies she'll catch up on. Fortunately, our housekeeper, Karina (who is a gem), can stay with Debby seven days a week, and our phone hasn't stopped ringing with family members and friends all volunteering to help in any way they can. All the casseroles that Debby has made for people over the years are going to be coming back (probably in the same containers).

Meanwhile, I was Mr. Mom today—fixing meals, running car pools, checking homework, making sure that teeth were brushed, etc. Breakfast looked like a scene from *Kramer vs. Kramer,* with dear old dad running around the kitchen completely lost and overmatched. Eggos were popping out of the toaster, macaroni was boiling on the stove (that's what Diana wanted for lunch), and cinnamon sugar was being liberally sprinkled over anything on a plate. We're talkin' hellzapoppin' here. But the kids seemed happy and secure, and that's all that matters. (Although, along with "Bugs Bunny vitamins" for children, I wish there were "Bugs Bunny Valium" for parents.)

Baseball: John Oates is no longer winless. The Orioles beat the Indians, 5–2. Randy Milligan crashed a three-run home run, and Roy Smith, recently rescued from Rochester, pitched very well. Hopefully, this victory will spell the end of the "Oates Diet." Since taking over the club and losing four straight, John has dropped eight pounds. When I get back, I'll have to tell him about Tommy Lasorda and Nutri-System. It's by far the safer diet.

Frank Robinson met with the front office, I understand. No decision has been reached.

My wife must think she's General MacArthur. Lying in a hospital bed, her leg in a mummy cast and an IV coming out of her arm, she proclaimed, "This will not be my last camping trip." Just how am I going to convince her that *Jews do not camp*???

Wednesday, May 29, Los Angeles

Debby got her permanent cast this morning. It's a little more comfortable than the temporary wrap, but so is having your leg wedged in the mouth of a bear. As she describes it, "I'm now lugging around this incredibly heavy fragile vase on my leg." She received her first lesson on the use of crutches and felt very shaky on the sticks. A walker is her preferred mode of transportation. Throughout, she remains in good spirits. (You're a better man than I, Gunga Debby!)

After getting the kids to school and visiting Deb in the A.M., I had lunch with my partner David. He's been doing a one-week polish on our movie that's lasted three months. Our producer always seems to have "one other thought." (The screenplay is loosely based on my adventures announcing minor league ball in Syracuse. Don't ask where I got the idea.) For the past couple of years, while I've been off doing baseball, we've taken script assignments and written drafts separately, shipping them off to each other for rewrites. When we're together, we write head-to-head, dictating the script to Sherry Falk, our secretary, but once a year we have always split up a script and written each half individually. That way we know we have the confidence to write on our own if need be, and our decision to remain as partners is one of choice, not dependency. Over eighteen years we have covered for each other on numerous occasions, and it has obviously worked out well (we're still together and our agent will take our calls). When the upcoming TV season gears up, I plan on doing a first draft of a *Cheers* and a *Wings* episode. David will first-draft another *Cheers*.

There's a lot that's cheap and phony about the entertainment industry, but I must admit I miss it and feel a little uncomfortable being out of the loop. I enjoyed catching up on the gossip, the scuttlebutt, the "dish."

I'm continually struck with how odd it is that a week ago I'm bouncing around Baltimore and Detroit, broadcasting baseball games around the world, and this week I'm back in my old neighborhood hanging out with people and frequenting haunts I've been to for years. It begs the question: If Dorothy could commute on a regular basis between Oz and Kansas, wouldn't the constant switching between color and black-and-white eventually drive her nuts?

I brought the kids to see Deb after school and they climbed on her bed to watch *Duck Tales* and *Chip 'n Dale Rescue Rangers*. We shared a nice low-key family day together. Too bad we had to do it in a hospital.

On the other side of the country, the O's made it two straight by shading Cleveland, 2–1.

Thursday, May 30, Los Angeles

Debby hit "the wall." We were forewarned that she would, but that didn't cushion the blow much. The prospects of what lay ahead began to really sink in. This vibrant, active person would be off her feet for a month. If there was ever a time that I wanted to quit, it was now. We were also told that this feeling of despair she's experiencing is temporary and lifts after a day or two, but that too was of little comfort. We hugged good-bye for what seemed like five minutes; neither one of us could pull away.

Friday, May 31, Los Angeles/Boston

The cab must've waited for ten minutes. One more kiss for Matthew, one more kiss for Diana. Then a final one for Matthew, a final one for Diana. Finally, a final final one for Matthew, and a final final one for Diana. When we eventually did pull away from the house and I saw the kids waving to me from the kitchen window, I almost burst into tears.

I called Debby from the airport at seven-thirty and was brightened considerably by the cheerfulness in her voice. She was feeling much more optimistic about things and was greatly looking forward to going home in a few hours (with my parents providing the shuttle). I phoned her again from the Boston airport upon arrival, and she was even more her old self. Armed with a stack of rental movies, books, an attentive housekeeper, and adoring children, she was anticipating a very pleasant weekend. (The painkillers didn't hurt either.)

I stepped out of the terminal into a light drizzle and took a "cab ride from hell" to Fenway Park. The traffic was bumper-to-bumper (how odd for five on a rainy Friday afternoon), and my driver spoke to himself in some foreign African tongue for the entire trip ("*Ooo choo choo wauka teeg teeg teeg*"). When we arrived, he wouldn't take me around to the main entrance since it meant one extra turn, so I had to lug my suitcase and carry-on bag halfway around Fenway until I found the press gate.

Al Conin, the Angels' announcer, told me that on his first

trip to Boston he walked over to Fenway at one for a seven-thirty game. He spent the entire afternoon just meandering and exploring this great old ballpark; immersing himself in the ambience and getting in touch with its many ghosts. For six months now I had looked forward to doing the same. Instead, I considered myself lucky to have arrived in time to go on the air.

Everyone was glad to see me and concerned about Debby. Jon had called her at the hospital a couple of days ago. Bob Miller even mentioned her in the Orioles "Game Notes"—"*Welcome back Ken*: Orioles' radio announcer Ken Levine is rejoining the team tonight. . . . He had missed the O's past four games when he returned to Los Angeles to attend to his wife, Debby, who suffered a broken ankle on a camping trip. . . . Her status is listed as day-to-day."

Chuck told me I had missed the best game of the year last night. Hey, great. The Birds beat Boston, 9–3, Jeff Ballard pitched well, David Segui had a timely two-out, two-run two-bagger, and Sam Horn belted a three-run homer. The highlight of the night, however, was the tribute paid Dwight Evans, who made his first return to Fenway after nineteen seasons with the Red Sox. When he ran out to his familiar right-field position in the first inning, he received a thunderous standing ovation. Then, in the second, when he led off for the Orioles, he received another standing O, this one for two and a half minutes. Dewey, a very shy man, doffed his helmet to the crowd, and the cheering wouldn't stop. At one point home plate umpire Ken Kaiser draped his arm around Dewey and said something to him. A full minute later the roar died down and Evans climbed in to take his at-bat. (He grounded to first, by the way. This is *non*fiction.) After the game, Chuck asked Dewey about the conversation with the umpire. "Remember that Chinese restaurant you sent me to ten years ago?" Kaiser apparently asked him. "Yeah?" answered Evans. "Well, I've been goin' there ever since, and it is one damn fine Chinese restaurant." Kaiser was trying to take a little edge off the tension, and it worked. Dwight broke into a wide, appreciative grin. On the one hand, I wish I had been here, but on the other, I'm quite content with where I was.

The press box at Fenway is hiiiiiiigh over home plate. Above the timberline. Several years ago the press box was reconstructed and moved up a level to accommodate a closed-in section of—guess what?—luxury seats. Jon tells of the old press box as being fantastic—perfect vantage point, just the right height. Oh, well. I'm waiting for the day Dyan Cannon pays enough and is given a seat on the dugout bench at Dodger Stadium.

The rain let up but not the cold. Game-time temp was in the high fifties under cloudy, clammy skies. The skyline of Boston is normally visible beyond the right-field line, but thick fog engulfed the tall shafts on this night.

Dewey received another standing ovation. Again he acknowledged with a doff of the helmet. It was another memorable moment in a ballpark that has seen so many.

As for the game, it's as if I'd never left. José Mesa was wild —the Orioles trailed, 6–1, by the time I came on the air for the third inning. BoSox rookie Mike Gardiner was as impressive as the Orioles were unimpressive and won, 7–2.

After a frigid season start, Jody Reed is starting to finally hit for Boston, but our rotisserie team is now thoroughly buried. We exchanged pleasantries at the batting cage during BP, but our relationship is certainly strained.

I checked into the hotel and phoned Debby again. She had a good day. I then prepared to settle in for a good night's sleep, unaware that that was an impossible task at the Boston Sheraton.

Saturday, June 1, Boston

Other than the team hotel in Des Moines, the Kirkwood (which had exposed light bulbs, no towels, and looked like the place Ratso Rizzo stayed at in *Midnight Cowboy*), the Boston Sheraton is the worst hotel I've experienced since doing baseball. It's overcrowded and understaffed. As opposed to the Ritz-Carlton Hotel, this is the Ritz-*Brothers* Hotel. My room was freezing and there was no heat. In the morning, after precious little sleep, I called down to the front desk. A maintenance man was dispatched. He told me their system allows for heat in the winter and air-conditioning in the summer, and since it's June that means air-conditioning. "Well, is there anything you can do?" I asked, expecting maybe a portable space heater might be procured. "Yes, there is," he said, "I'll have housekeeping send up a bathrobe." My shower leaks. A glass-enclosed shower and somehow it leaks. (No wonder the bath mat was damp and discolored.) I ordered a shrimp cocktail last night (which arrived in a brisk hour and a half), and its remains were still outside my door when I returned from the ballpark at five (and getting a little "funky," I might add).

Aside from the accommodations, the day was glorious. The clouds had moved on during the night, leaving clear skies and 70-degree temperatures. Daytime baseball in the sunshine at Fenway—the definition of perfection.

A fixture at the ballpark is P.A. announcer Sherm Feller. Since 1967, in a gruff, clipped voice thick in Boston accent, he has introduced the likes of Yaz and Rice and Evans, and has himself become a celebrity in Beantown. Jon does a great impression of him, as does Reggie Jackson. Feller has quite an interesting background. He has written over a hundred songs and even a full symphony. One of his tunes, "It's Summertime" ("It's summertime, summertime, sum-sum-summertime. . .") became a big pop hit in 1960. Feller, now in his early seventies, has also owned music publishing companies, managed artists, spun records on the radio, made and lost several fortunes, and was close friends with many greats in the music industry, including Arthur Fiedler, Frank Sinatra, and Nat King Cole. Currently, he has some ideas for movies and plays he wants to write. To look at Feller, you'd think he was a salty old sea captain who had just come ashore after one too many years on the ocean—the weathered face, the iron handshake, the missing teeth. But his spirit is youthful, his laugh infectious, and if even half of his stories are true, it would make for one helluva book. The next time you see or hear a game from Fenway, listen for the voice of Sherm Feller.

The Birds beat the BoSox, 3–1. Milacki pitched into the sixth, yielding one run, and the bullpen held 'em the rest of the way. Oh. While we're on the subject of the bullpen, it now has a name. (The new stadium doesn't, but the bullpen does.) The "Dirty Half Dozen," so coined by the Hick-man, consists of Mike Flanagan, Gregg Olson, Mark Williamson, Todd Frohwirth (the sidewinder just called up from Rochester), Paul Kilgus, and Kevin Hickey. A stabilized bullpen is the first step in Johnny Oates's rebuilding plan, and so far the "Dirty Half

Dozen" is holding its own. A solid pen keeps you in ball games and puts you in position to win with a key hit or two. I like the fact that not only does Johnny seem to have a plan, but it seems to be working.

This was another CBS Radio *Game of the Week,* and I was invited again to call the top of the fifth inning to a nationwide audience. Among the affiliates was KNX Los Angeles, so I was heard in my own hometown for the first time. (Whether anybody who knew me listened is another story.) For the second time in two hometown innings, I got lucky. In Seattle I called a six-run rally; today the O's scored only one, but there was a double, an error, a spectacular play, and an argument over a strikeout that nearly resulted in the ejection of the manager and a player. Johnny Bench was my color man, and we blended in well together, I thought. Bench is currently the spokesman for Toyota, and when I came on with him I said I was such an admirer of his that I just went out and bought a car solely on his endorsement.

After the game, Chuck, Dr. Paul, and I decided to walk back to the hotel since the weather was so magnificent (and we couldn't get a cab). We took our time, winding through Kenmore Square and the two-hundred-year-old residential streets. Being from Los Angeles, I can't get over seeing buildings that were actually built before 1940.

My dinner companions were Chuck, Dr. Paul, and Phil Itzoe, the traveling secretary. At Phil's suggestion we walked to nearby Morton's, a steak house. There was an hour and a half wait. We decided to stick it out, repaired to the bar (where we toasted Debby), and Phil excused himself to "use the bathroom." He returned and five minutes later we were seated. The wait was twenty minutes, not ninety. Phil insists he said nothing to the hostess, but I sure wish I knew what that nothing was.

After a delicious dinner I returned to my room at eleven to find last night's room service tray *still* in the hall.

Sunday, June 2, Boston/Minneapolis

The Red Sox sent two-time Cy Young Award winner Roger Clemens (who is 7–2) to the mound against the likable journeyman Roy Smith. Who do you think was favored? Who do you think won? Baltimore 5, Boston 1. Smith gave up one run in seven-plus, and the Rocket Man yielded three in eight innings —only two of them earned, but so what? This is Roger Clemens. Big hit of the day was by Dwight Evans, facing his long-time friend and teammate for the first time and tripling in a run. The crowd went gonzo.

Once a season the players' wives are invited on a road trip. This year it's this trip. So far, they're bringing the team something it has not had all year—luck. The Orioles flew on to Minnesota, having taken three of four from the Red Sox in Boston for the first time since September 1984.

Astute observation: It's a lot more fun being with a winning team.

Monday, June 3, Minneapolis

The Hubert H. Humphrey Metrodome, home of the Twins, has been described as looking from the outside like a giant Jell-O mold. Inside, it's like playing baseball in a space station—high tech, low charm. With all the rain and extreme weather this area sustains throughout the season, a stadium with a roof is unquestionably a must, but as people here say, "There will never be another perfect day for baseball in Minnesota."

As domes go, this is not the ballplayers' favorite. The Metrodome has a cream-colored tentlike roof that is murder on outfielders trying to pick up the flight of the ball. Also, with a big crowd, the arena can get verrrry noisy. The Twins have not enjoyed huge attendance figures over the last few losing seasons, but one only has to think back to the World Series in '87 to remember how deafeningly loud and distracting it can get in ol' HHH. One other factor: Why do you think they call it "the homer dome"??

The Twins took the first game of the series, 3–2. Kent Hrbek (who could use another vowel in his last name) ripped his thirtieth career home run off the O's in the fourth, then doubled in the winning run in the fifth. (What some guys won't do to be my postgame guest!)

Boston saluted Dewey, and Minnesota remembered Roy. Roy Smith, the former Twin (who was 5–10 last year and released) was greeted with two huge ROY banners draped from the upper deck tonight. Always the picture of "cool," Roy acknowledged that the banners "looked okay." He was very pleased.

The best story (or tall tale) of a visiting player being saluted at a stadium belongs to Nate Colbert. Supposedly, in 1969 while playing for the San Diego Padres, he had a career day one doubleheader in Atlanta. He had something like four hits the first game and three in the second, and when his name was announced to bat in the eighth inning, the large crowd rose to its feet and erupted in thunderous applause. Colbert was so moved he couldn't go right to the plate. As the ovation continued, he returned to Cito Gaston, kneeling in the on-deck circle. "Cito," he said, "this is the greatest thing that's ever happened to me. I mean, to have a day like this, and to be appreciated by this many people—" Cito held up his hand and stopped him. "Nate, look up on the message board," said Gaston. Colbert did and read the following message:

THE UNITED STATES HAS JUST LANDED A MAN ON THE MOON.

Tuesday, June 4, Minneapolis

Mazel tov to Frank Robinson! The Orioles announced today that he has accepted a newly created position as assistant general manager of the club. He'll be involved in player development and trades, and will consult on the new ballpark's baseball facilities. I'm very glad that he'll be remaining with the organization and hope he's happy in his new role.

I got a tour of the city and its outlying 'burbs today via my cousin Marty. Each sky-blue lake was more breathtaking than the last. (This is the "Land of Sky-Blue Waters," you know.) And the blue had nothing on the green. The entire region is one lush botanical garden. If only it didn't snow here nine months a year and have temperatures with minus signs in front of them. This and Seattle are by far the two most beautiful areas I've seen thus far on the circuit. Ironic, isn't it, that these are also the two stops with indoor stadiums?

This very promising road trip is starting to go up in smoke. Tied with the Twins at three in the tenth, the Orioles had runners at first and second with none out and didn't score, while in the bottom of the tenth, after two quick outs, Gregg Olson gave up a single and a walk, and pinch-hitter Randy Bush (who was hitting a stout .173) fisted a broken-bat single out into right field to score the winning run. And to make matters worse, Billy Ripken had to come out of the game in the third with a tight back. (It seems every time this club tries to turn the corner, it scrapes a wall and loses a fender.)

Obviously, there are some umpires who are better than others, and we're all only human, and everybody makes mistakes, and that's why they put those little pink erasers on pencils, and so on and so forth, but Dale Ford really did a subpar job behind the plate tonight. The cardinal sin for a home plate umpire is to not have a *consistent* strike zone. It's one thing if his strike zone is altered a bit, giving perhaps the high strike or squeezing the zone. At least both sides know the ground rules and can adapt accordingly. But when there's no rhyme or reason to why one pitch is called a strike and the identical pitch two seconds later is a ball, then there's chaos. That's what we had tonight. Jim Palmer called the officiating "disgraceful," and former major league pitcher Jim Kaat (now a broadcaster for the Twins and CBS-TV) agreed that the zone was all over the place. Most of the time I'd have to say that the umpiring in the American League has been top-notch, but when it's not, there should be some review system. Unlike the NHL, there is none. I think it's easier to get a job as the pope than to land a position as a major league umpire, and with hundreds of deserving individuals bouncing around for years in the minors, if an incumbent isn't up to snuff, he should be "tossed," as it were. Maybe Dale Ford just had a bad night. But it would be nice if someone were keeping track.

The Downtown Marriott is a much nicer hotel than the Boston Sheraton . . . except that the guy in the next room began practicing his trombone at eleven-thirty at night. Scales, up and down, for forty-five minutes. I wonder if he asked for that room specifically.

Wednesday, June 5, Minneapolis/Baltimore

Randy Milligan and David Segui hit back-to-back solo home runs in the ninth inning tonight. It was very exciting except that the O's went into the ninth trailing by three. The Twins swept the series. (So much for the "wives" theory.) At least the game was short (2:37). We flew home and I fell asleep only minutes after the sunrise. It was an even longer night for Ernie Whitt. He returned to Memorial Stadium from the airport only to discover that his Bronco 4 × 4 had been stolen from the stadium parking lot. The trunk was filled with his summer wardrobe, not to mention kitchenware and all of his dishes. So in a sense not only was his car stolen, his apartment was robbed too.

Thursday, June 6, Baltimore

All quiet on the homefront. Peter Casey, David Lee, and David Angell, the executive producers of *Wings* (another series that David and I consult on) sent Debby a huge floral arrangement with a card: "Heard you're going camping. Break a leg." She loved it.

In baseball there's an old expression (all baseball expressions are old), "The first day of a home stand is really the last day of a road trip." This old baseball expression is true. It usually takes a day to catch up on sleep, do laundry, etc. It isn't until the second day that everyone isn't dragging.

Toronto is in for a four-game series. The Blue Jays lead the A.L. East by 1½ over Boston. Both top teams have been struggling lately. The Jays have starting pitching woes. Dave Stieb —their big gun—is out with tendinitis. Jim Acker, a reliever by trade, started tonight, and rookie Juan Guzman will make his first big-league start tomorrow. One Toronto pundit has labeled the rotation "Three Men and a Maybe."

Well, the Orioles took advantage tonight, coming from behind twice to post a 6–4 win before 26,539 delirious fans. Dwight Evans had a clutch two-run hit, Sam Horn hit a ball to the moon, and Leo Gomez (just recalled this morning from Rochester) tripled and drove in a pair himself.

When Leo Gomez was sent down several weeks ago, he decided to drive to Rochester. However, he took a wrong turn off an expressway and got hopelessly lost. Today he had no trouble finding his way back to Baltimore.

To make room for Gomez, Jeff McKnight went on the DL. He sprained his wrist crashing into the wall in the "Metrodoom" Tuesday night. Opening Day third baseman Craig Worthington, who's been sidelined since Detroit with hamstring problems, remains on the disabled list. Oates claims he's only "ninety-five percent" ready and wants him to rehab for a couple of weeks down in the minors, where he can get his stroke back. Worthington, however, has to consent to this, and so far he is reluctant. In truth, he has no choice. The alternative is rotting on the bench. Another unresolved issue: Worthington would like to rehab at commutable Hagerstown. Johnny O would rather he go to Rochester, where the competition is much closer to the bigs. I suspect an underlying concern for Worthington is that if he goes to Rochester, it might be with a one-way ticket. After a great rookie season in '89, Craig had a terrible sophomore year in '90, and '91 has not been perfume. Gomez has been killing the ball in Rochester lately, and I'm sure Worthy feels that if Leo stays hot at the major league level, he'll be spending the summer in lovely upstate New York. This issue should be resolved within the week.

Worthington is just one of six Orioles currently on the DL. Brady Anderson (bum knee), Jeff McKnight (bad wing), Ben McDonald (elbow on the fritz), Dave Johnson (groinorrhea), and Glenn Davis (mystery neck tsuris) are the others. The Birds can ill afford to lose anybody else, but alas, that's the fate of a last-place club. Billy R. has missed two games with his stiff back, Dwight Evans is nursing an Achilles tendon problem, and tonight Randy Milligan dove for a line drive and sprained his left thumb. Other than Cal Ripken, the entire team is now patchwork.

Speaking of Cal, his great start is blending seamlessly into a terrific middle. He's the major league's leading hitter with a .362 average and he is among the A.L. leaders in ten offensive categories. It makes no difference who's pitching; he might as well be hitting off a tee—line shots, opposite field bloopers, bunt singles, towering home runs. The man is a machine!

Ralph Kiner hit over fifty home runs one year for the last-place Pirates and approached general manager Branch Rickey about renegotiating his contract. Rickey is reported to have said, "Ralph, we can finish last without you." God knows where the Orioles would be without Cal Ripken, Jr.

Friday, June 7, Baltimore

Another day, another bombshell. This morning's *Washington Post* broke a story that Orioles' owner Eli S. Jacobs is fielding offers to sell the team. The town went nuts. Painful memories of the Colts slipping out of town in the dead of night are still very much in the hearts and minds of the people of Baltimore. It is highly unlikely, of course, that anyone would want to relocate such a successful franchise (especially with a new stadium ready to open its luxury boxes), but local investors are scarce, and outside owners have outside interests, so there is always that doubt. Eli Jacobs is hardly beloved in this region; many believe he is unwilling to spend the money necessary to field a competitive ball club, his management team has been under a lot of attacks recently, and the local papers have claimed that he is more concerned about which political dignitary he can be seen with in his sky box than the fate of his investment. Yet still . . . "Better the devil you know . . ."

Jacobs purchased the club three years ago for a reported $70 million (although there were operating expenses and assumed financial obligations that certainly raised that figure). His asking price is around $120 million. That's not a bad profit for three years. When you consider what investors must pay to get an expansion franchise ($95 million plus enormous start-up costs, enduring years of a terrible product, *and* not sharing in national TV revenue the first year), $120 million starts to look like Filene's Basement. So far, no names have surfaced as potential buyers, and this could just be a trial balloon to determine the team's market value and whether a sale is advantageous at this time, but I suspect there will be more to this story in the coming weeks and months ahead.

Jacobs's reason for selling the club is still very vague. In the *Post* article today he claimed he was uncomfortable with the public limelight and wished to be involved in more low-profile pursuits. There's the potential to turn that quick $30 million profit. Also, a recent issue of *The Wall Street Journal* indicated that Jacobs is experiencing a number of very serious financial setbacks. Whatever the reason, it appears the seller is "highly motivated," as they say.

I had lunch today with Stan the Fan. Stan Charles, tall, Jewish, and approaching my age (middle) does a late-night sports call-in show on another station in town, WCAO. The show is much less polished than the 'BAL version but still quite fun. If you're familiar with *Diner,* Barry Levinson's brilliant depiction of life in Baltimore in the fifties, you'll have some idea of what the conversations are like on Stan the Fan's show. ("Hey, Stan, I wanna talk about Craig Worthington. . . . I mean, like, really . . . does he got a problem or does he got a *problem*? Personally, and it may just be me, but I think he's got a problem. Now am I off the pier here?") I've met Stan a few times at the ballpark and we arranged to get together today for lunch.

There's a reason why Stan's show sounds like *Diner.* He's living it. Stan was raised in this area and his attitudes are deeply rooted in Baltimore. The tour of the city Stan gave me included not the Inner Harbor or the aquarium, but neighborhoods and local fixtures. We ended up at Greg's Bagels for lunch. Greg is a fifteen-year advertising executive who said the hell with it and opened his own store (Elliott Gould will play him in the movie). This place is *Cheers* with bagels—filled with regulars where everybody knows your name. Greg (introducing me to a lanky forty-five-year-old customer): "Kenny, this is Neil. If your life had been a complete failure, this is who you woulda been." Neil (unfazed): "Hi. Nice to meetya."

After a bagel worthy of New York, it was off to P.J.'s. I told Stan I had been looking for somewhere to eat after the game, and this was his suggestion. P.J.'s is your standard pub—checkerboard tablecloths, wood-paneled, neon beer signs with electrical shorts and satellite TV. Exactly what I was looking for. Stan introduced me to the manager, H. That's what people call him, H. At a nearby table I overheard snippets of the following conversation by three overweight customers:

"I'm goin' down to Florida to get some crabs."

"There's no good crabs in Florida. You want crabs, you gotta go to Louisiana."

"Louisiana? You're nuts. Florida."

"How am I gonna prove it to you that Louisiana has better crabs than Florida?"

"Put me on a plane and blindfold me and take me to both places and feed me crabs. And then I'll decide that the Florida crabs are better."

"How much you wanna bet?"

"Both of you are nuts."

"Is that right?"

"Yeah. If it's crabs you want, you go to Alaska."

"Alaska??"

"That's right. Alaska."

"You don't get crabs in Alaska. You get crabs' *legs*."

And on and on and on.

This is what has been missing for me in Baltimore—tapping into the people, getting out of the malls and into the pubs. At least now I feel I have a starting point.

Debby had her stitches taken out and a new cast set today. Looking at the X ray with the plate and all the pins, she remarked, "Gee, it looks like I've got service for eight in there."

Two in a row for the Mighty O's! They're a juggernaut! For the second night in a row they beat league-leading Toronto, by the identical score of 6–4. Okay, so the Jays had a rookie pitcher, Juan Guzman, making his major league debut, and one of the runs was unearned and another was walked in; the Orioles still prevailed. Junkballer Roy Smith had another "banner" outing, to up his record to 3–0.

Saturday, June 8, Baltimore

So far, I have much preferred being on the road. At least on the road there's always someone in the traveling party you can pal around with, share some lunch with, take in a movie with. Here at home it's very lonely. I will often go until four without so much as speaking to a soul. The isolated, depressing bachelor life is not all it's cracked up to be.

I fill my days with movies when I can. Today's was *What About Bob?* with Bill Murray and Richard Dreyfuss. On the Levine Scale of one-to-ten (ten being a movie I wish I had written, one being a movie I *had* written), *What About Bob?* gets a six. I heartily recommend it if your family is miles away and you have absolutely nothing else in the world to do.

The long, arduous rehabilitation of Glenn Davis continues. The prognosis? No one knows. His injury is so mysterious, there is no precedent. On first appearance Glenn seems as strapping and healthy as an ox. But when you examine his right shoulder, it's a different story. Just above the collarbone there is an indentation, filled with a rather unsightly mound of flesh. As explained, the nerve injury has affected the sternocleidomastoid muscle, which runs down the right side of the neck, and the trapezius muscle, which affects the right shoulder and its ability to raise the arm. Glenn endures three-hour individual physical therapy sessions almost daily to strengthen the muscles in his neck and right shoulder. So far, there has been progress. In his words, the fleshy indentation "used to be a Grand Canyon." However, swinging a bat is still verboten. Glenn is a man of strength and conviction, dedicated to his family, his craft, and his faith. If anyone can overcome this obstacle, it is Glenn Davis.

So the Orioles can beat a converted reliever and a rookie. Can they best Jimmy Key, one of the premier left-handers in the game?

Not tonight.

The game was close until the eighth (2–2), and then a third of the Dirty Half Dozen, Paul Kilgus and Todd Frohwirth, combined to give up six runs, four hits, and four walks. Sam Horn homered in the ninth, so the Orioles lost 8–4, not 8–2. Jimmy Key picked up the win, his league-leading ninth.

Sunday, June 9, Baltimore

Today is an anniversary of sorts. Fourteen years ago today Debby moved out to California. I called 1-800-FLOWERS and ordered her a big floral arrangement to mark the occasion. They took down the information, my credit card number, billing address and phone number, etc., and said they would deliver the arrangement within a few hours. I spoke to Debby at the end of the day, and sure enough, the flowers had arrived. However, the surprise was blown. The florist had trouble reading the credit card number and called Debby to verify. Debby provided him the information, all the while thinking to herself, These flowers better be for *me*.

ESPN *Sunday Night Baseball* came to Baltimore. I commented to Jon that it must be great actually spending a Sunday at home, and he said, "Oh no. I flew to Toronto last night, got the paper, and came back. I don't want to get out of the groove."

The weather was perfect, Leo Gomez belted his first major league home run, and Jeff Ballard was hurling a perfect game into the fourth. Then Devon White hit only his second homer of the year, the wheels came off the wagon, and the Jays came away with a 3–2 victory. The Orioles were one for sixteen with men in scoring position. In five of the first six innings they got the leadoff hitter aboard, and only once did he advance (and that was Gomez, who moved around the bases because he had homered). At this point in the season it's no longer a matter of turning a corner. Now it's trying to make a U-turn with a battleship.

I did another hometown inning on the CBS Radio network tonight, this time with longtime Padre broadcaster Jerry Coleman. I was really looking forward to it, not so much to be heard coast-to-coast, but because the hometown inning seems to be the only inning in which the Orioles consistently score. Tonight: Melvin struck out, Billy struck out, Devo grounded out. I was on and off the air in four minutes.

Police file update: Ernie Whitt's car has been found. His dishes are still missing. No reward has been offered.

Monday, June 10, Baltimore

A day off. I went to see *Spartacus*. It was the longest movie I could find.

Tuesday, June 11, Baltimore

Craig Worthington begins his rehab assignment today in Rochester. Upstate New York is beautiful this time of year.

The Orioles took their team picture today. Two benches were placed out in center field, and at four-thirty players gathered in their home uniforms to be preserved in time. It goes without saying that they were as cooperative as could be. Julie Wagner, the O's community service director, was on hand to inspect and chide those making the obscene gestures.

The Kansas City Royals are in town. They're the only team in the league the O's haven't played. Like the Orioles, the

Royals are in last place in their division. This could be a chance for us to get healthy. Of course, they could be saying the same thing.

As it turned out, this was by far the worst night of the year (although I have an uneasy feeling even *worse* nights are ahead). José Mesa (who has gone from our most consistent to most inconsistent pitcher) was shelled in the third inning, and the Orioles trailed, 7–0, after two and a half. (Did I mention that Kansas City is in the cellar and the Royals are the one team we should be able to beat??) Then, in the seventh inning, with the score still seven-zip, it started to rain. After 1:17 of "Orioles Prattle," play resumed (before a crowd of about 117) and Kansas City added some "insurance runs" in the ninth—including a three-run homer by utility man Bill Pecota—to take a somewhat commanding 11–0 lead into the bottom of the ninth. Jon at least had a little fun with the predicament. With one out, Sam Horn singled. Jon made it sound like he had won the game. "Horn swings and hits it up the middle, *base hit*!!!!!" Everyone in the booth roared. The game mercifully came to an end around midnight.

Wednesday, June 12, Baltimore

I literally drove halfway across town to someplace called Essex to see *City Slickers* with Billy Crystal today. There were ten people in the entire auditorium.

And one of them was Jon.

On the Levine Scale—*City Slickers* receives an eleven (I'd be thrilled just to write the sequel). So far, it's the best movie I've seen this year, and remember, I've seen *Mannequin II*.

When the Orioles were 13–24, the manager was fired. Today they're 20–35 and the general manager has been given a two-year extension to his contract. Go figure. Roland Hemond is the world's nicest person, a forty-year baseball man, etc. But the decision to extend his deal at this moment in time has raised more than a few eyebrows. (The local ink-stained wretches are having a field day.) After all, it's not as if there are fifteen other clubs clamoring to steal Roland away. Also, two assistant general managers (Frank Robinson and Doug Melvin) can't be turning cartwheels. Melvin in particular is seen as a rising star on the baseball horizon, and the Orioles now run the risk of losing him to another organization should a juicier position open up before the end of 1993. All that having been said, I'm happy for Roland and wish him the best. P.S.: Through shrewd trades and savvy player moves, Hemond transformed the Orioles from one of the worst teams in the history of baseball in '88 to a club that was beaten out by Toronto for the divisional championship on the last weekend of the year in '89. Quite a turnaround in one year, no? I think he will continue to do a terrific job.

Sports Illustrated is preparing an article on Jon, and today a photographer was dispatched. He posed Jon sitting on the press box ledge with his legs crossed. For the rest of the night I called him "Buddha."

Space-age technology continues to invade the grand game. We can now track pitches the way we track incoming Scud missiles. Via cameras and computers, pitches can be timed in flight, and upon the ball's arrival to the plate its path can be accurately charted and any break or movement measured within an inch. The journey of the pitch is displayed on the screen through vivid graphic animation. It's the "Devil's Nintendo game." Three young geniuses are attempting to market the system and are giving the Orioles a free look-see during this series. It's almost as amazing as the events that occurred in tonight's game.

The Orioles were trailing Kansas City and premier pitcher Brett Saberhagen 8–1 going into the bottom of the fifth, but incredibly caught the Royals 8–8 in the seventh. "Sabes" came down with a mild stiffness in his shoulder and left after the O's posted five in the fifth, and Luis Aquino surrendered the other two runs—the tying one coming on a dramatic two-out homer by Dwight Evans in the seventh (my inning behind the mike). It was one of the miracle comebacks in franchise history!

But just to prove that this is real life, reliever Mark Williamson, after three shutout innings, served up a tenth-inning home run to Danny Tartabull (his second of the game and sixth RBI), and the Orioles lost, 9–8. After the game one of the reporters commented that maybe Roland Hemond should've gotten a *ten*-year extension.

Final note: the pitch that Williamson made to Tartabull—a fastball, straight as a string, 83 mph. Batting practice.

Thursday, June 13, Baltimore

Do you ever wonder how they get those people to sing the National Anthem before each game? It's simple. Ball clubs accept audition tapes from the general public. I had the chance to listen to a few sent in to the Orioles recently, and they were a howl. A few were decent, some even good, but most were just atrocious—out of tune, poorly recorded, with no musical accompaniment, done in styles that ranged from operatic to romantic ballad to folk singing. One guy must've thought he was Sinatra. "And the rockets' red glare, the bombs goin' crazy in the air . . ." Occasionally the applicants knew the words. Roseanne Arnold starts to sound pretty good after sampling a few of these babies. One was funnier than the next.

One of the Orioles' big problems lately is the woeful lack of quality innings from the starting rotation. No starter has gone seven in ten games. Rarely does a starter make it to the fifth. As a result, the Dirty Half Dozen are a taxed and beleaguered group in the bullpen. And although they're pitching well, they can't keep doing it forever. Williamson's home run yesterday is one example. Since his call-up from Rochester, Todd Frohwirth had gone 8⅔ no-run/no-hit innings out of the pen before giving up a knock, but when he finally did, it cost the Birds a game. Oates's game plan is to use his pen selectively so that specific pitchers can come in to face one or two specific hitters. But that plan is out the window when your relievers have to toil three innings a night. Mike Flanagan, the best bullpen lefty thus far, worked 3⅔ mop-up frames on Tuesday and now is effectively on the shelf for the rest of this series. That meant that in the ninth inning tonight Paul Kilgus, normally a middle guy, was forced to enter in a pressure situation instead of the more reliable and experienced Flanagan. The score was tied at four, and Kilgus (who was lit up Saturday night by Toronto in the eighth, turning a 2–2 tie into an 8–2 Blue Jay rout) gave up an infield single to Brian McRae, then a two-run homer to Kirk Gibson. The Orioles have now lost five in a row and have the worst home record in baseball. Hellllppppp!!!!!!

Friday, June 14, Baltimore/Toronto

We didn't actually fly to Toronto. We flew to Hamilton. The Toronto airport is fifteen miles from the hotel. Hamilton is sixty.

We went to Hamilton because it was quicker.

Customs and immigration at the Toronto airport are a nightmare, while it is a quick and organized affair at the smaller Hamilton. It took less time to clear customs and make the hour drive than it would have had we gone through Toronto International.

Toronto itself is magnificent. Modern yet charming, and spotlessly clean—almost an idyllic setting. The finest American city in North America may just be in Canada.

And then there's the Skydome.

The expression on my face when I first stood on the field and gazed up at the Skydome was probably the one I had when I saw my first breast. I was awestruck. I cannot imagine a more impressive facility. I suspect you've seen the Skydome on TV, so there's little need to describe it—the five seating levels, its numerous restaurants and bars, the infamous hotel that looks out onto the field and that the field looks into (two years ago during a game, a young lady with the help of her all-too-willing boyfriend demonstrated to 50,000 people the correct way to "attack a corn dog"), the Sony Jumbotron television board, which is three stories high by nine stories wide, and of course the world's largest retractable roof. Watching that roof open is an amazing experience—it's thirty-one stories high. You could put the Astrodome on the Metrodome and still not scratch the ceiling. It initially opens with two panels separating high above home plate. A brilliant slash of sunlight streaks across the field. It's as if the sky had opened up. Pure Steven Spielberg. And then silently two of the three sections roll back into each other while the final panel swings around the perimeter of the stadium and fits neatly into the other three. The entire process takes approximately twenty minutes, and when it's completed, all three sections remain above center field in a humongous half-shell reminiscent of the Hollywood Bowl. On days in which it is open, the roof is normally rolled back two hours before game time and it is closed after each game, usually well after the spectators have gone home so as not to cause major traffic tie-ups from the rubberneckers.

Everything about the Skydome is first cabin, from the press box to the dugouts to the locker rooms. The Blue Jays' clubhouse is unbelievable. Imagine the swankiest health club you possibly can—the plushest locker rooms, the finest training equipment. You've pictured the downtown Y compared to the Skydome. I don't understand how a Blue Jay player can be demoted to Triple-A Syracuse and not kill himself.

As for the field itself, the media guide boasts that 516 African and 743 Indian elephants could fit on its surface. The guide also claims that 396 million gallons of milk would be needed to fill the dome. That last statement I challenge, and I'm hoping that there's a fraternity out there somewhere willing to put it to the test.

The only blemish on the Skydome is that a thick wire cable used to support the backstop screen is attached to the top of our booth. As a result, my view is impaired. I can't see the pitcher. But he's only one of nine, so I really shouldn't complain.

Encouraging news on the Ben McDonald front: Big Ben threw a simulated game today (i.e., pitching off the mound to hitters for ten minutes, taking a break, then repeating the process for several "innings") and performed very well. He felt no discomfort, and take it from someone standing right behind the batting cage, his fastball had pop. Repeatedly, it exploded into the catcher's mitt, the sound reverberating around the dome. If the arm feels okay tomorrow (that's always the big test—how the arm feels the day after), he'll throw again in a couple of days, then go down to Rochester for a start or two and hopefully be back before the All-Star break. With the Orioles' bullpen now having worked more innings than any other pen in the league, a healthy McDonald could really turn things around for the club. It's not too late to win the division, you know . . . in 1992.

Dwight Evans went on the disabled list today. He has a strained left Achilles tendon and—with Brady Anderson ready to be activated and the Orioles slated to play seven of their next ten games on player-punishing AstroTurf—the club and Dewey decided he should go the DL route in order to open up a slot. So instead of having one of the great clutch hitters in the game (remember Evans blasted that dramatic game-tying home run against the Royals Wednesday night?), the Orioles have a

.147 hitter with no homers, a total of nine RBIs, and (for a speedster) as many caught-stealings as thefts (four).

The Orioles lost, 9–1. Starter Jeff Robinson was out on a shield after three-plus innings. Flanagan was forced into four innings of middle mop-up relief, thus perpetuating the bullpen's vicious cycle. The O's have now lost six straight, nine of eleven, and in six days have dropped five more games off the pace. But the Skydome is a pisser!

Saturday, June 15, Toronto

Cal Ripken could not be having a better year. An 0-for-3 night constitutes a prolonged slump. You talk about the model of consistency. Today he went two-for-three and drove in a pair of runs, lifting his average to .358 and his RBI total to 41. And it's awesome to imagine how many *more* ribbies he'd have if he were hitting behind, say, a Rickey Henderson, who's always on base. Watching Cal Ripken play every day (and he has played every day for 1,470 days) is truly a privilege.

Your heart has to go out to Billy Ripken, playing in the shadow of such an auspicious big brother. Billy's a damn fine glove man at second and at times swings the bat very well. But he's no Junior. (Of course, who is?) Personalitywise, Billy is very different from Cal, as you might expect. Whereas Cal is quiet and methodical, Billy is more boisterous, striving for attention and his own identity. If there is any jealousy or resentment toward Cal, it is not apparent. In fact, the two brothers seem very very close. (Interestingly, there is another brother, Fred, and there's also a sister, Ellen, in the Ripken family; neither are in baseball, but like Cal and Billy, they work together, at a motorcycle shop owned by Fred.) Cal Ripken, Sr., and, notably, Vi Ripken, did a Hall-of-Fame job of raising four youngsters.

For all of his heroics lately, Cal was upstaged today by the mighty bat of Bob Melvin. "Bo-mo," a backup catcher, collected five hits including a home run, to power the O's past the Jays, 8–4. Only twenty-eight times in Oriole history has a player accomplished that feat. After the game I asked Bob what he was going to do tonight to celebrate (the game being a day affair), and he said, "Order room service, watch a little TV." The man is an animal!

It used to be that there were team curfews at night on the road. Ballplayers not back in their hotel rooms by the prescribed hour were required to dig into their wallets. The practice no longer exists—today's highly paid athletes are just expected to conduct themselves responsibly and be ready to play by game time—but in the forties and fifties this was not necessarily the case. Stories abound of drunken players tiptoeing through lobbies or shimmying up drainpipes, trying to avoid their manager's detection. My favorite curfew story concerns either Leo Durocher or Casey Stengel (depending upon whom you hear it from). One night at curfew, Durocher-or-Stengel stepped into the hotel elevator and tipped the operator with a baseball in case he wanted autographs. The next morning Durocher-or-Stengel sought out the elevator man, made note of who autographed the ball, and then fined those players for being out after curfew.

Jon and I walked back to the hotel (the Harbour Castle Westin), taking a leisurely route along the lakefront (Toronto borders Lake Ontario). Sailboats lazily drifted by, street vendors peddled their appetizing wares, and families strolled along the shore, enjoying this sunny Saturday. I'm told that Toronto is the most expensive city to live in in North America (the taxes rival Robin Hood's Nottingham), but from what I've seen and heard, it also provides the highest quality of living. Plus, they throw in that Skydome.

Jon is flying to San Francisco tonight for tomorrow's ESPN game. He'll fly back to Baltimore on Monday. Over this eight-day period, he will be in Toronto, San Francisco, Baltimore, Kansas City, Detroit, and Cleveland. How he does it, I do not know. How his luggage doesn't wind up in Seattle, Oakland, Boston, and Milwaukee is an even greater mystery.

Went out to dinner at a place called Bigliardi's with Chuck Thompson and his wife, Dr. Paul, and traveling secretary Phil Itzoe. Superb meal, but I felt a little guilty. I shouldn't be having more fun tonight than Bob Melvin.

Sunday, June 16, Toronto/Baltimore

Father's Day, and I'm not even in the same country as my family. Depending on the day, I have the best or the worst job in the world.

Joe Orsulak hit his first major league grand slam today, and I was lucky enough to be behind the mike at the time. WBAL is replaying it every fifteen minutes. The Orioles went on to pound Toronto, 13–8. Two more hits for Cal (including another home run), and Leo Gomez went deep, extending his hitting streak to ten. (Craig who?) The Orioles have now won two in a row and head home to face Minnesota, a team that today posted their league-leading fifteenth straight victory. Oy!

Pitching coach Al Jackson told me to expect a fine from the next Kangaroo Court. Most ball clubs have these Kangaroo Courts. They're a great way of keeping the guys loose. A self-appointed judge will rule on such atrocities as giving up a hit on an 0–2 count, yawning in the dugout, walking the ninth-place hitter, etc. My infraction: During the seventh-inning stretch at the Skydome, instead of singing "Take Me Out to the Ballgame," everyone rises and does a little aerobics dance led by seven or eight cheerleaders. Feeling a little frisky today, I joined in. Unfortunately (and unbeknownst to me), my antics were shown on the massive Jumbovision board. Jackson and the others in the dugout went nuts. I can expect to be twenty dollars lighter.

One final thought about Kangaroo Courts: The Orioles hold theirs usually once or twice a month in a closed-door session before a game. Most teams conduct them *after* a game, and specifically, after a win. That way there is a little more incentive to win the game—a dangling carrot. Jim Palmer said that in the Orioles' championship years the postgame courts were responsible for sparking many a victory. Why aren't these trials still held after a game? Many of today's players are gone twenty minutes after the last out. Gee, I dunno, but that sounds like a felony to me.

By the time we arrived home (Baltimore is actually considered home now), it was after nine and I still hadn't eaten, so I zipped out to Ralphie's Diner in nearby-but-not-really Cockeysville. Owned by Hersch Pacino (of Hersch's Orchid Inn fame), Ralphie's is a terrific restaurant in an upscale diner motif. Unfortunately, by 9:42 it was closed. I wound up having my Father's Day dinner at Denny's. It was my second "grand slam" of the day.

5

Monday, June 17, Baltimore

The Twins are the hottest team in baseball. They lead the league in team hitting and pitching. During their fifteen-game winning streak they've outscored their opponents 87–39. Their starters routinely get into the seventh inning. As for the Orioles, well . . . they can suit up twenty-five guys.

The Twins were leading 5–3, going into the ninth. Rick Aguilera (he of the seventeen saves) came on to face the bottom of the Birds' order—bottom of the cage?? David Segui singled to center. Juan Bell came on to run for him. Brady Anderson, doing his best Dwight Evans imitation, followed with a clutch single to put the tying runs aboard at first and second. Mike Devereaux, not a good bunter, was asked to bunt anyway, and he laid down a doozy. Runners at second and third. Orsulak pinch-hit for Billy Ripken and flied deep enough to left to score Bell—5–4 Twins, two outs. Next up was Cal. Interesting dilemma for Minnesota manager Tom Kelly: Does he pitch to the hottest hitter in the game (Cal had already doubled and homered for the night), or break an unwritten rule of baseball that says you never intentionally walk the potential winning run? Kelly did what I would've done. He walked him—walked him without a second's hesitation. Randy Milligan, batting .115 lower than Cal, was the next batter. First pitch—a strike; second pitch—a ball; third pitch—a swinging strike, as Randy was badly fooled on a fastball way out of the zone. The Orioles were down to their last strike. Aguilera fired and Milligan drilled it up the alley in left. Anderson, the tying run, scored, Cal rounded third and headed home. The relay throw was not in time, Cal scored, and Memorial Stadium went nuts. Chuck called the play, and I swear I got chills. For ten minutes the spectators remained on their feet just yelling and cheering. Milligan was mobbed by his teammates, who remained out on the field savoring what I'm sure many considered might be *the* victory of the season. "Orioles Magic," at least for one brief moment in time, was back.

Tuesday, June 18, Baltimore

A potential buyer for the Orioles has surfaced. He is Leonard Weinglass . . . better known as "Boogie." The first day I arrived in Baltimore, Bonnie Levitt took me to the Cross Keys deli to grab a bite before going on to see my elegant town house. I spotted a gray-haired man in his late forties wearing a jeans jacket and sporting a ponytail. I was amazed. L.A., sure, but Baltimore? That was Boogie. If you remember the movie *Diner*, the free-spirit beautician/gambler character portrayed by Mickey Rourke was named "Boogie," modeled after director Barry Levinson's childhood chum Leonard Weinglass. Flash forward to the present and Boogie is a self-made tycoon worth over a hundred mil. He made his fortune selling attention-grabbing clothes for teenage girls in the late sixties. The Merry-Go-Round Boutique was his baby. He married, had children, sold his business for a king's ransom, and moved to Aspen, where he now operates a chain of fabulously successful restaurant/clothing stores—Boogie's Diners. (That's right. Fashion and food under one roof.)

Boogie would certainly make his stamp on the Orioles if he was to buy them, and although it's way too early to speculate on his chances, just the notion of his purchasing the team is an intriguing one. Also, it would be interesting to see how the other league owners take to a man who sports a ponytail.

Ben threw well in another simulated game today and will be off to Rochester tomorrow. He's scheduled to start Friday against Pawtucket.

The exhilarating momentum of last night's dramatic win did not carry over into tonight's. In fact, this was another one of those "worst nights of the year." First off, it rained. We had a 1:53 delay before we even started. That meant almost two scintillating hours of *Orioles Talk*—the root canal of broadcasting. Once we played, we lost. Twins 9, Orioles 2. Minnesota led,

6–0, after two. Roy Smith has been sharper. The Twins' starter, Scott Erickson, was another story. This twenty-three-year-old right-hander is leading the league in ERA with 1.60. Tonight's victory ups his record to 11–2, the eleven wins coming consecutively. He's got a devastating fastball that drops so sharply and with such bite that it's practically unhittable. Everybody talks about Ben McDonald becoming the next Roger Clemens, but it may well be Scott Erickson.

Here's how bad things went for the O's tonight: The highlight of the game was when rookie Juan Bell walked. It was his first walk ever in the big leagues, and it was obvious he doesn't draw many free passes, because when ball four was called, he remained at the plate. Home plate umpire Mark Johnson walked over to the plate and dusted it off (as umpires will normally do after a walk), and Bell just stood there. Johnson wondered if he himself had the count wrong, checked his little ball-strike clicker, and sure enough, the count was 4–2. He pointed to first base and told Bell to get his ass down there. No, Bell did not ask to keep the ball.

Wednesday, June 19, Baltimore/Kansas City

You've heard the expression "day/night" doubleheader? In a sense today we completed a "night/day" doubleheader. Last night's ugly affair didn't end until well after midnight, and today an afternoon game was scheduled. (The rare Wednesday matinee is to accommodate our flying to Kansas City upon its conclusion.)

To get people into the yard to see a last-place team in the middle of the work week, the Orioles staged a terrific promotion: "Turn Back the Clock Day." The idea was to bring back 1966—the year the Orioles won their first World Series. Bleacher seats went on sale at 1966 prices (seventy-five cents), popcorn was a quarter a bag, all fans received authentic replica (there's an oxymoron) 1966 Orioles caps, several members from the championship team were on hand to be saluted, longtime voice Chuck Thompson emceed, and the team wore authentic 1966 uniforms. Music from the era was played over the P.A., and old National beer commercials were reprised on the DiamondVision board. Everyone was asked to wear sixties-style clothing, and most of the secretaries came in miniskirts and mod outfits. Several of the beat reporters came as hippies, although some dress so slovenly anyway, it's hard to tell if they were in costume. Unfortunately, my Nehru jacket is still at the cleaners. Knowing that this was a travel day, I wore a jacket and a tie. A number of people stopped me and said, "Hey, is that what you wore in 1966?" to which I replied, "Yes, I went to a funeral that year."

The mood was very festive, and the excitement would build going into the ninth inning. The Orioles were leading Minnesota, 4–3, after a stirring comeback in the seventh. And in the eighth there was a spectacular catch by Devereaux to literally rob Shane Mack of a home run; Devereaux leaped and almost vaulted over the center-field wall to bring Mack's drive back into the ballpark.

But then the ninth.

Gregg Olson—the ace, the closer, the man, "Wild Thing"—was brought in to save it for Jeff Robinson, who actually got into the eighth inning. The first three batters singled, tying the game and putting runners at first and second. A wild pitch sent them to second and third. With first base now open, the batter was walked intentionally to load 'em up. Shane Mack stepped up. Before his at-bat would be over, all three runs would score. Here's how: Another wild pitch scored the first run. Olson scrambled off the mound to field it in an effort to throw the runner out at the plate. But the throw was wild, kicking off to the backstop. The second runner scored; the third runner was now at third. And then a *third* wild pitch scored that runner. Then, to add insult to ineptitude, Olson walked Mack, who scored all the way from first on a single by Kirby Puckett when Joe Orsulak threw to the wrong base. Five runs, four hits, three wild pitches, a throwing error, and a judgment error. The crowd of 44,742 saw the Orioles lose, 8–4.

In a sense, the Orioles turned back the clock to 1954; a year they won 54 and lost 100. Mr. Peabody will have to do some more tinkering with the Way-Back Machine.

Immediately after the game we flew out to Kansas City. The Orioles' private plane is scheduled to be ready following the All-Star break, and the company that'll provide that jet is furnishing transportation for this trip. Our buses took us onto the tarmac, past the terminals, to a plane sitting alone in the middle of nowhere. It was an Emerald Airlines (I'd never heard of them either) DC-9, a much smaller plane than we've ever employed before. We all looked at each other. Something did not seem right.

We boarded to find there was no first-class section and no overhead compartments. The seats were cramped and threadbare. I knew we were in big trouble when the safety instructions were in Spanish. The two stewardesses were inexperienced and completely lost. It was as if someone went into Arby's and said to the first two waitresses he could find, "Hey, how'd you like to make some extra money tonight and get to see Kansas City?"

Standard procedure is for soft drinks and beer to be available upon boarding. Today there were none. Pitching coach Al Jackson asked for a beer and was told by the stewardess that they didn't want to serve anything until after they had taken off. There was a near riot. After "permission" had been secured from the captain, a chest of beer was slid down the center aisle. I asked the stewardess where I could get an application form to join Emerald Airlines' frequent-flyer program, and she had no idea I was joking. Apparently, this is a chartered airline. One of the stews said they recently had the Ice Capades on a flight, "and it was really funny because we had all these big ol' props and things, and we even had to strap in some animals in the main cabin." Ha ha ha.

We sat for close to an hour while they loaded the luggage, and then realized the plane was too small to accommodate it all. Some was then FedEx'd to K.C., and the rest was loaded into our cabin. With no overhead compartments on the plane, we all had bags and carryons stuffed under our seats, and now luggage was coming aboard. Johnny Oates, who traditionally sits in the front row, was asked to move back; his space was needed for suitcases. The pilot—who had been loading luggage—finally walked in, surveyed the scene, and muttered to himself, "I sure don't like the looks of this." Imagine how comforting *that* was to overhear.

We finally took off, and dinner was served. Lasagna. I don't have to tell you how delicious it was. Salad was included, with a stewardess going down the center aisle flinging salad dressing packets out of a garbage bag. I asked for a Coke and was given Shasta Cola.

I really felt bad for our traveling secretary, Phil Itzoe. None of this was his fault. He was more surprised and horrified than anyone. This same aviation company is supposed to provide a DC-9 to Cleveland on Sunday and another DC-9 home next Thursday night. I suspect some changes will be made.

We were supposed to land in Kansas City at 7:45. Obviously, if the game had gone long, that arrival time would be later. Today's game finished in 2:48—one of our shortest this year. We arrived in K.C. at 10:05.

The hotel we stay at here, the Adams Mark, is within walking distance of the ballpark but convenient to absolutely nothing else. The city of Kansas City is miles away, and the airport is farther still. The bus ride to the hotel was an hour. By the time I got in my room and got my luggage, Wednesday was Thursday. Of course, I was one of the lucky ones. I *got* my luggage.

After the team de-boarded the pride of Emerald and bused off into the hot Missouri night, the baggage compartment was emptied into the team truck, which sped off to the hotel and ballpark to make its drop-offs. The plane then refueled and taxied down the runway en route to its next destination. Just before it rolled into position for takeoff, one of the copilots noticed that all the luggage loaded into the cabin was still there. They had to turn the plane around, unload, and find taxicabs to transport everything.

I've come up with what I think is the perfect slogan for this airline, and it's welcome to use it for free.

> EMERALD AIRLINES—FLY US AND KNOW WHAT IT'S LIKE TO BE GREEN.

Thursday, June 20, Kansas City

Royal Stadium is as beautiful a ballpark as you'll ever see. It's hard to believe it is nineteen years old. The stadium looks brand new. Shea Stadium in New York is only nine years older but looks fifty. The waterfalls and grass embankments against a setting of pastoral rolling hills provide a lovely, serene backdrop, and although I hate artificial surfaces, I must admit the emerald-green carpet is a striking sight.

The press lounge was amazing. Dinner entrées were not hot dogs and meat loaf (normal media-guzzler fare), but steak and frog legs. (That's right. Frog legs.) Next to the lounge in Detroit (yes, Detroit) this is the best in the league so far. I haven't sampled Cleveland, New York, or Oakland yet, but I've got a feeling Kansas City is a good bet to keep the title.

The view from the booth was spectacular. Unfortunately, I had to watch the game. The Orioles lost in ten innings, 3–2. Brady Anderson misjudged a fly ball in the tenth, which resulted in the winning run crossing the plate. One disgruntled member of the media had this to say: "If I were the general manager of this team for ten minutes, the first thing I would do is send Brady Anderson so far down to the minors no one would ever find him. Then I would have Juan Bell carry his bags and send Tim Hulett out looking for them." The truth is, although they're nice guys all, the Orioles have been reduced lately to a club largely consisting of castoffs, nonroster invitees, and Triple-A journeymen. It's the "Dirty *Two* Dozen Plus Cal." They're all doing the best they can; it's just that their best is the league's worst.

Reliever Mark Williamson received a scare in the seventh when hitter Terry Shumpert lashed a drive back to the box that struck him on the right forearm. He dropped to his knees to retrieve the ball and couldn't get his fingers around it. He was taken immediately to the hospital for X rays, and fortunately the results were negative. It was just a bad bruise. You can literally see the imprint of the ball on his arm. I'm surprised you can't see the league president's signature stamped on his arm as well. Last year Mark broke his finger in a game at Oakland, but he said this injury was much more painful and far more frightening. This time he thought his career might be over. Words can't express his relief upon learning it was not.

Friday, June 21, Kansas City

I hear K.C. is the barbecue capital of the world, Oates Brothers' and Bryant's the two standouts. Someday, if I'm ever *in* Kansas City, I'll have to try them.

Jon and I went to see *The Rocketeer,* which opened today at our nearby outpost theater. It's based on a comic-book hero, and the nice thing about this movie is that you really don't have to read the book first to enjoy it.

A severe thunderstorm ripped through the area during the early evening, wiping out the ball game (after a tedious two hours of *Orioles Talk* with your pals Ken & Chuck). The game will be made up Sunday as part of a double dip. José Mesa was tonight's starter and gave up three quick runs in the first inning (the rains came in the second). Fortunately for José, the game is thrown out with the rainwater.

Mesa remains a big mystery. For some reason, he is now afraid to throw his change-up and slow curve during a game. Hitters sit on his fastball and (when he gets it over the plate) light him up. During warm-up he'll throw change after change, but once "Play ball" is called, he relies on his heater. Earlier in the season, when he was the Orioles' best starter, he would routinely throw the curve or off-speed pitch 2–0 or 3–1 in the count, but now when he falls behind, you can bet the farm on the fastball. It's interesting that a pitcher will lose confidence in a certain pitch if, say, he's been taken deep a few times, yet that rarely applies to the fastball. Most pitchers will continue to serve up their fastballs regardless. Oates has maintained that Mesa has one of the best arms in the organization, and he's sticking with him, but many—some teammates included—are wondering just how long the team can afford to suffer with Mesa every five days until he regains his confidence and form. Isn't that what the minor leagues are for? they wonder. Mesa is scheduled to start again in the makeup game on Sunday.

Speaking of the minors, Ben McDonald started for Rochester tonight against Pawtucket. He gave up two runs, four hits, a wild pitch, and made 43 pitches in the first inning. He settled down somewhat in the second and third and came out after 68 pitches. There was some talk that Ben might be back with us next week; now I'm not so sure.

From the idiocy file comes this: The baseballs used at the major league and Triple-A level are not the same. The majors use the Rawlings model, while the minors employ the Wilson ball. There is a big difference. The Wilson ball has raised seams. As a result, a number of big-league pitchers have come down to Triple A for rehab and have developed blisters that've retarded their progress. Ben McDonald fell victim last year. The pitchers in the minors who are used to the raised seams have a huge adjustment gripping the ball when they get to the majors. Imagine practicing the piano your entire life, and when you finally get a chance to perform a concert at Carnegie Hall, you learn the piano you'll be using only has eighty-seven keys. For the life of me I cannot understand why major league organizations don't insist their minor league affiliates employ the same balls they do. It sure seems like a no-brainer to me.

Saturday, June 22, Kansas City

Our hotel is hosting the contestants for this year's "Miss Teen America" contest. That's just what you want—hundreds of perky little teenage girls and a team of professional ballplayers on the road.

A group of us went to see *Robin Hood: Prince of Thieves*. It had action, suspense, scope, fine performances, and even Sean Connery. Why didn't I love it? However, on the Levine Scale: ten. (The movie took in $27 million its first weekend. If I had written it, I might be as rich as one of the players I saw it with.)

The forecast was not promising, but the rain stayed away. Bob Milacki pitched his guts out, and the Orioles led 1–0 going to the ninth. Although he had thrown only 72 pitches (50 for strikes), Oates elected to bring in Olson to start the ninth. After his disastrous outing Wednesday against the Twins, Olson needed to "get back up on the horse," so to speak, and had one base runner gotten aboard in the ninth, Milacki would've been gone anyway, making Olson's task that much tougher. So the skipper opted to make the move. We all held our collective breath.

Olson got 'em out in order—two strikeouts to boot. This was the first 1–0 Oriole victory since July 6, 1986. That may seem hard to believe, but . . .

Sunday, June 23, Kansas City/Cleveland

. . . this was the first Sunday doubleheader at Royal Stadium since 1974. With today's economics in baseball, scheduled doubleheaders are about as rare as U.S. presidential resignations—and when was the last time you can remember one of those?

Today's agenda: the twinbill, then a flight to Cleveland. Estimated arrival at Hopkins Airport, Cleveland: 8:45 P.M.

A low, overcast, gloomy sky served as our roof all afternoon. The threat of rain was ever-present, but none appeared.

Chuck was my partner today, but only till five. He has an appointment tomorrow morning in Baltimore he must keep, and the last flight out of Kansas City is at six. With a single game originally scheduled, that posed no problem, but now. . . .

I told him not to worry, I'd be happy to finish up the second game. I even enlisted the K.C. announcers, Denny Matthews and Fred White, to come in and each do an inning for me. With a little luck, the games would speed along and I'd end up doing maybe three or four additional innings.

Wrong!

The doubleheader began at 1:05. Kansas City jumped out to a 4–0 lead in the second. It was two o'clock. The pace picked up. The Orioles trailed, 8–1, going to the eighth. Oh well, at least no extra innings. They scored three runs; 8–4 Kansas City, heading to the ninth. Four o'clock. Still, we should be well into the second game by five. And even if the finale goes three hours plus the postgame show, I'm signing off well before eight.

Take it to the bank!

Billy walked; Brady and Cal singled. The bases were loaded with one out for Chris Hoiles. He hit a grand slam. I didn't know whether to cheer or plotz. A miracle comeback.

Of all the times!

We did go into extra innings . . . at 4:25. Tim Hulett led off the tenth with a home run. Devereaux singled and Brady hit his first homer of the year. Olson pitched a perfect tenth and the O's won it, 11–8 . . . at 4:49. Chuck left a silver bullet and was gone.

I turned the program over to our local stations for ten minutes between games, all the while scrambling for lineups, game notes, and a urinal. (David Glass, the former San Francisco Giant announcer, once called games for Jacksonville, residence of the great Red Barber. He had occasion to meet Barber that summer and asked if Barber had heard any of his broadcasts. Barber responded that he had, so Glass asked if he might be so kind as to give him a critique. Barber said, "You work those games alone, don't cha?" Glass replied yes and waited anxiously for this legend's sage advice. "Then never miss a chance to use the bathroom," Barber said, and moved off.)

Game two began at five-twenty. The big crowd of 30,000 had all but left (following Chuck's lead). José Mesa rediscovered his curveball and gave up only one run and five scattered hits through five innings. We were cookin'! A double and two singles to start the fifth and he was gone; 6:45. The Orioles broke a 3–3 tie with two in the second and two more in the eighth. Juan Bell had three hits and three RBIs (Anderson, Bell, and Hulett all had good days). At 8:05 we went to the ninth. Orioles 8, Royals 3.

Mark Williamson was pitching. After getting struck on the forearm only four days ago, he was, it was nice to see, already back out on the mound . . .

. . . until he gave up back-to-back singles and a walk. Goodbye, Williamson, hello, Olson. Gregg's first batter, Danny Tartabull, singled to right; two runs scored, 8–5 O's. Still no problem. Olson uncorked a wild pitch (shades of Wednesday vs. Minnesota). Runners now at second and third. Warren Cromartie hit a sacrifice fly—8–6 Orioles, but now with one out. Kevin Seitzer singled. Royals at first and third, with the tying run on base. I glanced back at Dr. Paul. This couldn't be happening. Brent Mayne stepped up to the plate. Mayne's a reserve catcher who doesn't often play and doesn't have a high average. He's a great candidate to hit into a double play.

Mayne singled to right. Tartabull scored, Seitzer to second—8–7 Baltimore. All of a sudden I was in a Stephen King novel.

Bill Pecota was next. Base hit to left. Seitzer crossed the plate with the tying run. I was in shock. The Orioles had blown a five-run lead in the ninth. Jim Eisenreich followed, and Olson let fly another wild pitch. Runners were at second and third. Eisenreich was then walked intentionally to load the bases in favor of Brian McRae. Finally, a good curve, and McRae chopped it to Cal. He threw to the plate for the force. Two outs. Kirk Gibson (the eleventh batter of the inning) then lined out to Anderson, and for the second time in the doubleheader we plunged into extra innings.

At 8:35.

One thought kept going through my mind: Keep the energy level up. I took it as a personal challenge not to sound fatigued. If someone was just tuning in, I wanted him to be amazed at how I was still maintaining my sense of enthusiasm. Besides, if I did a good job with this, I could always get a job hosting a telethon.

The Orioles got two on in the tenth and couldn't score. The Royals got a man on in the eleventh and couldn't score.

It was 9:25.

With one out in the twelfth, Cal walked. Randy Milligan then hit his fourth consecutive single (worth noting because I like Randy). David Segui flied out, and Joe Orsulak—whom I could kiss—singled to right to score Cal. Paul Kilgus came in and hurled a one-two-three inning, and the marathon was finally over. The Orioles had swept the Royals . . . at 9:46.

I did the postgame show and signed off nine and a half hours after I had signed on. Till the very end my energy level never flagged. I was exhausted but very pleased.

What better way to unwind after a lonnnnnng day than to fly to Cleveland? And what better way to do it than on Emerald Airlines? We checked into the Cleveland Sheraton at three-thirty. Jon Miller called the Angels-Tigers ten-inning game from Detroit tonight on ESPN and he arrived at 3:25. He would've been here earlier except his driver got lost.

Monday, June 24, Cleveland

An off-day in Cleveland. So much to see, so much to do. Actually, from what I did see and do, Cleveland is not that bad. It is certainly one of the most maligned cities in America (ugly, polluted, skyline of smokestacks, those idiots eating dog bones at the Browns' games), but recently Cleveland has taken steps to clean up its act. In a sense, Cleveland is fifteen years behind Baltimore. The major face-lift that Baltimore underwent in the eighties is just now on the drawing board in Cleveland. Lakefront development (the city is situated on the shores of Lake Erie) is in the planning stage. The downtown section has been improved tremendously over the last few years. Where the old train station stood is now the Tower Center, a most impressive high-scale indoor mall with the obligatory nine-screen theater. New construction is definitely on the rise in the town Randy Newman immortalized as "Cleveland, city of lights, city of magic."

I really only had a half day off since I slept until 11:45. I set out for the Tower Center and saw *Thelma & Louise*. A recent *Time* magazine article about the film said its popularity was clearly delineated along gender lines; women loved it while men hated it. Well, there must be something wrong with me. I liked it—liked it a lot. However, I'm not going to spread that around the clubhouse—although I doubt many of the Orioles will see *Thelma & Louise* . . . especially with *Terminator 2* opening soon.

The rest of the afternoon was spent at the computer. Currently, I'm writing the first draft of a *Wings* episode. David worked out the story with the producers and FedEx'd me the outline last week. I'm enjoying the process. Not only is it refreshing to have something to take my mind off baseball for a few hours a day, it's also gratifying to be working on a project where I can draw upon eighteen years of experience instead of three.

What do ballplayers do on their day off? Many play golf. Some are hermits who never come out of their rooms. The Orioles held a voluntary workout at Cleveland Stadium, and eleven attended. I asked John Oates which eleven, and he didn't know. It was his day off too, you know.

Assistant PR director/new best friend Bob Miller has several cousins who live in the area, and I joined him as he joined them for dinner. We zipped out to the "Flats," a redeveloped section of restaurants and clubs along the mighty Cuyahoga River, which separates East and West Cleveland. The weather was ideal—clear, temps in the eighties, low humidity—so we found ourselves eating outside in a seafood place with a delightful view of the river and many passing ships. The atmosphere was better than the food. A member of our party chipped a tooth . . . while eating a salad. Either the lettuce was too fresh or the croutons were from hell.

After dinner (and an exchange of phone numbers), we were treated to a tour of Cleveland and some of its residential areas. Shaker Heights and a few of the 'burbs even farther out were really eye-popping—huge, stately homes framed by lush green weepy trees. And the prices! We cruised by one home that looked like Bruce Wayne's stately manor in *Batman*: an enormous Tudor mansion that must be sitting on three acres of land. The asking price: $700,000. In Los Angeles that's what you'd pay for the driveway.

I'm starting to worry about my taste. It's one thing, I suppose, to like *Thelma & Louise*—but Cleveland???

Tuesday, June 25, Cleveland

My son, Matthew, started a weeklong baseball camp offered by Gary Adams, the head coach of UCLA. Matty was enrolled in Elrod Hendricks's camp but had to beg off when Debby's ankle required her and the family to stay in Los Angeles for another month. Matt was a little leery at first. Elrod's brochure said that soft drinks were provided, but the UCLA pamphlet said "nourishing drinks" would be served. Be that as it may, Matt went the Bruin route and enjoyed his first day. The highlight: He learned how to switch-hit. To get to the camp, Debby put Matthew and our housekeeper, Karina, in a taxi. UCLA's stadium is right across from a V.A. hospital and an expansive V.A. cemetery. Row after row of identical white tombstones stretch out for what seems like miles. The taxi driver made a wrong turn, taking them through this cemetery, to which my eight-year-old said, "What is this? Am I the only live person in the *Field of Dreams*?"

If I were a young man in Cleveland and I wanted to take my girlfriend out for a nice quiet evening, someplace dark where we could be alone, I'd take her to an Indians' game. This is what I said tonight on the air. Cleveland Stadium is a gigantic, cavernous ballpark that seats 74,483 for baseball but barely cracks the 10,000 mark per game. The park is dark, imposing, and quite honestly, depressing. The fact that the worst team in baseball plays there doesn't help either. The Indians are two and a half games behind the Orioles, fourteen games behind league-leading Toronto. They have lost four straight, and sixteen of nineteen. They have scored fewer runs than any team in the league, and in 35 of their 66 games they have posted two or fewer runs (winning only five of those games). Their big home run and RBI threat was talented but troubled Albert Belle, who on June 6, despite leading the club in both of those categories, was exiled to Triple-A Colorado Springs for disciplinary reasons. Several reported incidents contributed to the demotion. In May he fired a baseball at a heckler, drilling him in the chest (resulting in a league suspension), and the following month he failed to run out a double-play ball in a crucial late-inning spot. Manager John McNamara and general manager Hank Peters agreed it was time for "Snapper," as his teammates call him, to pack his bags.

The Indians' preseason game plan was to build the club around speed and defense. To that end their linchpin was to be Alex Cole, a Vince Coleman–type player with blazing speed. Cole stole 40 bases in only 63 games last year while hitting a cool .300. Since the Tribe didn't figure to hit too many home runs anyway, they decided to ensure that the competition wouldn't either, and moved the fences back during the off-season. It is now 400 feet to the power alleys and 415 to straightaway center. Unless you pull the ball right down one of the lines (320), you need a bazooka to hit one out at Cleveland Stadium.

The result: The Indians have been hoisted on their own petards. Cole separated his shoulder in spring training, has never gotten on track, and has stolen a grand total of seven bases while getting caught nine times. Yesterday in Toronto, representing the tying run in the ninth, he was picked off first to end the game. Earlier in that same game he caught a ball for the final out of an inning but fired a beebee into second base, obviously thinking it was the second out. This is not the guy you want to build your franchise around. As for the distant fences, the effect has been demoralizing for the home team. Indians routinely blast the ball for outs. They round first, see that the ball has been caught, and scuttle back to the dugout with their heads down in frustration. At the plate they either try to pull everything or hit the ball even harder, two real good ways to lower your average.

The team has given the county a self-imposed June 30 deadline to commit to a new stadium, and if agreement isn't reached, the team could be heading the way of all elderly East Coast Jews—to Florida. June 30 is just around the corner, although I hear the prospects of the Tribe staying are good. For the fans' sake, I hope so, because if the Indians desert, there will not be another team taking their place here in Cleveland.

Final note on Cleveland Stadium: NBC is making a TV movie on the life of Babe Ruth. Over the upcoming weekend they will be filming it here at Cleveland Stadium. So, in order to make the park look like 1927, they're sprucing it up a little.

In yet another marathon, the Orioles won, 5–3, in twelve

innings. Time of game: 4:01. The Tribe stranded sixteen men. The last time the Birds played three consecutive extra-inning games was April 29 to May 1, 1977. Of course, as long as we keep winning them, so what?

Wednesday, June 26, Cleveland

Albert Belle is back! The Cleveland bad boy has served his penance, was a model prisoner with the Colorado Springs Sky Sox, and was back in the starting lineup tonight. Belle is quite an enigma. Off the field, he's soft-spoken and articulate. On the field, it's like a light goes off and he becomes James Cagney in *White Heat* upon learning that his mother died. People who follow the club say he just cannot accept failure, even to the smallest degree, and in a game where the very best hitters fail seventy percent of the time, it's impossible to be that tough on yourself and still survive.

Well, his return was a triumphant one. In his first at-bat he doubled in two runs off Jeff Ballard. In his next at-bat he singled in another.

Both at-bats were in the first inning.

The Cleveland Indians, baseball's most anemic team, scored nine runs on eight hits in the first inning. With the bullpen so beleaguered, Ballard had to suck it up and stay out there. He finally left after three, trailing 10–1. Flanagan then pitched five brilliant innings in garbage-time relief as the O's lost, 10–4, to snap their season-high four-game winning streak.

Meanwhile, in Rochester, Ben had his second outing. P, and might I say, U. Syracuse scored five runs in four innings, Derek Bell hit a 421-foot homer, and McDonald developed a blister on his pitching hand. Seventy-five pitches, only 45 strikes.

Tom Hamilton, one of the Tribe's radio announcers, was in Triple-A Columbus a couple of years ago when I was in Syracuse and Tidewater. We got to be pretty good friends. After the game tonight we got some dinner, along with Jon, at the Grand Slam Grille down at the Flats. A good time, a lotta laughs, and prices that couldn't be beat—I was Tom's guest on his pregame show and received a fifty-dollar credit to the place. With that kind of meal ticket we were able to order the full "shitload" of ribs instead of just the half-shitload.

Thursday, June 27, Cleveland/Baltimore

Ballplayers (and announcers) talk of the mid-season blues. They say a second wind comes along about late August, but around this part of the season the daily grind really begins to take its toll. I'm finding that to be true. Not that it isn't still fun, but long separations, and late-night flights, and rain delays, and noisy hotel rooms, are starting to take the luster off the job. I'm "Baseball Numb," as Angel manager Doug Rader calls it. Four months ago I never believed I would be saying, I CAN'T WAIT FOR THE ALL-STAR BREAK!

The Indians made a long-anticipated blockbuster trade with Toronto today. The Tribe sent thirty-four-year-old premier knuckleballing right-hander Tom Candiotti and a minor leaguer to the Jays in exchange for young outfielders Glenallen Hill and Mark Whiten, lefty pitching prospect Denis Boucher, and the dreaded "player-to-be-named-later." Candiotti's contract is up at the end of the year, and the Indians made it clear they weren't about to pay him what he desired. (See the Ralph Kiner/Branch Rickey "We can finish last without you" story.) It appears to be a good trade for both concerns. The Indians have not been able to (a) hit the ball, and (b) catch the ball. Hill and Whiten will help. The Jays have a wealth of outfielders in the wings—in particular, Derek Bell (no relation to Juan, George, Jay, Gus, Ricky, Archie, or Tinker), plus they can afford a Candiotti. Cleveland traded for the future, Toronto dealt for the present. And if it doesn't work out for one or both sides, hey, that's what radio call-in shows are for.

On this date in 1939 the very first night game was played at Cleveland Stadium. To commemorate that event, they had a power failure tonight. No foolin'. Just before game time (and remember this was a getaway night), the lights went kaput. For fifteen minutes Chuck and I read scores, promoted the upcoming home stand—"Squeeze Bottle Day on Sunday, so you'll wanna make your plans," etc.—and reread the scores. Finally, the lights returned and the game began. Bob Milacki turned in his second straight fine performance, spreading out ten hits and only two runs through 8⅔ (with Olson getting the final out) as the O's whupped the Sons of the Wigwam, 7–2. Randy Milligan had four hits, Cal only had three.

The Orioles thus ended their best road trip of the year. They won five while losing only two.

I got to sleep back in Baltimore at four. It would've been a respectable 3:45 if it weren't for that damned power failure.

Friday, June 28, Baltimore

The Red Sox are in town for a big three-game series. Crowds of over 40,000 are expected for each game. The weather forecast: hot tonight, hotter tomorrow, Dante's Inferno on Sunday. As for humidity: yes!

Among the dignitaries meandering about the batting cage was the honorable commissioner of baseball, Mr. Fay Vincent. He graciously agreed to be my guest on the warm-up show. We discussed expansion, the fate of Pete Rose, teams relocating to other cities, and in general, the state of the game. It was a very comprehensive two and a half minutes.

Does Pete Rose deserve to be in the Hall of Fame? That's a question you'd think would be hotly debated in the clubhouse but is not. (Yesterday's topic instead was which American League stop had the most "mullions"—ugly women. Milwaukee won, followed by Cleveland.) Personally, I feel Rose should be in Cooperstown but only after a lengthy waiting period. There may be Ten Commandments in life, but in the Great American Pastime there is but one:

THOU SHALT NOT BET ON BASEBALL GAMES, DUMMY!!

No one, not even Pete Rose, is above the game. He stepped over the line. I think the punishment is appropriate. As for Milwaukee vs. Cleveland? There are some topics that are just too controversial.

José Mesa started for the Orioles and looked great for two innings. If only he didn't give up six runs in the third. Final: "Those Big, Bad Beantown Dudes" (as longtime broadcaster Red Rush used to call them) 9, "The team with the worst home record in baseball" (as everyone calls them) 3.

Letters, we get letters. From Easton, Maryland, comes a ten-page handwritten opus on legal paper from "B.B." B.B. is the Cliff Clavin of the Chesapeake. He sends these outrageous angry letters to us announcers, Roland Hemond, and Jeff Ballard (the team's player rep) on a very regular basis. Usually, they begin with, "I have submitted fifteen letters to date and have yet to receive a response." B.B.'s current targets are hitting coach Tom McCraw and pitching coach Al Jackson. Four pages of his most recent tirade center on that topic. The pitching staff is critiqued, and here are some highlights:

Olson—Please hire a pitching coach to at least teach Olson to learn one new pitch. Fire Jackson now!

Flanagan—Old. Once fine pitcher. Now hanging on. Not the kind for rebuilding. Allow him to retire gracefully.

Hickey—Please, this joke is on Oriole fans. Send to Hagerstown. Keep the Mountain People happy.

Kilgus—A monstrosity. What can you do with such a loser? Get job with Baltimore Sanitation Department.

Johnson—He says he gets "no respect." Has made the so-called "groin" injury famous. Do him a favor. Send to team (minor league) near Mayo Clinic.

Williamson—Kerosene Man. Trade quickly. He is a total loser.

McDonald—A worried man. May never return. Remember the quotes of F. Robinson, that McDonald's arm was sound, and look what happened. Robinson should be kicked out of his office job just as he was as manager. Also goes for Jackson.

Mesa—Probably the dumbest pitcher ever to come into the majors. Learns nothing. Send to Canary Islands.

Robinson—Sparky's revenge. Probable record: 9–17. Is this a rebuilding pitcher? Trade quickly.

Smith—This guy couldn't pitch in the Three-Eye League. A waste of time. Back to Rochester.

As you can see, all constructive suggestions presented in a very thoughtful manner. Beware, dear reader—these people are out there.

On the other hand, another listener sent me a hand-made clock. He's retired, makes wooden clocks (little radish-head nebbishes with clocks in their centers), and enjoys my broadcasts. I am sure glad *he* sent me the ticking package instead of B.B.

Saturday, June 29, Baltimore

The Orioles were on the CBS-TV *Game of the Week* today. Well . . . the CBS-TV *backup Game of the Week.* In any event, they looked good. Roy Smith (who couldn't pitch in the Triple-Eye League but holds his own in the American League) outdueled Danny Darwin, and the O's won, 7–3. Darwin makes over $3 million a year, Smith makes cab fare, and Smith now has more victories than Darwin. Home runs by Cal and Randy, and two doubles by former Red Sox (or is it Red Sock?) Sam Horn contributed to the thunder.

The Orioles topped a million today in only their thirty-fourth home date. They're on a record-setting attendance pace despite the fact that no team in the majors has won fewer games before the home folks than the O's. Some may claim that the final year of Memorial Stadium is bringing 'em out in droves, or perhaps Cal Ripken's boffo year, but I like to think it's the radio broadcasts. Fans will do *anything* to avoid having to listen to the games.

Sunday, June 30, Baltimore

Roger Clemens was supposed to start for Boston but came down with a stomach flu. He was replaced by Joe Hesketh. On the air I noted that many in the big crowd of 47,274 were probably disappointed that Clemens didn't pitch. I likened it to getting tickets to see *Phantom of the Opera* only to learn just before curtain that the part of the Phantom would be played by John Davidson instead of Michael Crawford.

Clemens's absence was just the start of the Orioles' good fortune. Carlos Quintana, a first baseman by trade, played in right for the BoSox and dropped a routine fly ball to allow the winning runs to score for the O's; 6–4 was the final.

Worth noting: Boston rookie Mo Vaughn hit his first major league home run, a majestic blast that almost cleared the right-field bleachers. No one has ever cleared right field, and only one man, Frank Robinson, ever sailed one over the left-field bleachers. Vaughn came within thirteen feet of hitting a historic home run. There is a flag in left signifying where Frank's went out. It reads: HERE. After the game I kidded him that a companion flag of THERE almost had to be commissioned.

The Orioles finish June 15–13. Cal and Randy each homered for the second day in a row. Although Cal continues to lead the league in hitting, Milligan is even hotter of late. He's batting over .500 the past week and becoming the most popular "Moose" since Bullwinkle.

Craig Worthington's twenty-day rehab assignment is up. To the surprise of no one, Mr. Worthington has been optioned to Rochester indefinitely.

Dave "Groin" Johnson will make a couple of rehabilitation starts in Hagerstown this week. If all goes well, he could be back after the All-Star break.

And then there's Ben. Oates said that he'll start tomorrow . . . either in Rochester or Baltimore. So make your plans.

Most Sunday nights we're in the air, but with the home stand continuing through Wednesday, I got a rare night off. Bonnie Levitt invited me to her home for a family cookout, which I enjoyed thoroughly. By force of habit I tipped her.

Monday, July 1, Baltimore

Ben got the start, his first since May 22, when the Tigers shelled him in the second inning. After he had two very unimpressive outings in Rochester, no one was expecting much at all—especially not eight shutout innings of two-hit, no-walk, seven-strikeout ball over Detroit. Big Ben hurled a masterpiece. He was the Ben McDonald of old, a completely dominating pitcher. Suddenly, the prospects for a better second half seem considerably brighter.

The offense was in bloom as well; the O's won, 10–2. (Reliever Paul Kilgus gave up the two runs in the ninth, in case you're dying to know.) The Orioles have now won three straight, four of five, and eight of ten. We're so hot we're now six and a half out of last place! (Cleveland is house-sitting the cellar.)

Randy Milligan was named the American League Player of the Week. I'm not sure what he gets for that. It's either a trophy, a plaque, or a free oil change at Jiffy Lube.

To make room for McDonald on the roster, José Mesa will

join Craig Worthington on the Rochester team bus. (Note: Players are given a couple of days to report to their new assignment. From Boston to Pawtucket—the Red Sox Triple-A affiliate—is about forty miles. For some reason, it takes an hour to get from Pawtucket to Boston but two days to get from Boston to Pawtucket.)

People magazine wants to do an article about me. I guess I've now officially entered the world of "pop culture." A reporter was dispatched to observe me in action tonight. After watching Jon and me trade barbs for several innings, she turned to Dr. Paul and said with great sincerity and self-importance, "I'm going to make these two guys famous!"

Get real, lady!

Tuesday, July 2, Baltimore/Washington, D.C.

Several weeks ago I received a call from an ad executive representing a regional supermarket chain, Giant Foods. They're a participating sponsor on Orioles' games and wondered whether Jon and I would agree to record several commercials for the chain. I would be paid $1,200. (Debby: "Oh, good. That'll just about cover the anesthesiologist.") Today was the day, and the limo pulled up at eight o'clock. (The recording studio was in Washington, and transportation to and from was part of the deal.) I shared the limo with Jon and his wife, Janine, and had a very pleasant trip to D.C., getting a complete tour of the city and Georgetown as our driver, "Captain Wrongway Peachfuzz," made one wrong turn after another. The commercials themselves were utterly ridiculous but fun to record. Jon's teenage daughter Holly described the campaign as "two stupid baseball announcers who get so excited when food platters from Giant are brought into the booth that they forget about the game." That pretty much sums it up. Fortunately, they let us play the commercials tongue in cheek. Otherwise, we would've been in trouble big-time. How do you say this with a straight face?

JON: Here's the pitch . . . it's a fastball.

KEN: That's not a fastball. It's a cheeseball . . . from Giant Foods!

So after an hour of doing what hookers do when they spread their legs, we finished the spots and dashed off to lunch at Duke Zeibert's. Duke Zeibert is a Washington institution. He's probably been in town since Roosevelt was president (and I'm not sure which one). Spry and sharp as ever, he presides over THE power restaurant in THE power capital. Duke and Jon are close. Of course, Duke is also close with the other members of our party—Larry King, and Stan Bromley, the GM of the Washington Four Seasons Hotel. Lunch was tasty, as was the conversation. Larry King had just returned from spending a week in Montana at the home of Ted and Jane. He fished with Ted, went shopping with Jane. They all went out to dinner; they spent some nights eating at home. Very relaxing, very downhome.

By the way, Ted is Ted Turner, Jane is Jane Fonda, and Ted's home in Montana is larger than Rhode Island.

Just plain folks.

Over the past several months, I've gotten to know Larry King a little, and I must say I find him as charming and ingenuous as he appears on his many many many many public forums. He travels in the highest circles, but somehow you get the feeling he's still just that street kid from the corner who likes to talk. (I would've given anything to see him fly-fish.)

The limo deposited me back home by two. There was time for an hour's nap before heading out to the park. The O's lost to Detroit, 4–3. Home runs by Cecil Fielder and "Sweet Lou" Whittaker did 'em in. I made the comment on the air that all athletes named Lou, it seems, become known as "Sweet Lou." "Sweet Lou" Whittaker, "Sweet Lou" Johnson, and on and on. That nickname doesn't translate to other professions, however. Take the practice of law. "Sweet Lou" Nizer just doesn't have the proper ring.

Wednesday, July 3, Baltimore/New York City

Fireworks night at the ballpark, so the place was packed. For some reason, whenever there's a big crowd, the Orioles not only lose, but lose badly. Tonight was no exception. The Tigers embarrassed the good guys, 8–2.

Our charter was waiting after the game to take us to New

York City. In a stroke of scheduling genius we're slated to play a day game after a night game in another city. To ensure that we wouldn't get caught in the postgame traffic, a police escort led the way to the airport. The comment was made on the media bus that after the way the team has played these last two days, they *need* a police escort to get safely out of town. They're a cruel but honest bunch.

By the time we arrived at the Grand Hyatt Hotel, it was one o'clock. I turned on the TV, and my name flashed on the screen. The late-night movie was playing *Volunteers,* the film David and I had written. In only five years it had sunk to this—showing in the same movie package as *Gidget Goes to Rome* and *Beyond the Valley of the Dolls.* In any event, it was fun to see my name, especially in this case, supered over Roger Maris hitting his sixty-first home run at Yankee Stadium (used as part of the opening credits sequence). A fitting welcome to Gotham, no?

Thursday, July 4, New York City

When I first got the job, I envisioned one day in particular. On the Fourth of July, I would be broadcasting a major league baseball game from Yankee Stadium, the ballpark of the ages. This was the day.

Gee, what a disappointment.

Not that Yankee Stadium doesn't symbolize all the tradition and lore and majesty that makes baseball the great game it is; that stuff's all there—the monuments, the distinctive, arching outfield facade, etc. But the big ballpark in the Bronx is also in the middle of a war zone, is unreachable by taxi (cabbies either refuse to go out there or don't know where it is), and the broadcast facilities are the worst in the league. Our tiny booth is strewn with exposed wires and recessed far back from the action. This is where Mel Allen and Red Barber used to broadcast??? (Actually, no. Before the stadium was renovated, the radio booths were suspended below the upper deck. According to old-timers, they went from being the best to the worst. Progress.)

After a game it is *imperative* that you catch the team bus back to the hotel. If it's hard finding transportation *to* the stadium in the supposed safety of daylight, imagine trying to find a way back at midnight. Catching the team bus is literally a matter of life and death. Dave Niehaus, the Seattle broadcaster, tells of busing back to the hotel with the team one night. The route took them through Harlem. Dave was sitting next to coach Vada Pinson, who is black. Kiddingly, Dave said, "If the bus breaks down here, you're my best friend," to which Pinson wryly replied, "If the bus breaks down here, I don't know you."

In fairness to Yankee Stadium, I'm sure my expectations were just too high. I will say this. Actually standing on the playing field was a thrill. For all the "improvements," Yankee Stadium is still very much hallowed ground.

The weather was perfect, the crowd large and festive, and Bob Shephard was on hand to announce the "Yan-kee" starting lineups, as he has for over forty years, and introduce Robert Merrill singing "our National Anthem on this July the fourth." (Merrill, by the way, was there in person, not just on a recording. And he sounded great . . . even if he did foul up the lyrics.) The ambience, thank goodness, was still there.

The day belonged to New York, and save for a home run by Chris Hoiles, the big crowd had lots to cheer about. The Yankees won, 3–2, to extend their winning streak to six.

On the team bus back to the hotel, Kevin Hickey was waxing nostalgic about growing up in Chicago and playing with fireworks as a kid—wistful stories of friends getting their eyes blown out, etc. He extended an invitation to fellow reliever Todd Frohwirth to see his old neighborhood the next time the club is in Chicago, "if I'm still on the team." Frohwirth said that would be great, "if *I'm* still on the team." Ballplayers all say they "take things one day at a time." Some mean it more than others.

My wife's sister, Mitty, and her fiancé, Alan, picked me up for dinner, and afterward we sauntered down to the East River along with 2.1 million other saunterers to watch the big Macy's fireworks show. It was, of course, spectacular. Say what you will about New York, it is a decayed and dying city, but it does have superb pyrotechnics. The fireworks were synchronized to music, and the last song was Whitney Houston's stirring rendition of "The Star-Spangled Banner." Alan said, "The grand finale *should* be, 'Macy's, we're a part of your life!' "

The crush of humanity made its way back to its cars and homes (or street corners). Two notable scenes: (1) a homeless man sitting on the street bundled in a tattered blanket watching a portable TV (I felt as if I were trespassing through someone's living room), and (2) a parking lot removing its sign that said JULY 4TH PARKING $12.95, and replacing it with ALL DAY EVERY DAY PARKING $4.00. Now *there's* the holiday spirit.

The evening was capped off with drinks and pithy conversation at the musty but nostalgic Algonquin Hotel.

Friday, July 5, New York City

Rain was predicted, and although the skies were leaden and gloomy, the precipitation never materialized. (Good news for someone who hates *Orioles Talk* as much as this young lad.)

I walked into the clubhouse before the game, just as Roland Hemond was marching into John Oates's office trailed by Ernie Whitt. It didn't take a rocket scientist to figure out what was going on behind that closed door. The last original Blue Jay was given his release. This is the inevitable day that all ballplayers dread and all believe is still a year away. If Ernie Whitt does not latch on with another club (which is doubtful), expect to see him back in the big leagues in the near future as a manager. A damn good one. You heard it here first.

Filling Ernie's spot on the roster is Chito Martinez, who's batting .322 at Rochester while leading the International League in home runs with twenty. In that league twenty home runs is an ungodly amount. With a little luck he'll hit four for us.

Talk about paying your dues, Martinez is getting his first shot at the big leagues after seven years in the minors (up until this year, all with the Kansas City chain). And still, he's only twenty-five. Reynaldo Ignacio "Chito" Martinez was born in Belize, Central America (the first major leaguer to hail from that part of the world), but was raised in New Orleans. He speaks no Spanish.

If you think I was amazed walking onto the field in Yankee Stadium for the first time, you can imagine Chito's reaction. He just stood in the dugout dumbfounded. That morning he had been in Pawtucket preparing to fly back to Rochester. Instead, he was in the Baltimore Orioles' starting lineup, playing in the most famous ballpark in the history of the game. Seven years. That's a long time to wait by the phone.

The O's snapped the Yankees' winning streak by posting a 7–4 win. Heroes included pitcher Jeff Robinson, Sam ("There's a long drive to right and that ball isssss gonnnnne!") Horn, and Chito Martinez, who got his first major league base hit.

Rotisserie update: Me and David are in last place. The Pit's fireworks show did not go well. Issuing fireworks to all in attendance was an ill-conceived idea.

Saturday, July 6, New York City

The National League owners officially approved Denver and Miami as their new franchises. The Colorado Rockies and either the Florida or South Florida Marlins. I don't quite know why teams are reluctant to be identified with their cities as opposed to regions, especially when they are set in large metropolitan centers. Someone said the problem with the New Jersey Nets (an NBA team that plays in the Meadowlands) is that they're not associated with one big city but fifty little ones. The team should be called the Exit 16W Nets. As for the names the new N.L. entries selected? They're okay, but I would've preferred the Miami Retired Jews and the Denver Omelettes.

"Another One Bites the Dust" Department: The Cleveland Indians fired John McNamara. There are still two or three teams he has not managed yet, so I'm sure he'll be back soon. New Indian skipper is coach Mike Hargrove, a very nice man. Of course, considering Cleveland's current talent base and the organization's penchant for not spending a lot of money, I wonder if instead of a new chief they need a medicine man.

The Orioles let a 5–3 lead slip away in the sixth and lost, 13–5. Matt Nokes hit two home runs and drove in six. Ben McDonald, so brilliant last Monday against Detroit, was shaky from the get-go today. Is he real or is it Memorex?

I had dinner with my sister-in-law, mother-in-law, and fiancé-in-law, and came down with maybe the worst case of food poisoning I've ever had in my life (and I've been to Mexico). I spent the entire night in the bathroom hoping that a serial killer would break into my room and kill me. I should've known something was amiss when we went to dinner at a French restaurant that stays open twenty-four hours.

Sunday, July 7, New York City/Los Angeles

After three hours' sleep and barely the energy to carry my bags, I dragged myself onto the team bus and set out for Yankee Stadium, praying that I wouldn't have to ask the driver to stop and try to find a bathroom for me somewhere in Harlem.

Today's plan: ball game, then a ride to Kennedy Airport from Debby's relatives (who attended the game as my guests), followed by a seven-thirty flight to L.A. By eleven o'clock West Coast time I should be home. If life could only imitate plans.

Another advantage of traveling with a professional ball club is that when your stomach explodes, there's a trainer who can give you Lomotil not Tums. I know from my experiences south o' the border that Lomotil is the ultimate cork. After a delicious lunch of saltines and club soda, I headed up to the booth to do my fifteen minutes of exhaustive preparation. Just as we went on the air, it started to rain. (This was not in the forecast, understand.) An hour and a half of dreaded *Orioles Talk* and the game finally began. The Orioles won, 5–3, capping off the first half of the season in fine fashion. I rushed through the postgame show and dashed out of the stadium at five-thirty. Traffic leaving the park was unbelievable, of course, and getting on the Triboro Bridge was a treat not to be missed. I arrived at Kennedy at seven. With ten minutes to spare, I approached the boarding gate, only to learn that the emergency lights in the plane weren't working. Maintenance people were looking into the problem, and they hoped to have it resolved soon so that the flight (completely overbooked) would not have to be canceled. CANCELED?! That's all I would need. Fortunately, the malfunction was corrected and we took off . . . an hour and a half late. I arrived home at two A.M. I hugged my wife and children till three, then passed out.

Bring on the All-Star break!

6

Monday, July 8, Los Angeles

Debby is now in a walking cast. It ends below the knee and allows for somewhat greater mobility. She can even drive. In Southern California that means a pardon from the governor. What's scary is to see her maneuver around on her crutches with more grace and greater dexterity than a number of Orioles' prospects.

I did a double-take when I saw our postman this morning, but then remembered that the All-Star break is *not* a national holiday.

Today is our twelfth anniversary, and in light of all that's happened in recent months, we decided to really "blow it out." We went to a drive-in theater and saw *Robin Hood* (Debby hadn't seen it). We had more laughs, more fun, and yes, even more romance, than if we had gone to some candlelit restaurant. (Plus, I still couldn't eat.)

Tuesday, July 9, Los Angeles

During the course of the New York trip, I finished the *Wings* script. David and I rendezvoused at the office to give it one final polish before turning it in. He's about to write a draft of *Cheers,* so the next script up is mine. Like that guy on *The Ed Sullivan Show,* I continue to spin the plates.

CBS carried the All-Star game this year, and I must say I loved the pregame show.

I was on it.

The program opened with a montage of great play from this current season, and the first one up was a thrilling Cal Ripken home run . . . WITH MY CALL. I was astounded. I had no idea it was coming. Matty and I were sitting on the couch when suddenly there was my voice. Now I'm used to hearing Mel Allen, and Russ Hodges, and Vin Scully on those montages, not *me* for God's sake. Of the millions of people who heard it, maybe three recognized me, but it was quite a thrill nonetheless.

The game itself was most satisfying. The lone Oriole to compete, you-know-who, singled and homered and was named the MVP. (The day before, he won the home run hitting contest, belting 12 of 22 pitches out of the park. He was so impressive during his at-bat that they literally changed the rules on the spot to let him keep hitting. He was supposed to get only ten swings.) If ever a player deserves to be called a superstar this year, it's Cal Ripken the Younger.

Wednesday, July 10, Los Angeles/Anaheim

I plan to take Matty with me tomorrow to Oakland, so I wanted to give Diana a special day as well. Today she and I went to Disneyland. There is no better way to see the Magic Kingdom than through the wide eyes of a four-year-old. I cannot think of a more gratifying feeling in the world for a parent than to see his (or her) child so utterly and thoroughly happy. It's hard not to get emotional. I'll admit it: I actually got a little choked up in "It's a Small World."

Debby thinks this is a day Diana will remember her entire life. I know her dad will.

Thursday, July 11, Los Angeles/Oakland

Matty and I were off to Oakland. The last time he was this excited was his first day of Little League, when he slept in his uniform all night. Besides his clothes, he had his backpack filled to the brim with necessary items (e.g. Gameboy, Travel Battleship, score book, etc.). He also wanted to take along a wooden pistol from the Old West that he fancied, but I thought that might not be a good idea for the plane.

Brady Anderson was on our flight, and after picking up the

rental car in the Oakland airport, we gave him a lift to our hotel. Matty was blown away to have an actual major leaguer in our car. After months of separation, I was quite jazzed just to have Matty in the car. Brady was very sweet with him, and the two had a lively discussion of Nintendo games.

The Oakland Alameda County Coliseum is the last venue in my tour of the league. In 1974, when I was a disc jockey in San Francisco, I frequently went to A's games here. It was their third straight championship season and yet the park was always empty. The Charles Finley era was not embraced by the Bay Area. Some of the greatest games I've ever seen, I've seen alone. On the plus side, however, if I had a ticket and knew I was going to be late, I could always call ahead and they'd hold the game for me.

The visiting broadcast booth is separated from the main press box (which is rather odd). You have to exit the press box, walk down a flight of stairs, wind through a public concession area, and then hike up a flight of steps to get to our little cubbyhole. Once inside, it's fine—more than enough room for two announcers, an engineer, and a very happy little boy.

Matty wasn't allowed into the press lounge, so today began a four-day diet of hot dogs and licorice ropes. Matty had the same.

Glenn Davis is here and has begun taking batting practice. He's even throwing a little on the side. This is one happy camper. A month ago he could not lift a glass to his lips or (as he says) he could not reach over in the car and turn me off on the radio. Glenn admitted that playing again seemed like a miracle several weeks ago, but now he's confident he can return. The sooner the better, Glenn!

Kevin Hickey will not be able to show Todd Frohwirth his old neighborhood the next time we're in Chicago. The Hickman has been "designated for assignment." (Dwight Evans has been activated.) What that means in real-people-talk is that the O's have ten days to assign him somewhere in their system (or finagle a deal) or they must give him his release. Kevin was very philosophical about it (it's not like this hasn't happened before . . . a lot). "For every car door you step out of, you step right into another one," he said while starting a roller-hockey game in the locker room. I do hope he lands on his feet again. He's got a terrific attitude, keeps the clubhouse loose, and is a *left*hander. Southpaws are always at a premium, so as long as he can lift his arm over his shoulder, he's got a chance.

For the benefit of those Oriole fans who didn't want to stay up too late to learn the outcome of the game (first pitch is at 10:35 back East), Jeff Robinson and the Birds gave up five runs in the first inning. The game was decided by eleven. Final score: 8–1, the Orioles' only run coming on rookie Chito Martinez's first major league home run.

Early in the game Billy Ripken made a nice diving catch. I described it, then swiveled to the monitor to see the replay. Here was my call: "Great play by Billy! Taking another look, I see . . . that Homer is opening his mail." Matty had switched the TV to *The Simpsons*. It was a good episode. Very funny.

There's a saying in baseball: Every team is going to win 60 games, every team is going to lose 60 games. It's what you do with the other 42 that matters.

This was game 81 for the Orioles, the exact halfway point. Their record: 39–44. They've already lost most of the 42. In the East, Toronto is starting to pull away from the pack, with Boston still in pursuit. In the West, it's a five-team race between Oakland, Texas, California, Chicago, and Minnesota. And even Seattle is within striking distance. I sure hope none of their announcers are writing books.

Friday, July 12, Oakland/San Francisco

Matty loved San Francisco—the cable cars, winding down Lombard Street (see the chase scene in *Bullitt*), Fisherman's Wharf, and first and foremost, the candy factory at Ghirardelli Square. As we were driving over the Bay Bridge back to Oakland, he turned to me and said, "Dad, why don't you get a job announcing for the Giants?" I was thinking the same thing.

Chuck Thompson is working this entire West Coast swing with me. Jon is taking a well-deserved week off, which he is spending with his family in Naples, Florida. (The Orioles will fly an estimated 34,000 miles this year. I bet Jon will log 50,000.) Matty left his jacket in the car, and it started getting chilly around the third inning. Uncle Chuck walked him to the car to retrieve it. Why is this man not in the Hall of Fame???

Rarely does a player come to bat in the later innings needing just a triple to complete hitting for the cycle. Tonight the Orioles had two. You're probably saying, "Cal Ripken and who else?" Chris Hoiles was the other. Neither succeeded, but their combined thunder sparked a 6–3 win over Oakland. Ben McDonald looked nifty through eight innings, so who knows? The O's are undefeated in the second half.

Shortly after the game John Oates was rushed to the emergency room. He was passing a kidney stone. Having passed one myself (on a plane between Pittsburgh and Syracuse), I can tell you that there is no greater hell. I'm told that women experience similar pain during childbirth, but I have my doubts. If they did, there would be no such things as siblings. In any event, John did pass it in a couple of hours and will be in uniform for Saturday. I don't expect him to pitch batting practice.

The only thing worse than being sick is being sick on the road.

Saturday, July 13, Oakland/San Francisco

There are so many days I've been away, and too many school plays and Little League games I've missed, but when Matty thinks back to this year, I hope those recollections fade and he is left instead with the memory of this one day. As the expression goes: "They couldn't write it any better in Hollywood."

After a room-service breakfast (Matty's favorite thing in all the world), we set out for the ballpark on a crystal-clear day. First stop was the Orioles' clubhouse, and the guys could not have been nicer. Roy Smith even taught Matty how to throw a change-up. Next was the dugout, where Matty and John Oates engaged in a lively conversation. Dwight Evans wasn't playing enough for Matty's satisfaction, but John assured him that he'd be back in the lineup real soon. I introduced my son to José Canseco at the batting cage. They shook hands and Matty told him to keep hitting those home runs—"You're on my dad's rotisserie team, you know." I then was able to take pictures on the field of Matty with Jim Palmer, and Matty got a ball autographed by both Palmer and fellow Hall-of-Famer Brooks Robinson.

The game featured Eric Show vs. Bob Milacki. Through four

innings the game was scoreless. Barry Salberg, a longtime friend from college, came by to visit me in the booth, and after I wrapped up the fourth, he was about to return to his seat. Chuck turned back to him and said, "Where're you going? You can't leave. We got a no-hitter going." And indeed we did. Bob Milacki had not allowed a hit. For the good of the Orioles, Barry decided to stay.

The Birds jumped ahead, 1–0, in the fifth as Hoiles singled in Martinez, who had doubled. (Chito Martinez, by the way, became the first Oriole rookie *ever* to hit in his first six games. So far, I love this guy.) The no-no was still in effect in the sixth when Willie Wilson hit a shot back to the box that struck Milacki's pitching hand and fortuitously ricocheted right to first base, where Milligan recorded the out. Milacki was able to finish the inning, but that's all. His hand swelled up to the size of a mitt and he was lifted after six despite not giving up a hit. (X rays were negative, just a bruise. He hopefully will not miss his next start.) Mike Flanagan came on in the seventh, allowed a two-out walk but nothing more. Meanwhile, Mike Devereaux homered to up the score to 2–0.

I had never seen a no-hitter, and amazingly, neither had Matty. There's always the question of just how an announcer should call a potential no-hitter. One school of thought is not to mention it at all (so as not to be a jinx), and the other says the broadcaster *must* discuss the situation. It is his responsibility to alert the audience to the potential historic feat. Chuck, who has seen and called many a no-hitter, has a way of splitting the difference. He will say anything but the words "no-hitter." He will inform the listeners that the Orioles have yet to give up a hit, that the A's are hitless, that they're looking for their first base knock, etc., but he will not utter the phrase "no-hitter." I followed that policy as well.

Mark Williamson came on in the eighth. In his last outing, Thursday, he had given up four hits and two runs in one inning. Mike Gallego popped out to first, Rickey Henderson grounded out to third, and Willie Wilson (after fouling off four pitches) bounced out to second. Eight innings in the book.

Matty said his stomach was "all scrunched up." So was mine. I turned the mike over to Chuck for the ninth and held my breath like everyone else. Gregg Olson was summoned to work this inning. Big Dave Henderson led off. On a 1–1 pitch, he grounded the ball to the hole. Cal sprang to his right, made a backhand grab, and rifled a hurried throw to first. Out by half a step. Shortstops will tell you there is no tougher play than on balls hit deep into the hole. Shortstops will also tell you no one makes that play better than Cal Ripken. One out.

José Canseco was next. With the count 1–2, Olson delivered a wicked curve, and Canseco swung so hard he almost came out of his spikes. He was nowhere near the pitch. Strike three. Out two.

Matty was holding my hand.

Harold Baines, the Maryland native, stepped up to the plate. Baines was 14 for 24 against Baltimore going into the game, with four home runs and thirteen RBIs. Olson, who normally is a slllllowwwww worker, seemed to take forever between each agonizing pitch. Finally, the count advanced to 2–2. Olson looked in for the sign, nodded, swung into his windup, and let 'er rip.

A fastball . . .

A half swing . . .

Strike three!

And for the first time today Chuck Thompson said it, he used the words: "Four Orioles pitchers combine for a *no-hitter.*"

Matty was jumping up and down and screaming so loud it's a wonder he wasn't heard over the air. I took pictures of the last strike and the subsequent celebration on the field, but like an idiot I neglected to get a photo of the scoreboard.

The celebration itself was rather interesting. It was somewhat subdued. No one really knew whom to congratulate. Had one pitcher accomplished the feat, there would've been a mob scene, but with four, there were more handshakes than hugs.

Regardless, for only the second time in the history of baseball four men combined for a no-hitter. (The other was in 1975 and occurred right here in Oakland, of all places.) In a sense, five men contributed to today's masterpiece. Bob Milacki, Mike Flanagan, Mark Williamson, Gregg Olson, and Foster City's own Barry Salberg.

That night Matty, Chuck, Dr. Paul, Phil Itzoe, and I went into San Francisco to have dinner at Phil Lehr's Steak House. (I'm being treated to all of Chuck's favorite haunts.) On the ride home Matty led us all in several rousing choruses of

"She'll Be Comin' Around the Mountain When She Comes." Chuck was great. Dr. Paul and I need to work on our harmony.

Sunday, July 14, Oakland/Los Angeles

After the wondrous events of yesterday, I prefer to skim over today. Suffice it to say the Orioles took a 2–1 lead into the bottom of the eleventh, and Gregg Olson (working his fourth consecutive day) gave up three hits and a wild pitch, and on a jam-shot single by Canseco with two outs, the A's prevailed, 3–2.

The team went on to Anaheim, while Matty and I flew back to L.A. On the plane he hugged my arm and said, "Dad, this has been the best road trip of the year!"

On Friday, Debby had another appointment with her orthopedic specialist, who reduced her walking cast to a Velcro brace. It now looks like she's wearing Conan the Barbarian's sandal. The brace is lighter, more maneuverable, and most important, removable. Debby is allowed to go cast-free for several hours a day now. Walking must still be done with crutches, and stairs are no picnic, but all things considered, this is a *big* improvement.

Monday, July 15, Los Angeles/Anaheim

Allan Mallamud, my favorite sportswriter in the world, concluded his column in the *L.A. Times* today with this:

> HOW MANY BALTIMORE ORIOLES DOES IT TAKE TO THROW A NO-HITTER? FOUR.

After a lovely day at home, Matty and I set out for the hour-and-a-half, freeway-clogged drive to Anaheim Stadium at two-thirty. I still can't get over how weird it is to sleep in my own bed and then broadcast a game back to thirty-three stations on the East Coast.

Since I knew that I'd have tons of requests for tickets from friends and coworkers while I was in Southern California, I decided before the season to organize one night to accommodate everyone. My secretary, Sherry, working with the Angels' group-ticket representative, Lynn Biggs, coordinated the effort. And tonight, ninety-five people were coming on my behalf. (In Cleveland that would double the attendance.) Among them was George Wendt (Norm on *Cheers*), and in the third inning he joined me on the broadcast. It went very well. I had him read the Esskay Out-of-Town Scoreboard, we chatted about *Cheers,* his love of the White Sox, and what it was like doing a movie with Annette Bening (*Guilty by Suspicion*). You know, the usual baseball banter.

I spent the fifth and sixth innings with my group and found myself feeling very homesick even though I was home. It was also quite odd to be watching an Oriole game from the stands.

The O's were down to their last out in the ninth, trailing the Angels 1–0 with their ace, Bryan Harvey, on the mound. Randy Milligan kept it alive with a single to center, and then Chito the Magnificent belted a homer to right (only the third allowed by Harvey this year) to give the Birds a 2–1 lead. Sidewinder Todd Frohwirth struck out Winfield and Parrish and got Gaetti to ground out to post his first major league save. After the tough loss yesterday in Oakland, this come-from-behind victory couldn't've come at a better time.

By the way, when Chito hit his dramatic home run, I glanced up at my section and saw that at least twelve of the ninety-five people were still there to witness it.

Tuesday, July 16, Los Angeles/Anaheim/Kansas City

My final day home until the end of the season (almost three months away). I spent it having breakfast with my father and daughter, conducting loose-end errands with my wife, and playing ball with my son. Steve Leon, my sportscasting compadre who shared my first microphone in the upper deck of Dodger Stadium in '86, gave me a lift to Anaheim Stadium. (Steve, by the way, will hopefully be doing NBA basketball within the next few years. If not, there is no justice. He is excellent. And I'm not just saying that because he gave me a ride.)

Yesterday Billy Ripken stepped into the batting cage during BP experiencing a little discomfort in his right side. On his fifth swing he was jolted with such pain that tears came to his eyes. Today Billy was placed on the fifteen-day DL with a muscle strain in his rib cage. Rookie Juan Bell will finally get his chance to show what he can do.

Tonight's game was almost the mirror image of last night's. The Orioles took a 1–0 lead into the eighth, and the Angels scored twice, to triumph, 2–1. Juan Bell was the goat. Covering first on a sacrifice bunt in the eighth, he dropped the throw for an error. The tying and winning runs were both unearned as a result.

After the game the team took the hour bus ride to Ontario Airport to take the three-hour flight to Kansas City to take the hour bus ride to our hotel. This was my first flight on *Orioles One,* our new plane. The good news is that all the seats in this 737 are first class with scads of room, and card tables are scheduled to be added along with VCR entertainment units. The bad news is that there is no hot galley yet (so the food is served on lovely white china, but cold) and the pickup airport crew of former circus roustabouts doesn't have a clue as to how to load the aircraft ("Whaddawe do with these bats?"). Both in Oakland and here, the team sat on the ground for an hour before taking off. Usually, it's fifteen, twenty minutes. We arrived in Kansas City with the sun and staggered into our hotel rooms at six-thirty.

It's important to point out that this is not the Orioles management's fault. They entered into this chartered-plane business with the best of intentions. Their goal was to provide luxury conditions and a sense of familiarity. The front office sure can't be faulted for that. Unfortunately, the plane we've been given is not the one we had been promised. Apparently (and I know this sounds straight out of a B novel), two businessmen from Indonesia with (literally) a suitcase full of cash came over to the United States and bought our plane right out from under us. The company then had to scramble to find us an alternative. That's why our plane wasn't ready in June as promised (necessitating Emerald Airlines), and that's why all the fabulous amenities are not yet in place. But it should be made clear that in no way were the Orioles trying to cut a corner or save a buck with this venture. If anything, they should be applauded for trying to give their players a little something extra.

Wednesday, July 17, Kansas City

After a fitful day's sleep, I wandered over to Royal Stadium at four-thirty. "Summer in Kansas City." Air temp was 97, and on the AstroTurf surface near 110. Two weeks ago during a scorcher the carpet temperature was showing 154. It must've been like playing on a pancake griddle. Where's the Players' Union when they need it?

Sometimes a team exhausted and beleaguered from a night of no sleep will go out and score a ton of runs. They're loose, they're playing on fumes, and a blowout is the result. That was the case tonight with the Orioles as they jumped out to a 7–0 lead. Other times, however, a team can come out flat after a night of bone-weary travel, and that unfortunately was also the case with the Orioles. The Royals tied the game 8–8 in the ninth. Juan Bell's throwing error in the ninth (three bounces to third, six bounces past third) allowed the tying run to score after the O's held a two-run advantage going into the frame. (Jon, getting a tad carried away, as he occasionally does, called it "the worst throw in the history of baseball.") Incredibly, the Orioles and Royals have played four extra-inning games—each one tied 8–8 after nine innings—and three in a row (counting the recent doubleheader).

The Royals finally won it 9–8 . . . in fifteen innings. That's right. Fifteen. Bill Pecota drove in George Brett at 1:06 A.M. Time of game: 5:32—only fourteen minutes shorter than the longest game in Baltimore Oriole history. Total time of the last three 8–8 extravaganzas: 13:43.

Fred White, one of the K.C. broadcasters, was waiting at the elevator with me after the game. As the doors opened he slung his heavy travel bag over his shoulder, glanced back at me, and said with a wry smile, "You gotta love ball. You *gotta* love ball."

I'm sure Juan Bell and Sam Horn found the evening even longer than the rest of us. Bell's worst throw in the history of the game led the way for the marathon, and Sam Horn struck out six consecutive times, tying a dubious major league record. And the only time he did hit the ball—a majestic blast to right in the fifteenth—he stood at the plate to admire it. Unfortunately, the ball hit the wall and stayed in the ballpark. Turning on the jets, Sam barely made it into second ahead of the throw. After the game, Chuck and I rode up the elevator with Sam (a rather awkward position for us, you can imagine), and to the big man's credit, he was very cool.

"Man, I stunk out there tonight, didn't I?" he asked.

We sorta cleared our throats and politely mumbled, "Well, yeah . . . y'know . . . these things happen . . . I mean . . ."

"Nope. I stunk," he repeated, "but tomorrow is another day." His final words as he stepped out were: "And I'm going to be runnin' 'em *all* out from now on."

Thursday, July 18, Kansas City/Baltimore

You really have to feel sorry for Juan Bell. He's not well liked on the ball club, doesn't have many friends among his teammates, and now is in the barrel, expected to prove himself at the big-league level while playing an unnatural position (shortstop is his forte, not second base) and hitting every day after making only cameo appearances for the entire first half of the year. (Bell is out of minor league options, meaning that if the Orioles wish to send him down, they run the risk of another club claiming him on waivers. That is why he has been here all season despite playing just slightly more innings than the batboy.) If Bell is a little tight, a little tentative, I think it's understandable.

Bob Milacki was our Loyola Federal Peak Performer of the Game tonight, despite the fact that he gave up four runs in the fourth and was the losing pitcher. (Says something about our choices, doesn't it??) Other than that one clunker inning, he pitched well and gritted out a complete game. (But, as longtime manager Dick Williams used to say, "So what if he pitched great for eight? It's a nine-inning ball game, you know.") The O's lost, 5–1, but Milacki's performance gave the bullpen a much-needed night off after toiling a combined 11⅓ innings the night before.

There was another very positive note to this evening's loss. The O's went down quickly; 2:23 and we were back on the bus. Still, we did not touch down at BWI until five A.M. On the bus back to Memorial Stadium (where some of our cars were hopefully still parked), Cal Senior loudly expressed his displeasure with the travel schedule. "Look at that," he barked, "the god-damned cows have come home before us!" At daybreak we pulled into the stadium, thus ending the Orioles' longest road trip since 1982.

My night, however, was to prove far from over.

Friday, July 19, Baltimore

I walked into the town house a trifle before six. The maid I'd hired had apparently been there. The place looked clean, almost as if a slob did not live there. With the family due to arrive around seven tonight, I wanted to make sure that everything was just so. Right before turning in for the night (or should I say "day"?), I decided to inspect the entire apartment. Did a lamp need a new bulb? Was there toilet paper in all the bathrooms? All was in order until I stepped into the kids' room.

There, in one corner, were 300 dead bees and the remainder of a hive. I almost passed out. Imagine finding hundreds of dead bees strewn about your children's room. Remember now, Debby had loathed the summer in Syracuse with every fiber of her being, and I was determined to make this year the complete opposite—'91 in Baltimore was going to be pleasurable, exciting, fun. A houseful of bee corpses was not a great kickoff.

I got on the phone to Bonnie Levitt. She was aware of the problem but thought it had been rectified. The maid discovered the live hive yesterday while cleaning. On her way out of the apartment (at 90 miles per hour), she notified the condo association, which sent over an exterminator. It seems a warped board in the roof provided a hole from which the bees were able to enter, and with no one home for two weeks, they had ample opportunity to set up shop and declare statehood. So the bees were exterminated, but the hideous mess remained. And call me paranoid, but I thought I detected one tiny buzz. Bonnie was as incensed as I that the condo association had not fully corrected this rather urgent problem, and got on the phone to them. Moments later she assured me that the exterminator would return, a carpenter would fix the roof, and a maid would completely clean and vacuum the area all within that morning. Three questions remained. One: Would all of that really be done by noon, or is this the real world? Two: Could the family spend the night in the condo after it had been exterminated for bees? And three: I had now been up for twenty-two hours. Where was I going to sleep, if at all? The answers: One: blind faith. Two: assurance from the exterminating company. Three: I checked into the Cross Keys Hotel and told the association to expect the bill.

At nine A.M. I crawled into bed. By noon I was up. I drove back home to find, to my relief, that everything had been taken care of. By now Debby, the kids, and our housekeeper, Karina, were in the air en route to Dulles. The limo I had ordered was on its way to pick them up. A stop at the market to get a few necessities, and then it was off to the ballpark. Expect a *great* broadcast tonight.

I called home every fifteen minutes, and finally, at seven-fifteen, Matty answered. They had arrived. It was an uncomfortable flight for Debby and her ankle, of course, but they were there safe and sound. The association had left a basket of fruit and flowers with a card, and Debby wanted to know what this "Laura person" meant by "Sorry you had to spend the day in a hotel." I'll fill her in later.

That crisis over, I turned my bloodshot eyes to the field and one of the most memorable events of the season. This was Cal Ripken Night, celebrating his two most recent accomplishments—MVP of the All-Star Classic, and reaching his milestone 1,500th consecutive game. A crowd of almost 40,000 turned out in sweltering 97-degree weather to salute him. And then, in the third inning, with yours truly at the mike, he hit a home run. The stadium went nuts. For ten minutes the fans stood on their seats and roared. This man definitely knows how to throw a party!

Baltimore beat Seattle 4–1. Finesse pitcher (hurler/thrower/chucker/twirler/slabsman) Roy Smith picked up his fifth win. Save number 20 for Otter.

I returned home to find my eager, wide-awake family. They were still on California time; I was on either Hawaii or Switzerland time. But it didn't matter. This was one all-nighter I actually found replenishing.

Packing tip (although you might not want to try this yourself): Debby found she had a lot more room for her other items by packing only right shoes.

Final postscript to the road trip: Cal Senior, now in his thirty-fourth year of pro ball, said that the last three days from Anaheim to Baltimore were the worst, most strenuous he had ever experienced. What a rube I am. I thought this was the way it always was.

Saturday, July 20, Baltimore

Usually, Baltimore will have thirty days a year in which the mercury tops 90. Today was day 32 and the really "hot" season is not until August and September. And heat is not the half of it. It's the humidity that's the killer. Sultry, sticky, sweaty—this region is like living in Noriega's mouth. Thank God for air-conditioning!

Seattle evened the series with a 5–1 victory. I came an eyelash away from seeing (and calling) my first triple play. Gomez stepped on third for one out, fired to second for two, but the relay to first was just a whisker late. Other than that, this was just one of those games that fills out a 162-game schedule.

Sunday, July 21, Baltimore

Big day for Matty. He didn't just get his Orioles' press pass. He got his LAMINATED Orioles' press pass—good for the entire year, every game. The pass also gave him access to the clubhouses, which we immediately put to good use. Matty's been dying to meet Ken Griffey, Jr. (Griffey and Jim Abbott of the Angels are Matty's two favorite players/trading cards.) Junior (as he's known) was very approachable and charming. They must've talked for ten minutes. Matty asked how Junior liked being in the All-Star game, what does his candy bar taste like, etc. I don't know how Griffey is with adults, but with kids he's the league's MVP. (Of course, at age twenty-one he's not too far removed from being one himself.)

Next stop was the Orioles' clubhouse, where we chatted briefly with today's starter, Jeff Robinson. I asked what his game plan was, and he said he was going to try not to lose too much weight. (Another scorcher was predicted.) Matty then chimed in with: "Yeah, and I know another thing you should do. Try not to pitch like you did in Oakland." (Matty was referring to that recent disastrous outing in which Jeff gave up five runs and five hits on only thirty pitches in the first inning.) He was right, but still! Jeff, to his credit, smiled and said Matty wasn't the first person to say that. Matty didn't make the suggestion in a mean-spirited way, but I greatly appreciate Jeff's being a good sport. A *very* good sport.

Game-time temperature was 101 degrees—a new record. On the field, the mercury topped 115. Robinson pitched well until the fifth, when his fastball began to rise like the heat. Ken Griffey, Jr.'s three-run homer tied the game at 4–4, and moments later Mike Flanagan surrendered a two-run homer to fellow lefty Alvin Davis. Final: Seattle 6, Orioles 4.

The good ones'll get you. They always do. The superstar hitters always seem to prevail, no matter how you pitch to their weaknesses or pitch around them. Ken Griffey, Jr., homered against the O's today. He joins the list this year that includes Cecil Fielder, Mickey Tettleton, Mike Greenwell, Jack Clark, Kirby Puckett, Kent Hrbek, Don Mattingly, Joe Carter, Danny Tartabull, Kirk Gibson, Harold Baines, Dave Henderson, and Wally Joyner, among others. (Conspicuously absent is José Canseco, but that's because he's on my rotisserie team.) You have to marvel at the ability of these men, even though they make ungodly sums of money and get free athletic footwear.

I took the family to Ralphie's Diner for a real pseudo-authentic Baltimore dinner. What a treat to (a) spend an evening with the family, and (b) not be flying to Cleveland.

Jon Miller's *Sports Illustrated* article is out now. It's very flattering despite the fact that they used one of the "Buddha" photos. I'm briefly mentioned in the article as Jon's "radio foil." Actually, that *is* what I have become on those broadcasts when I work with Jon. Jon seems to have the need to get in the last word. As a result, over the past few weeks I've found that if an amusing line or thought should come to me, I will usually wait until a night with Chuck before airing it.

Monday, July 22, Baltimore/Annapolis, Maryland

Yesterday Baltimore was the second-hottest spot on the earth; edged out by some desert in Africa. No relief is in sight, but at least we have an off-day. Since Debby can't (or actually shouldn't) walk much, we took a drive to nearby Annapolis and spent a very pleasant day winding through its eighteenth-century streets (where historic redbrick buildings now house such American treasures as Crown Books and Sam Goody Records), lunching on the waterfront, touring the Naval Academy, and not discussing a certain baseball team's woeful lack of pitching. A good time was had by all.

Tuesday, July 23, Baltimore

No letup on the inferno. To beat the heat, we all went to see *Naked Gun 2½* in air-conditioned comfort. On the Levine Scale: either a ten or a six, depending upon which Levine. (Matty gave it the higher of the two.)

The Orioles continue to find new and exciting ways to lose. The California Angels, a team that has fallen from first place in the A.L. West on July 3, to fifth, seven off the pace, staggered into town to play three. Their problem has been hitting or lack thereof. They've scored barely two runs a game the past month, and haven't hit a homer since July 6.

But then they came to Baltimore.

Ben McDonald tried to get by primarily on just his fastball, a risky proposition in the big leagues, and the Halos (as they are unfortunately sometimes called) jumped on him for five runs, including three home runs. It's bad enough that Dave Winfield and Gary Gaetti went deep, but Luis Polonia? He hadn't homered in a year. (And, of course, I was on the air dazzling the audience with my knowledge of the game, going on and on about his lack of power when *bang!* he lofts one into the bleachers.)

When an announcer anticipates a certain play or a manager's move, he sounds like a million bucks. However . . . when he guesses wrong, he can *really* make an idiot of himself. It's a risk you take, and usually it's a safe one if you've done your homework and have a passing knowledge of the game, but there are those times . . .

Here are a couple of mine:

"You can bet the farm Cuyler's not going on this pitch . . . and there he goes!!"

"Here comes Robinson with the hook. That'll be it for Bautista. With the left-hander Palmeiro comin' up, Frank is going to go to the pen . . . and leave in Bautista."

. . . and finally . . .

"Bunting situation. Everyone in the ballpark knows that. Billy is up there to bunt. Now the pitch home . . . swung on and there's a fly ball to deep left field. . . ." (I don't feel so bad about that one. Everyone in the ballpark was wrong.)

With the Angels leading, 5–0, in the bottom of the eighth, Randy Milligan socked his first-ever grand slam (off ace closer Bryan Harvey, no less). The crowd went nuts. What a great moment. A cherished moment. Just the kind of moment that can turn a club's fortunes completely around.

The Orioles lost, 5–4.

After the game a fan approached me and wanted my autograph. "Do you know who I am?" I asked. "Sure," he said, "you're Leo Gomez." I took his program and next to Gomez's picture signed "Hola! Leo Gomez."

Phil Itzoe, the traveling secretary, tells of the time several years ago he was walking out of Memorial Stadium after a game and a youngster approached him for his autograph. Phil politely told him that he didn't really want his autograph, but the youngster persisted.

Phil asked the same question I did. "Do you know who I am?"

"No," said the kid, "but I do know you're *somebody*."

"How do you know that?" Phil wondered.

"Because you're wearing white shoes."

Wednesday, July 24, Baltimore

The heat wave finally broke as overnight thunderstorms drenched the area. Now that we can step outside for more than six minutes without collapsing, the family headed to the Inner Harbor for a pleasant lunch.

Debby and Diana plan on attending a game or two over the weekend, but for now are staying home where the air-conditioner is. We rented *The Sound of Music* for Diana and was it ever a hit. She watches it over and over. In two days she has the songs memorized. A few story points are a little difficult for my four-year-old to grasp (she surmises the Nazis are robbers, and is completely baffled at the notion of nuns), but still, I bet her fondest recollection of Baltimore this sweltering summer will be its breathtaking snowcapped mountains.

Facing a tough customer in premier lefty Chuck Finley, the Orioles prevailed, 5–2. Rookies Chito (this guy might be for real) Martinez and Leo Gomez each homered. Cal drove in a run with a double, but his average has slipped to .331, and he is now second, behind Danny Tartabull. Kirby Puckett is right up there as well. I suppose this is not a good time to mention that Cal is the coverboy for this week's issue of *Sports Illustrated*.

As I mentioned, Matty's single favorite player in the whole world is Angel pitcher Jim Abbott, the young man born without a right hand. Matty is astounded that someone could rise above such an enormous handicap to be a major league pitcher. Since the day Abbott first donned an Angel uniform, my son has followed his career diligently. He'll rarely miss watching or listening to a game in which Abbott pitches, and his room is filled with Jim Abbott trading cards, articles, and posters. Well, today may have been the highlight of his summer. I introduced him to Jim Abbott. Matty was in complete awe. Abbott could not have been nicer. The two talked for quite a while. Abbott told Matty how, as a kid, he used to practice throwing a ball against a wall and catching it, moving up each time so that the ball would ricochet faster and his reactions would have to get quicker. He even showed Matty how he transfers his glove back and forth from his left hand to his right arm. He left Matty with two pieces of advice, both of which I approve of heartily: (1) work hard and practice, and (2) be nice to your little sister. How can you *not* idolize this man???

P.S. He also tried to sell Matty on the University of Michigan.

Tonight's comedy corner: In the third inning I mistakenly called Luis Sojo (Angel second baseman) Luis Polonia. I then covered by saying the Angels lead the league in Luises and for the rest of the half-inning proceeded to call every Angel Luis. "Luis Winfield takes his lead from first. Luis Joyner at the plate. Luis Finley looking for his fourteenth win . . ." (I have this fantasy of somebody driving along an interstate tuning in my broadcast for the first time and saying to himself, "What the *fuck* is this??")

Play of the night: A foul ball shot into the Angels' radio booth and, after careening off a wall or two, clonked broadcaster Al Conin on the head. I reported it on the air and said he was fine (which he was) "although for some reason he's now calling the game in French."

Foul balls can be nasty business. From what I've observed, the best way to snare one is to let the mullethead sitting in front of you attempt to catch it. When it invariably bounces off his hands (leaving them swollen the size of Goofy's), you just play the carom. Depending upon which section you are seated in (lower levels especially), always be on guard for these lethal souvenirs. You just never know.

The strangest foul-ball story I've ever heard involved former Phillies' outfielder Richie Ashburn. He once hit a foul ball that struck a woman in the stands, causing a rather serious injury. As she was being led up the aisle to the hospital, Ashburn hit another foul ball, and wouldn't you know, that one hit her as well.

Thursday, July 25, Baltimore

After fourteen years with the same hairdresser, I find seeking a temporary replacement as traumatic as seeking a new dentist. I hadn't had a haircut since our California swing in May and needed one desperately. I was teetering on the edge of "sixties throwback." The lady recommended to me turned out to be a major neurotic with numerous phobias (elevators, crowds, certain cars). How nice of her to describe them all in full detail while sharp instruments were whizzing about my head. The end result was not terrific, but who's going to see me here in Baltimore?

Answer: the world.

People magazine still wants to do a profile on me and chose tonight to send a photographer. Great. I can only hope that through lighting and the proper angle I don't look like Jack Lord.

The Orioles took their first series of the month, beating the fallen Angels, 8–4. Cal went one for two to stay among the batting leaders.

Another positive to the monster season Cal is enjoying is that it finally lays to rest the notion that by playing every day his performance has suffered. Last year he got off to a horrendous start (on June 13 his average was .209), and although he finished at .250, he was the subject of quite a bit of criticism. He was selfish for not taking himself out of the lineup, he was tired, he was pressing, etc. Cal maintained throughout that his consecutive-game streak had nothing to do with his mulligan season, and the results this year are certainly supporting his claim.

Friday, July 26, Baltimore

Right-hander Dave Johnson has finally returned. He's been gone (or "groin") since May 19. For the past month he's been on rehab assignments with Hagerstown and Rochester, but on the big-league level "there's been no room at the inn." D.J., you'll recall, led the club in victories last year with 13. This year 13 seems like 25. Thus far, our two leaders are Bob Milacki and Jeff Ballard, with six. (Milacki is 6–4, Ballard 6–10.) The problem for Johnson is that he doesn't throw particularly hard on a staff filled with finesse pitchers. If he were a flamethrower, he would've been back weeks ago. In any event, an opening now exists as Oates has decided to return to a six-man Dirty Half Dozen bullpen (Oriole relievers lead the league in innings pitched, a marvelous distinction). However, it's a pen rather lopsided to the right with Johnson, Frohwirth, Williamson, and Olson all throwing from that side, and only two lefties in Kilgus and Flanagan. (To make room, infielder Shane Turner, who was called up a week ago, has been told to finish his cup of coffee, leave his dime on the counter, and return to Rochester.)

The Oakland A's are here over the weekend. The three-time defending American League champs are currently in the unfamiliar position of playing catch-up. (I know. Where's the violin music??) They began the night in fifth place in the A.L. West, five games behind Minnesota. Carney Lansford's miracle comeback from a serious snowmobile accident has stalled, and after coming off the DL only two weeks ago, he's right back on it with recurring soreness in his left knee. His replacements, Ernest Riles and Vance Law, are hitting a combined .211, so the A's went out and traded a couple of minor leaguers today to Cleveland for Brook Jacoby. Jacoby must feel he's died and gone to heaven. An Indian since 1984, this will be the first time he's ever been with a contender. Games in August and September will actually count. Jacoby has several days to report, but my guess is he'll be here tomorrow—six hours before the grounds crew.

The trading deadline is July 31 (after which players traded must clear waivers, a risky proposition). Contending teams will often make one or two eleventh-hour swaps to shore up for the stretch run. That usually means pitching. Former Oriole, now with Montreal, Dennis Martinez is a name frequently mentioned. So is California's Kirk McCaskill. The problem in making deals today is that club owners are not negotiating players, they're negotiating contracts. Will the player be a free agent after this season? Is he a ten-and-five man with trade approval (ten years in the majors, five with the same club)? Are there trade restrictions or bonuses built into his contract? Is his multiyear deal too great a risk for the future? Does he want his money all in nickels? These are the major considerations today, not "Can he throw his slider over for strikes?" or "Can he work out of the pen every third day?"

How the Orioles figure in all of this remains to be seen. There is some scuttlebutt that the Mets are interested in Mike Flanagan, and Texas manager Bobby Valentine very casually asked Jon recently about Mark Williamson and how he's been throwing lately. Dwight Evans would also be a tasty catch. For now, though, negotiations are in the exploratory rumor stage.

This had all the earmarks of a long, lonnnnngggggg night. After the second inning (with the Orioles already trailing 2–1), the game was halted due to rain. For an hour Jon and I conducted *Orioles Talk* (which is fun, but not as much fun as, say, having a prostate exam). Play finally resumed and the A's scored another quick run.

Dave Johnson got his feet wet in a hurry. Oates summoned him to relieve starter Jeff Robinson in the fifth. The score was 3–3, one out, the bases loaded, with slugger Mark McGwire coming to the plate.

D.J. struck him out swinging. Welcome back, Dave!

Next up was left-hander Ernest Riles, who was 6 for 58. He hit a grand slam. Yes, welcome back indeed.

Remember when I listed all the superstars who had homered

this year against the Orioles with the exception of José Canseco? Add him to the list. His "big fly" off Johnson was followed by one by Harold Baines (his fifth of the year against the O's).

The Orioles trailed Oakland and Dave Stewart 9–3 going into the bottom of the seventh. Time to head for the exits?

Not yet.

Chito Martinez led off with a walk. Leo Gomez doubled him to third. He scored a moment later on Bob Melvin's sacrifice fly, 9–4. Ho-hum.

Devereaux's single to center scored Gomez to make it 9–5. At least the big crowd of over 43,000 had a little something to cheer about.

With a lefty—Orsulak—due up, LaRussa went to the pen for veteran left-hander Rick Honeycutt. Oates lifted Orsulak for switch-hitter David Segui. Segui promptly legged out a base hit. The O's had runners at first and second for Cal. Honeycutt walked him. The bases were loaded for Sam Horn, who all of a sudden represented the tying run.

Oates again went to the bench. Right-hand hitter Dwight Evans bounced out of the dugout with a bat. LaRussa followed suit by handing the ball to right-hander Gene Nelson.

With the count 1–1 here's what happened, as described by Baltimore Oriole announcer Ken Levine: "So Dewey Evans, who throughout his career just thrives on pressure situations, is in one here. Nelson holds the ball behind his back, straightens up, and the pitch . . . swung on and belted! . . . To deep left field! . . . In the corner! . . . That ball is a . . . *slammmmm!!!!*"

Memorial Stadium exploded in jubilation. It was one of the most exhilarating moments of my life. When you dream of being a baseball announcer, *this* is what you dream of—calling that truly amazing dramatic play. Sure, this was not a home run that will rival Bobby Thomson's 1951 "Shot Heard Round the World" or Bill Mazeroski's Series winner in '60, or Kirk Gibson's Game One blast in the '88 Fall Classic, but still, for me, Evans's slam was almost mythical. The next time you come over to my house, I'll have to play it for you.

Too bad the Orioles went on to lose the game, 12–9, in the ninth inning. (How it happened is unimportant, and I'm sure Gregg Olson would agree.)

Tonight's Orioles' loss was not the most crushing defeat of the night. Not by a long shot. At Dodger Stadium rookie Mark Gardner of Montreal pitched a no-hitter through nine full innings, but since there was no score, he was forced to work the tenth, where he gave up two hits and lost the game, 1–0.

Saturday, July 27, Baltimore

Another train wreck for the Orioles and Jeff Ballard. Oakland needed just thirty pitches in the first inning to collect four runs on five hits. Todd Frohwirth gave up another three runs in the second, and the A's breezed to a 9–1 rout. It's the twenty-eighth time that the Orioles have been behind by at least three runs by the fourth inning. This does not make it easy for the announcer whose first inning of the night is the third. I was talking recently with my counterpart on the Angels' radio team, Bob Jamison, and asked him how often he's had that experience. His answer: never.

Repeat after me: PITCHING IS NINETY PERCENT OF THE GAME. AND RELIEF PITCHING IS THE OTHER TEN.

The weather, for a change, was beautiful, and WBAL was throwing a "bullpen party" before the game. There is a large picnic area between the left-field bullpen and scoreboard, which 'BAL commandeered this evening to throw a big bash for staff, sponsors, and announcers' families. Debby, Karina, and the kids had a swell time.

The Orioles have really rolled out the red carpet as far as Debby is concerned. The tickets they provide her are directly behind home plate, with a minimum number of steps required. When she arrives early, she's ushered into the executive lounge, and today before the party, a team representative escorted her and the troop over to the picnic area. Like I told her, "This *is* the big leagues."

Sunday, July 28, Baltimore/Sioux Falls, South Dakota/Seattle

Kevin Costner took batting practice with the Orioles today. He and Jeff Ballard have a mutual friend who made the arrangements. You can never really tell about an actor until he's on the stage or set, but from all appearances, Costner seemed very down-to-earth. After he completes his current project in the D.C. area—*JFK*—he plans to rent a Winnebago and just get lost with his family for a month in the Pacific Northwest. For most stars of Costner's caliber, getting away from civilization means having the entourage stay on a different floor of the Ritz-Carlton.

The players feigned ultracoolness in the clubhouse around Costner, giving him shit for his shower shoes, etc. A few asked for autographed balls, and I must say he was more gracious than some of them are when fans make the same request.

On the field he stretched and ran wind sprints with the rest of the squad, doing his level best to just blend in with the crowd. It was an impossible task. The alerted media were there in full force. The Orioles' PR department calls this a "Foof" event, meaning that pseudomedia types who never come out to the park suddenly appear in droves, milling about as if they're on the trail of an important story or have a crucial deadline to meet. In truth, their only function is to get in everyone's way.

Costner looked pretty good in the cage. He actually cleared the fence once, but even more impressive were eight or ten line shots right over shortstop. Dwight Evans told me he was pretty capable with the glove as well. I invited Kev to read the Esskay Out-of-Town Scoreboard in the third inning, but he had to decline, having made previous plans—he was playing golf this afternoon with the president of the United States. Boy, am I getting tired of *that* excuse. Of course, the reality is, he *is* playing golf with President Bush. I just wonder if Dan Quayle has been enlisted to caddy for Costner.

One final note on Kevin Costner: He's a lot shorter than I thought.

In the first inning, Ben McDonald threw a curve that got away and strafed José Canseco's back as he was ducking out of harm's way. Canseco, who got in a shouting match with a sixty-year-old woman in the stands the night before, trotted to first, yelled out something to McDonald, then started for the mound. This naturally caused both benches to clear. Cooler heads prevailed, and no punches were thrown. Everyone stood around for the obligatory five minutes, then returned to their stations. The thought that McDonald would be throwing at Canseco is ludicrous. José was the first batter in 782 that Big Ben has plunked. And if he *was* out to drill him, it sure wouldn't be with a tumbling curveball.

Canseco grounded out to third the next time up, and needless to say, the crowd loved it. Unfortunately, José got his revenge in the sixth with a game-tying three-run homer off McDonald. Rickey Henderson belted a solo shot in the eighth that proved to be the game winner: 4–3, Oakland.

In other baseball news: Two days after Mark Gardner no-hit the Dodgers for nine innings in Los Angeles, Dennis Martinez hurled a perfect game against "the Bums." And Montreal is looking to unload this guy??? I'd be surprised to see him traded this week.

At five-thirty the Orioles headed off to the airport to begin their Sunday night journey to Seattle. We boarded *Orioles One* at six-fifteen, then sat for an hour while the Neanderthals loaded the plane. Fortunately, Larry Lucchino, club president, was on the flight and was livid at the length of time it took to throw a few bags and trunks into the belly of an aircraft. He was even less thrilled when our little 737 had to make a refueling stop in Sioux Falls, South Dakota.

That part of the trip, I must admit, I enjoyed. Several of us got off the plane just to say we had actually set foot in South Dakota. I stood on the tarmac with Dwight Evans, watching a breathtaking purple sunset, the kind they only get here in "Big Sky Country." Reflecting on the day and the appearance of Kevin Costner, Dewey was saying how little he enjoyed the "fame" aspect of his career. He's a shy man by nature, and his sole pleasure in baseball is playing the game. It's not the thunderous ovations, the recognition, even the money. It's standing in right field and at the crack of the bat racing toward the line to make the catch. Evans said he can't imagine not "playing the game." Even after his career is over he'll be out there on Sunday mornings playing softball. Somehow Evans's reverie on the purity of the game, spoken against this backdrop of golden wheat fields and a crimson sky, made it all the more poignant.

In half an hour the plane was refueled, the pilot given his complimentary glass tumbler, and we were off to Seattle.

One in-flight story: The Orioles treated two of their clubhouse attendants to this road trip, one of whom is Fred (the name has been changed to protect the embarrassed). Fred is probably in his early twenties, gangly and awkward, but very sweet-natured. He is constantly razzed by some of the players, and it doesn't help his cause that he is, well, let's just say "gullible." He was with us in Florida and took his first plane flight ever when he caught the team charter back to Baltimore in April. As a result, he does not have what you'd call "savvy" in terms of air travel. Several of the players have convinced him that the plane will be refueled in midair and that he, as the new guy, must assist in that procedure. Even the crew was in on the gag. After about two hours in the air the pilot announced that it was time for the midair refueling and would Fred please report to the cockpit. He was scared shitless. They had him believing he was to walk out on the wing. (When I said "gullible," I meant GULLIBLE.) Finally, after much taunting, he made his way up the aisle to the cockpit—Tom Dooley walking that last mile. He entered the cockpit, closed the door, and a minute later came bursting out. "No way!" he screamed. Based on what he saw peering out of the cockpit windshield, he exclaimed, "We're going so slow we're not even moving!"

We touched down in Seattle at eleven—two A.M. Eastern Time—and checked into the Crown Plaza an hour later. Once in my room, I noticed a huge swelling on my neck. I had a mosquito bite the size of an apricot. And I'd been worried I wouldn't have time to get a souvenir of Sioux Falls.

7

Monday, July 29, Seattle

I took advantage of a gorgeous clear day in Seattle by sleeping till the early afternoon, getting lunch, then heading out to the domed yard.

The poor Seattle Mariners. They've never had a .500 club. Ever. This year they're 52–47, playing the best ball in team history, boasting some outstanding players such as superstar Ken Griffey, Jr., drawing well despite playing indoors in an outdoor paradise, and yet they are a franchise in deeeeeep trouble. Mariners' chairman Jeff Smulyan is trying desperately to keep the ship afloat and keep it in the Seattle harbor, but he expects to lose $5 million this year, not to mention a onetime penalty fee of $10.7 million as his share of the collusion damages (although he did not own the team during the collusion period). They're hurting because of the market size and the corporate community. Consider their radio-TV package. It's less than $2 million. The average is between $10 and $12 mil. And then there's the Yankees. Thanks to a deal masterminded by Mr. Steinbrenner, they earn $50 million. The other big source of revenue is luxury boxes, but there are very few takers in Seattle. With St. Petersburg, Florida, making a big play to get a team to occupy its "White Elephant Dome," the Mariners' future in the Northwest is somewhat shaky. Remember when drawing two million people a year meant a successful franchise? Not anymore. Ask the Mariners.

One thing the M's have going for them is a great broadcasting team. Dave Niehaus has been their voice since game one, and in my opinion he's one of the best. Colorful, enthusiastic, highly excitable—no one can make a game come alive any better than Niehaus. (And considering the dogs he's had to cover for nineteen years, that's no easy feat.) His partner, Rick Rizzs, is smooth, solid, and the perfect complement to the "Veteran Spieler," as Niehaus kiddingly calls himself. There are other broadcast teams in the league perhaps as good (Mark Holtz and Eric Nadel in Texas for one), but few better. Unfortunately, they receive very little national exposure, being way off in the mountains and forests of the Northwest. (Which brings to mind a question: If you call a home run and no one hears it in the forest, is it a home run?)

Before the game, John Oates announced that Jeff Ballard and Jeff Robinson have both been bumped from the starting rotation to the bullpen. Dave Johnson rejoins the rotation Wednesday, and the last spot is still open. I think that means Mike Mussina, the hot prospect having a great year in Rochester, but nothing has been announced.

With the score tied 4–4 in the seventh, tonight's starter, Bob Milacki, gave up a one-out double to Greg Briley. Exit Milacki; enter Ballard. Jeff promptly walked the number-eight and -nine hitters in the lineup, then gave up back-to-back two-run doubles. Larry Lucchino in the press box, I understand, was ready to explode. Paul Kilgus then came on and gave up two more consecutive doubles. (Four straight doubles by the M's, five in the inning—one shy of the record set in the 1930s.) When the inning was over, Seattle had scored seven times. The Orioles lost, 11–4. Baltimore's record: 39–59 (still a good five games better than Cleveland, so you can *imagine* how bad they are).

One high note: Juan Bell hit his first major league home run. When he rounded first and saw that the ball cleared the twenty-three-foot wall in right, he leaped in the air and thrust his fist in triumph. He was like one of those game-show contestants who had just won a Nissan Stanza. He did everything but kiss Erik Hanson, who had given it up. It was refreshing to see such a genuine show of emotion. The amazing thing about the home run is that Johnny Oates had predicted it. Talking to Jon Miller before the game, he said that, based on Bell's batting practice that day, he wouldn't be surprised if Juan went deep. Once Bell crossed the plate, Oates popped his head out of the dugout, looked up to the booth at Jon, and the two traded "thumbs up." What's not surprising is that Bell, a switch hitter, hit it from the left side. That is clearly his best side of the plate. From the right he's batting .154, but from the left .155.

Tuesday, July 30, Seattle

Sweeping changes in the pitching staff! Jeff Ballard and Jeff Robinson were demoted yet again. This time to Rochester. (What does it say about the kind of year a team is having when its Opening Day pitcher and team leader in victories—albeit with a 6–11 record—is sent to the minors?) Also jettisoned was lefty Paul Kilgus, who was "designated for assignment." Taking their place will be left-hand reliever Jim Poole, right-hand reliever Stacy Jones, and, as predicted, right-handed starter Mike Mussina. Poole and Jones will report immediately. Mussina will join the club Friday in Chicago and start Sunday against the Sox.

A disgruntled Ballard has asked to be traded. He'll be back, I'm sure, September 1, when rosters expand to forty, but Robinson, I believe, is toast. Apparently he had an angry exchange with Lucchino in the hotel lobby this morning, and when chased down at the airport by Peter Schmuck of the *Morning Sun,* he was asked how he felt about the demotion to Rochester, to which he replied, "Rochester, Baltimore. It's all the same. It's all Triple A." I don't think the local talk shows are going to be wanting for calls.

Who are the new guys? Jim Poole is twenty-five, raised in Philly, blue eyes, baby face—looks kinda like a Cabbage Patch Kid. He began the year in the Texas organization after being traded during the off-season from the Dodgers. His Opening Day was with Triple-A Oklahoma City, then he was promoted to the Rangers briefly in May, pitched well enough to get kicked back to the minors, where he was picked up by the Orioles off the waiver wire. From there to Rochester and now Baltimore via Seattle. (Yes, you do need a map.)

Right-hander Stacy Jones is six-foot-six, 225, the first major leaguer from Gadsden, Alabama. He was Otter's roommate in Auburn. His nickname is "Country," and from what I hear, he's a delightful fellow. He supposedly is on a crusade to prove that Elvis is alive. I hope Stacy's car breaks down someday in Dunedin, Florida.

Twenty-two-year-old Mike Mussina is another Stanford grad. (Stanford University is becoming a Baltimore farm club.) He was the Orioles' first-round pick last June and will be making his M.L. debut Sunday after only one year of pro ball. (Of course, it only took him three and a half years to get an economics degree at Stanford.) I didn't get to know Mussina real well in spring training, but my one memory is of him sitting at his locker in the crowded clubhouse, nose buried in a book, while the rest of the players whooped it up, snapped towels, etc.

Mussina throws a fastball, change, and two knuckle curves (the pitch Burt Hooten of the Dodgers made famous in the seventies). Since Mussina couldn't perfect a normal curve in high school, he taught himself the more unorthodox pitch and has been a shooting star ever since. I'm anxiously looking forward to his debut on Sunday.

Both Poole and Jones got their feet wet right away, and both were impressive in their initial outings. Poole retired the last ten he faced, striking out six. Jones hurled two perfect innings. If only starter Roy Smith hadn't given up six runs in the first two innings, including a grand slam to Ken Griffey, Jr. Seattle breezed, 8–2. This was the thirty-first time the Orioles have trailed by three or more runs by the fourth.

One of the features they have at the Kingdome is "Comedy Clips." Once a game, between innings, they show a comedy snippet from a movie or TV show on their DiamondVision Board. It's quite a popular feature (and makes a lot more sense than idiotic dot racing). Tonight they showed a clip from the *Simpsons* baseball episode David and I wrote last year. Rarely have I gotten the chance to hear 20,000 people laugh at one of my jokes . . . or, in the case of tonight—chuckle mildly. I'm told that on Opening Day they showed another segment from our show—the blues singer taking twenty minutes to perform a wildly improvisational version of the National Anthem—and they received calls and letters of complaint. I dunno, as an artist I feel it's important to challenge the audience, be controversial, take risks no matter what the cost . . . especially when writing cartoons.

I saw *Terminator 2* today. I always knew that Arnold Schwarzenegger could beat the shit out of me, but now I think Linda Hamilton could as well. Still, an eight-plus. I may have even gotten a new home run call as a result of the film. As a ball sails over the fence I say in a slow, bludgeoning voice, "Hasta la vista, baby!"

What do you think???

Wednesday, July 31, Seattle

Jon Miller awoke with a start this morning, bolted up in bed, and shouted in horror, "Oh my God! I missed my flight!" Which flight and to where, he could not recall. After a minute things came back into focus and he realized this was not a travel day. He was in Seattle and could sleep as late as he wished. Again, I do not envy the man his schedule.

Had a great lunch with PR maestro Rick Vaughn and several of the Orioles' "ink-stained wretches" at Cutters down at Pike Place Market. Spectacular view of Puget Sound and maybe the best salmon I've ever eaten. (I'm gonna order a steak in Seattle?)

The trading deadline is midnight East, nine P.M. Left Coast time. Trade speculation in *USA Today* said the Orioles were offering Mark Williamson for ANYTHING. Gee, Mark must've enjoyed getting up in the morning, having a refreshing glass of orange juice, sitting down to peruse the paper and reading *that*. Mike Flanagan is hoping that he won't be dealt off. He's emotionally attached to the Orioles and Baltimore, and would love to pitch in the final game at Memorial Stadium. For him to be traded would be another case of "no good deed going unpunished." Dwight Evans, on the other hand, is intrigued with the notion of perhaps joining a contending club. He told me before the game he was just trying to remain focused, but his bags were packed for anywhere.

Dave Johnson made his first start since my mother's birthday (April 29, of course) and was fairly effective. He didn't allow a run until the fifth. He left the game in the seventh, trailing 2–1 (the difference being Jay Buhner's home run . . . which didn't go 500 feet, like the rest of his have lately, so that's a major achievement). Since this was getaway night, you could almost count on extra innings, and sure enough, there were. The Orioles tied the game in the ninth on a leadoff single by Horn and a single by Milligan that left-fielder Greg Briley played into a triple—charging and letting the ball bounce high over him. Flanagan (so far still an Oriole) pitched 3⅔ shutout innings, and the Birds broke through in the eleventh with a bloop single by Chris Hoiles to drive in two with the bases loaded. Final: Orioles 4, Mariners 2.

The trading deadline passed. The Dodgers got reliever Roger McDowell for two minor leaguers, starter Ron Darling went from Montreal to Oakland for prospects, and veteran right-hander Jim Clancy moved over from Houston to Atlanta for a minor leaguer and the famous "player to be named later." Do you see a pattern here? Pitching, pitching, and more pitching. Meanwhile, Flanagan, Evans, and even Williamson remain with the Orioles.

John Oates has said on a number of occasions that he'd gladly stay up all night if the Orioles could get a win. Well, tonight he got his wish.

Thursday, August 1, Seattle/Sioux Falls, South Dakota/Chicago

Our destination is Chicago, where, after an off-day today, the Orioles begin a weekend series with the hottest team in baseball. Our buses arrived at Boeing Field outside of Seattle a little after midnight, which was already past two A.M. in Chi-town. Naturally, we sat on the ground for forty-five minutes while the village idiots loaded *Orioles One*. We then weren't in the air ten minutes when the pilot came on the P.A. and announced that one of the grounds crew members forgot to secure a back-door hatch and thus the plane would have to return to the field. Forgot to secure a hatch?? (I suggested Fred go out and do it while we were in midair.) Back on the ground, the problem was corrected in fifteen seconds, followed by a half hour of preflight safety checks. At one-thirty we took off again, this time rising above a thousand feet. Lindbergh could make it all the way across the Atlantic on one tank of gas, but we had to stop in Sioux Falls again to refuel. (United Airlines planes can go nonstop. So can Emerald's.) Dawn broke as we landed in "Outlaw Country." This time I stayed on the plane and watched as the mosquitoes hurled themselves violently at the window trying to get me.

Unfortunately, I am one of those people who cannot sleep on a plane. I've tried every kind of pillow and sitting position possible, and short of being shot by a stun gun, I cannot doze off. By the time we landed in Chicago at eight A.M. local time, I had been up twenty-one hours straight. Our parade of zombies boarded the buses and headed for the city just at the height of rush-hour traffic. Did I mention I can't sleep on buses either? I got to my room at the Westin Hotel at nine-ten. It should take a good two days to recover from my day off.

One final thought vis-à-vis our charter: This is the same plane used by the Sacramento Kings of the NBA. Didn't they have the worst road record in sports last year???

Friday, August 2, Chicago

I'm recalling that bus conversation in New York: Kevin Hickey didn't make it to Chicago, but oak-jawed Todd Frohwirth did. Actually, Todd's been one of the team's better acquisitions . . . and there've been *many* new faces. The only pitchers left from the Opening Day roster are Dave Johnson, Gregg Olson, Mark Williamson, and Mike Flanagan.

Note to hotel room designers: Place the phone near the bed. My phone at the Westin is on the desk on the other side of the room. I left a wake-up call and almost got a hernia groping for the receiver. Toilet paper is near the toilet. It's the same principle.

Lunch at Gino's East. Best Chicago-style deep-dish pizza east of the original Gino's.

For some reason the new Comiskey looked better to me this time in (especially after three games in the "Dome of Kings"). I sense an air of excitement at the park, and it's due to the team. The Go-Go Sox are going better than they have in years. Currently, they're on an eight-game winning streak, averaging a whopping nine runs per game. They've shot up to second place, only two games behind Minnesota. Already this season they've won twenty-five games in their final at-bat, and their third baseman, Robin Ventura, is coming off a career month in which he hit .357, belted twelve home runs (including two grand slams) and drove in 33. It doesn't hurt, of course, that the Cubbies are odoriferous this year, but still, you can sense it everywhere you go—Chicago loves them Sox!

Another reason why I'm warming to Comiskey is that I love Nancy Faust. Bar none, she is the best stadium organist in baseball. The key to becoming a good organist is being inventive and versatile without being intrusive and insufferable. Knowing when *not* to play is as important as knowing when, and Nancy seems to walk that fine line with the best of 'em. You don't hear "charge" between every pitch, you don't hear the "Mexican Hat Dance" on an endless loop, but you do hear *The Addams Family* theme when Leo Gomez steps to the plate, and one hell of a cookin' version of "Runaround Sue" when a pitcher is lifted. I can't fathom why many organizations have abandoned stadium organs in favor of prerecorded rock 'n' roll (Memorial Stadium included). Organ music at a ballpark adds as much to the overall experience as a soundtrack to a movie, and Nancy Faust is Henry Mancini, John Williams, and Max Steiner all rolled into one.

And besides, haven't we heard "We Will Rock You" just one too many times???

Remember which team snapped the Twins' fifteen-game winning streak? Well, the O's did it again, this time to eight-straight Chicago—3–0 was the final. The Orioles set a club record as five pitchers combined for the shutout. Ben started and yielded just four hits in 5⅔ innings to record the victory. More impressive than the win, however, was the fact that he displayed a good change-up tonight. Although Ben's fastball has been top-notch, he has not been able to get his curve over for strikes. The word is out in the American League, and hitters will no longer offer at it. Thus, Ben gets behind in the count with breaking balls out of the zone and must come in with the old "number one." In the big leagues you can't get by on just a fastball, no matter how good it is. Sooner or later these hitters are going to catch up to it, and when they do—"Hasta la vista, baby!" Now, with a change-up to complement the heat and a curveball that will, in time, be back on track, Ben might live up to his enormous potential and blossom into one of the more dominant pitchers in the game.

Severe thunderstorms were predicted for tonight, but not until after midnight. They arrived early. In the fifth inning tremendous streaks of lightning tore through the sky. They were almost as impressive as the Comiskey Park exploding scoreboard complete with its flashing lights and rotating colored disks. The wind, which had been blowing from right to left, suddenly changed direction and began gusting straight out. In anticipation of the rain—but before a single drop had fallen—the crowd rushed up the aisles for cover. We continued to play (because there was no rain), and in five minutes the winds calmed, the lightning subsided, and the spectators cautiously returned to their seats. There were no further almost-interruptions all evening.

Working with Jon is great fun but at times can be challenging. I've learned over the last few months to let him initiate any witty repartee between us. When he's in a frisky mood, we joke around; when he's not, we don't. Also, I've discovered, when we do trade barbs, it's usually best to give Jon the final joke. Tonight, however, I just couldn't resist. During one of my innings we were discussing Ken "Hawk" Harrelson, the very colorful TV voice of the ChiSox. The Hawk has this catchphrase, "Yes!" He uses it frequently to punctuate a good play or a big hit for Chicago. Jon noted that he too needed a catchphrase and came up with "Hello!" After every pitch I called, he blurted out "Hello!" This went on for seven or eight straight pitches and it started getting tiresome. "Here's the one-two delivery, fouled away."

"Hello!"

"Next pitch is low, two-and-two."

"Hello!" Finally, Jon said, "So do you think it'll catch on, 'Hello!'?"

"Yes, Jon," I said, "pretty soon people will even be answering their phones with that." Dr. Paul and Chuck both burst out laughing, and Jon didn't say a word to me for the next three innings.

Yes, I was a little devil, but it was worth it.

Saturday, August 3, Chicago

The storms did visit overnight, cooling off the "Hog Butcher to the World" considerably. The high today was a very pleasant 80 degrees.

There is some alleged espionage at the New Comiskey. The Orioles suspect that the White Sox may be stealing signs via video-monitoring eqiupment. John Oates believes there are TV cameras in the center-field scoreboard, one trained directly on him. Also suspicious is "the room." During our April trip John and the coaches were afforded a tour of the ballpark. They were ushered into every room in the stadium (lounges, training facilities, broom closets), all clearly marked. But directly off the White Sox dugout was a door that was conspicuously unmarked. Not thinking much of it, John opened the door. Instantly, the tour guide and two others blocked his passage, slammed the door shut, and shouted at him to "Stay outta there! That room's off-limits!" He was never given an explanation as to the purpose of that mysterious room, and his feeling is that it houses television monitors. How angry is he over this situation? Not very. Stealing signs is a part of the game. So too now is technology. When he starts to believe that these cameras are trained on him *after* he leaves the ballpark, then it'll be time for concern.

It should be noted, however, that the White Sox deny any wrongdoing and contend that the Orioles are the only team making these charges.

Jack McDowell, the ace of the Sox staff, could not get into the third inning. The Orioles had touched him up for six runs and ten hits. (Maybe we were stealing their signs?) Cal was back on the beam with two doubles and two RBIs. Meanwhile, Bob Milacki pitched very well and the O's hung on to win, 6–3.

Elsewhere in baseball, the Twins are in Oakland for a big showdown series with the A's. The A's were leading 5–0 going into the eighth, but Minnesota scored seven times. The A's bullpen is Swiss cheese. But 7–5, Minnesota, would not be the final score. At game's end Oakland would have six home runs . . . and lose, 8–6. That's right, six solo homers but nothing else. That's the type of game late in the year that can break a team's back. I'll be interested to see if the A's can recover. (By the way, I wonder if in their game notes they will include: When the A's hit six home runs they are 0–1.)

Jeff Ballard, Jeff Robinson, and Paul Kilgus have now reported to the Rochester Red Wings. Of all the places to join the club, they hooked up with it in Toledo. You talk about a comedown! Ballard (who's been making noises in the papers lately about not being appreciated and wanting to be traded—in other words, the "usual") made his first start tonight in the International League. He worked five innings and gave up ten hits and three runs. Kilgus came on and in less than two innings surrendered four hits and another two runs. I think the numbers speak for themselves.

Rotisserie update: Gee, it's nice and cool here in the cellar. There have been complaints about sign stealing at the Pit, notably last week when someone ripped off the Budweiser sign from the scoreboard. That's the trouble with letting people into these stadiums.

Sunday, August 4, Chicago/Baltimore

Mike Mussina made his major league debut today, only fourteen months removed from Stanford University. Was he nervous? As Don Knotts used to say on the old *Steve Allen Show*—"N-N-N-N-ooooo." At Rochester, Mussina averaged only 1.9 walks per nine innings, an excellent ratio. With a crowd of over 41,000 looking on at Comiskey, he walked two in his first inning. Did he settle down? "Yessssss." Mussina got into the seventh inning giving up only one run, a homer by Frank Thomas (who hits them against everybody). His debut was a rousing success. Okay, the Orioles lost, 1–0, but it was still a great day for the organization. With McDonald starting to come around, and now Mussina, the light at the end of the tunnel might not be an oncoming train.

Footnote on today's game: Credit where credit is due to Charlie Hough, whose knuckleball completely befuddled the O's. He posted his twelfth career shutout; a five-hit complete game. Hough is forty-three and made his major league debut when Mike Mussina was twenty months old.

The trip home on *Orioles One* was without incident or fuel stop (although I was a little concerned when we hovered over Canton, Ohio). The plane did land in a remote part of the airport, and buses were needed to transport players to another remote part of the airport where wives who were lucky enough to find it were waiting.

My happy homecoming took place at ten o'clock.

Debby has a close cousin from Long Island with two kids our kids' ages staying in town the last few days. That meant museums, aquariums, Babe Ruth's house (he wasn't home, by the way), and standing on her mending foot for long stretches of time. Now that Simon Legree has returned, she will once again be forced to stay off her feet and relax. I know that's cruel, but that's my nature.

Monday, August 5, Baltimore

Spectacular weather! Blue skies, temps in the eighties, low humidity. It's almost California weather.

Debby's physical therapy continues. Three days a week now she "works out with the team," as she says. The Orioles' trainer steered her to the club's therapist; she now bikes, stretches, and wonders whether she'll be assigned to Rochester for a month of rehab.

Big doings at the stadium. It's the battle for fifth place. The Orioles host the Milwaukee Brewers for four, a team only one and a half games up on the Birds. The Brew Crew's problems have been injuries (the team fight song is the theme from *M*A*S*H*) and a generous bullpen. Since the All-Star break, the bullpen ERA is a stout 7.61.

Matty has made himself right at home at the ballpark. While I did my pregame interviews, he sat directly behind the Orioles' dugout with his cousins, watching batting practice. Through the course of BP he called over Frank Robinson, Brady Anderson, and John Oates to introduce them to his guests. You'd think he was Sinatra at Jilly's.

Roy Smith started, and for the second outing in a row left after 1⅔. By the time I hit the air in the third, the Orioles were down 5–0. Familiar patterns continued, and the Orioles came back to tie the game in the eighth . . . only to lose in the ninth. Mark Williamson (who has pitched well enough lately to qualify as a Brewer reliever) gave up a single to Darryl Hamilton and a double to Robin Yount and that was all she wrote. Final: Fifth Place 6, Mired in Sixth Place 5.

Bright Note Department: Juan Bell continues to benefit from playing every day. Over the last eleven games he's batting .324, and his glove work has shown steady improvement. Billy Ripken, who's still nursing that rib-cage injury, is being given all the time he needs.

Tuesday, August 6, Baltimore

Chuck Thompson has been raving about this hamburger joint called Alonzo's. Today, with the family and Debby's cousins, we decided to give it a shot. The prices seemed reasonable—$5.95 for a burger and fries. When the orders arrived, our jaws dropped—which was helpful in eating—because each burger was a full POUND. This must be the "Hungry Heifer" we refer to on *Cheers*—enormous portions at reasonable prices. Alonzo's, however, uses beef, whereas the Heifer featured "beff," a beeflike substitute, the perfect complement to "loobster."

Be it duly noted that my almost-five-year-old daughter, Diana, is quite the little swimmer already. She and her dad had much fun at the pool.

The Orioles exploded for a 13–5 drubbing of the Brewers this evening. A six-run fourth inning was the spark. With the team leading 10–5 in the sixth, mild-mannered Johnny Oates was ejected by home-plate umpire Derryl Cousins for trying to stand up for Senior (Cal Senior), who had been popping off in the third-base coaching box on a few questionable calls on Junior. It was the first time Oates has been tossed as a manager. Odd that it should come on a night when his squad was leading by five runs.

Postgame quote: Brewer manager Tom Treblehorn on his team's recent pitching woes—"It has just been ineffective lately. But from the other side, it has been exciting."

The best moment of the night came in the eighth when a Milwaukee Brewer stepped up to the plate. Ten-year Oriole veteran Rick Dempsey, now with the "Brewskies," received a thunderous ovation. Baltimore fans are among the most loyal in the world!

My favorite Rick Dempsey story: One afternoon at Memorial Stadium he was at the plate and fouled a pitch off the plate. The catcher and umpire, as they usually do, instinctively turned away so as not to be hit by the ball. In this case, however, the ball bounced straight up, slowly, and Dempsey caught it. Quickly, he hid it in his armpit, and when the umpire and catcher turned back, the ball was nowhere to be found. The big crowd roared with laughter, and Dempsey, completely deadpan, just stood idly by as the catcher and umpire whirled their heads from side to side in search of the missing sphere. Baseball people will tell you the trouble with the game today is there are not enough pitchers. I say there are not enough Rick Dempseys.

Third baseman Leo Gomez has been mired in a terrible

slump. He has a hole in his swing—fastballs up and in give him fits. Originally, pitchers were feeding him breaking balls, knowing he's got good power. But all too quickly they learned that he's a breaking-ball hitter. They adjusted by busting him back with fastballs and have enjoyed success as a result. Now it's Leo's turn to adjust, and lately he's been cheating in, holding the bat back a little farther to get around better on the inside heat. So pitchers have reverted to breaking stuff low and away, and Gomez is lunging over the plate trying to make contact. The words of Kermit the Frog apply to the rookie Gomez: "It's not easy being green."

Wednesday, August 7, Baltimore

Last night I had a dream that my wife was having an affair with her physical therapist. Hmmmmmm? What could *that* mean, Dr. Freud?

Tonight's game was another one of those "fill-out-the-schedule" contests. Milwaukee won, 4–2, Ben McDonald struggled with his mechanics again, a couple of Birds got hits and two of 'em scored, which was two too few.

Thursday, August 8, Baltimore

I'm published! A recent magazine article I've written has made its way into print. You'll find it in the August/September issue of the Orioles game program/scorecard. (Okay, so it's not *The New Yorker*.) Several months ago I was asked to contribute an article on *Cheers* (why come to *me* on the subject of baseball?) and thus: KEN LEVINE'S OTHER JOB. My angle was: "The questions most frequently asked of me about *Cheers*." To capsulize some of my answers (so you never have to go through the trouble of finding it): No, there are others responsible for the success of the show as well. . . . The real *Cheers* bar is the Bull & Finch in Boston. . . . Shelley Long left the show to pursue a movie career. . . . No, that's not real beer Norm is drinking—it's warm, nonalcoholic, and best used for shampooing your dog. . . . The hardest aspect of writing a *Cheers* script is finding a good story. . . . Story structure can be taught, but not a sense of humor. Jon Miller could write a *Cheers* if he so desired. Same with Mike Flanagan. Members of the Secret Service? I'm not so sure. . . . *Cheers* is filmed at Paramount Pictures in Hollywood, and free tickets may be obtained from NBC in Burbank. . . . And finally, the show should stay on the air at least until Nolan Ryan retires, which I estimate at another ten or fifteen years.

Debby and Matty went outlet-store shopping while Diana and I took in *101 Dalmatians*. On the Levine Scale: a nine-plus. All those spots! How many animators went blind to provide us with an afternoon of frothy entertainment?

Without question these last few weeks have been the best of the season. Having my family here makes all the difference in the world. It's as if I actually have a life. They return to Los Angeles next Thursday, and already I'm dreading the separation and loneliness. As a kid, I thought of baseball as the window to heaven. It symbolized everything great—summer, no school, playing games, mythical heroes, exotic locales, a shared interest with my parents. These feelings still resonate within me, and it's times like this that I have to reach down and draw upon them, because for all the fantasy aspects of being in the game, I'm paying a mighty dear price. Time was I'd sing "Take Me Out to the Ballgame" with everyone else during the seventh-inning stretch, and really mean it when I belted out the line "I don't care if I never get back." Well, now I have something to get back to.

Kevin Hickey is back with us, pitching batting practice, still hoping to land a September spot on some major league roster. His chances? Roland Hemond says he's already had nineteen lives, why not twenty? The Hick-man, as usual, is philosophical. "I used to think that only two things were certain in this world, death and taxes," he said recently. "Now I know there are three things—death, taxes, and my unconditional release."

Another potential buyer of the club has stepped forward. Two of Baltimore's most celebrated TV pitchmen have expressed interest in joining to purchase the Orioles. Jack Luskin, who owns a chain of discount appliance stores and is the self-proclaimed "Cheapest Guy in Town," has gotten together with attorney Steven L. Miles, the only lawyer in Baltimore who advertises on radio and TV. The other interested party, remember, is Boogie Weinglass, who currently operates a group of combination teen clothing stores and diners. I find it interesting that this is the type of entrepreneur who can afford a $120 million purchase today, while Donald Trump now has to save coupons.

The Brewers made it three out of four, winning tonight 6–4. Highlights: no players' cars were stolen and Sam Horn crushed a 461-foot home run to straightaway center. The park record is 471 by Harmon Killebrew. I didn't ask him, but I assume he got good wood on the ball.

Friday, August 9, Baltimore

On and off rain all day long. I took the kids to see *Hot Shots* with Charlie Sheen and was pleasantly surprised. It was a spoof on those *Top Gun* teen macho/action/male fantasy pictures that do so well each summer, and although it wasn't as funny or silly as *Top Gun* itself, the picture did have its moments.

One problem with being a sportscaster is that if you forget to pay a bill, sometimes you are on the road when the "final notice" reminder arrives. Our phone service was cut off today. Getting it restored took the better part of my morning.

This was just one of those nights. Nothing went right . . . not for the Orioles, who lost to Chicago 7–4, not for rookie sensation Mike Mussina, who gave up five runs and eleven hits and was finished in his Memorial Stadium debut by the fourth inning, not for the fans, who were rained on for forty-six minutes at the start of the game, and certainly not for me. I was a disaster on the air tonight. If a fielder moved to his left, I said it was his right. I had averages wrong, scores wrong, you name it—I misnamed it. This game was that first waffle you make on Sunday morning that you toss out.

Saturday, August 10, Baltimore

Bo knows Matty! At least now he does. Bo Jackson, who is making an extraordinarily difficult recovery from a serious hip-pointer injury, is traveling with the White Sox and taking BP. Matty *had* to meet him, which was fine by me because, again, how often does a father get the chance to make one of his son's fondest wishes come true? Off the field, Bo is quiet, private, and possesses a very wry sense of humor. I introduced him to Matty, who extended his hand. Bo shook it and said, "That'll be twenty dollars for shaking my hand." Matty smiled and said he didn't have twenty dollars. "What do you have, then?" Bo asked. "Life Savers," Matty replied. "Okay, I'll have one of those," said Bo. Matty then emptied his pocket, and Bo noticed a pack of gum. "Red Stick! You've been holdin' out on me." Matty offered a stick, and Bo said no, he'd still like a Life Saver. Matty quickly and happily obliged. They chatted for a few minutes about his injury and when he'd be able to play again ("I don't know when, but I do know this: I will be back"), and shook hands for a second time (this time costing Matty fifty dollars). I thanked Bo for his time and shook his hand as well, charging *him* ten bucks for the privilege. We parted before payment schedules could be arranged.

Without Bo, the Sox won tonight, 6–4. Ten years ago today Cal Ripken, Jr., made his major league debut. He celebrated tonight by getting three hits, including his twenty-fourth home run. Chicago got homers by Carlton Fisk, Frank Thomas, and, of all people, Ozzie Guillen (whose last home run came one year ago today against Nolan Ryan).

The good news is that Glenn Davis received the green light to play again. The game plan is to send him to nearby Hagerstown tonight to be the designated hitter. He'll return to Baltimore tomorrow to be reevaluated, and if all is well, he'll spend a few more days in Hagerstown not only DHing, but playing a little first base as well. He could be back in an Oriole uniform as soon as this weekend in Milwaukee.

So how'd Glenn do tonight? Two groundouts and two fly outs, but one of the flies was a 400-footer. General manager Roland Hemond looked happier than I've ever seen him following an Orioles loss.

Sunday, August 11, Baltimore

Debby's mother is in town from Brooklyn, much to the delight of her two grandchildren. Somewhat reluctantly, she agreed to go to the game today. It was her first since Ebbetts Field. All in all, she enjoyed the experience. The weather was nice, the atmosphere pleasant.

And she did see a no-hitter.

Two years ago a nineteen-year-old left-hander from Venezuela made his major league debut. He was pitching for the Texas Rangers against the Toronto Blue Jays. That was *not* a day to remember. He faced five batters, retired none, gave up three runs, including two home runs. Until today, there had been no second appearance. After today, there will be many more. Wilson Alvarez became the second-youngest pitcher (behind Vida Blue) to hurl a no-hitter.

With composure and precision he mowed through the hapless Oriole lineup inning after inning. There were only two scares. Center-fielder Lance Johnson made a dazzling diving catch to rob Chris Hoiles in the eighth, and the official scorer kept the no-hitter afloat by ruling a throwing error on catcher Ron Karkovice on a bang-bang bunt play involving Cal.

By the eighth inning and with the score 7–0, Chicago, the crowd of over 40,000 had shifted its allegiance to the young left-hander. Alvarez received a tremendous ovation as he took the mound for the ninth. Chuck Thompson, veteran of many of these potential no-hitters, was as nervous as I've ever seen him. Or heard him.

Mike Devereaux led off. A fly ball to fairly deep center. Lance Johnson made it one out.

Juan Bell worked the count to 3–2, then struck out. The ball was dropped by Karkovice, who recorded the out at first.

Alvarez was one out away from baseball immortality. The crowd rose to its feet. Wouldn't you know it—Cal Ripken would be coming to the plate. For the first, and I'm sure the only, time in Memorial Stadium history, the fans were rooting *against* Cal Ripken. Shortstop Ozzie Guillen went out to the mound to remind Alvarez that Ripken was the O's' most dangerous hitter. Don't give him anything good. Alvarez heeded the advice. Cal was walked on four pitches.

Dwight Evans now stood in his way. Another veteran clutch hitter, another walk.

Randy Milligan was next. With the count 1–2, the Moose took a mighty rip and came up empty. Wilson Alvarez had his no-hitter . . . and reacted in the most unusual manner I've ever seen. Instead of spinning on the mound and leaping in the air with exultation, Alvarez calmly walked off the hill. Just another day at the office. My mother-in-law was more excited, and she still didn't know what exactly had happened.

The kids spent the night with "Bubbe" ("Grandma" in Brooklynese) while Debby and I dined at Hersch's Orchard Inn, where the food is excellent and my picture is now displayed in the foyer. Hersch took the photo of me and Jon last December during my interview stay. He said at the time he would put it up with the others (Jim Palmer, Brooks Robinson, Liberace, etc.) and I thought, gee, if I don't get this job, what will the caption be: "Jon Miller with failed applicant"?

Monday, August 12, Baltimore

We took Bubbe to lunch and bumped into John Oates and his wife, who were celebrating their twenty-fourth wedding anniversary. They were in search of a two-hour reprieve from baseball. We congratulated them and let them be. Matty, good-naturedly, did ask John one baseball question, however: "What did you think of the no-hitter?" John tactfully said he's liked others better.

It's getting harder and harder for *me* to ask John questions these days. Before every game, we do the five-minute "John Oates Report" (catchy title, no?), and with the team losing night after long night, how often can I delicately say: "The starters shouldn't give up five runs in the first two innings every night, should they?" And how many times can John repeat: "We've got some good young players who just need time. We're working on this with X and that with Y." I will say this—John is always accessible to do the show and will answer any question. You can't ask for much more than that . . . except for an occasional win (or, after yesterday, maybe a couple of hits).

Tonight's game featured the strangest umpiring decision I've ever seen. Every season has one or two sticky little "knotty problems," but nothing like this.

The Orioles were batting in the fourth inning against Chicago. One out. Randy Milligan was at third, Chito Martinez on second, and Chris Hoiles at the plate. Hoiles hit a big bouncer up along third. Milligan returned to the bag as third-baseman

Robin Ventura gloved the ball. Third-base umpire Jim McKean immediately signaled "Foul ball." Ventura, not taking any chances, after making contact with Milligan as he was returning to the base, threw on to first, but late and up the line. But, of course, none of this should matter, right? The ball had been ruled foul.

Not tonight.

The umpires had a conference, both managers sprang out of their respective dugouts, and Jon and I tried to speculate on just what was happening. We concluded that perhaps Milligan had interfered with Ventura's ability to field the ball. If so, Milligan would be out. Except that the ball had been clearly designated foul. After a long discussion, Randy Milligan *was* ruled out. Oates then snapped. The most mild-mannered manager in the game exploded and, natch, was given the heave-ho, but not before he ripped off his cap, kicked dirt over the third-base bag, and gave all four umpires a nose-to-nose earful. Happy anniversary.

Oates finally left. Milligan left. And then Hoiles was awarded first base. Huh?????

Here's what happened. Home plate umpire Vic Voltaggio overruled Jim McKean's foul call. McKean then claimed that Ventura tagged out Milligan before he returned to the bag. Hoiles was then awarded first on a fielder's choice. But closer examination reveals this to be a fiasco. First off, a fair or foul call is made by the home plate umpire until the ball passes first or third base. Usually, however, the home plate umpire will defer to the base umpire, who is two feet away from the play, whereas he is ninety feet from the action. In this case both umpires signaled, which led to complete chaos. Milligan had his back to home plate. In clear view he saw and heard Jim McKean signal foul. Milligan thus thought he was entitled to return to the base without fear of being tagged out. Hoiles is lucky he ran out the ground ball. Had he returned to the plate (thinking the ball was foul), he could've been doubled up at first. (Are you still with me?)

Did the ball pass the third-base bag? The replays showed that it did. Was Milligan tagged before he reached the base? The replays suggest no.

And things get even murkier. The umpires felt that because of the fair/foul confusion, the White Sox were hindered in their ability to get an out. They might not admit this, but someone had to go. Hoiles clearly had beaten the inaccurate throw to first, so that left Milligan.

All of this could've been so easily avoided if the umps just stuck with their original call—foul ball.

Jim McKean, normally a fine umpire, had a bad night all around. In the second inning "Palehose" Warren Newson hit a foul ball that drifted toward the third-base stands. Leo Gomez chased after it and at the last was blocked out by McKean, thus preventing him from making the catch. McKean was in the wrong place. Given second life, Warren Newson then homered.

In the end, however, the night belonged to the Orioles. A game-tying homer by Hoiles in the ninth and a game-winning home run by Gomez in the eleventh sent the crowd home happy. Gomez's shot, a majestic blast into deep center field, was ruled fair.

Tuesday, August 13, Baltimore

The Orioles and the Texas Rangers played a double dip tonight. The first game started at 5:05, the second game ended at 12:52. (Matty diligently scored every inning of both games. He has better concentration than I do.) There were no rain delays. Just extra innings, and a lot of runs, and a whole lot of pitchers. The O's tied a major league record for most pitchers in a doubleheader with thirteen. (One—Mark Williamson—hurt a muscle in his side and had to depart. He may wind up on the DL.)

The upside is the Orioles won both games. They took the finale 8–7 and the opener in twelve innings, 4–3. That first game had a wacky finish. Leo Gomez led off with a routine ground ball to shortstop Mario Diaz, who bobbled it for an error. Bob Melvin was asked to bunt and did so. Catcher Geno Petralli took a chance and tried to get the force at second. Too late. Now with O's at first and second, Juan Bell laid down a bunt. Pitcher Kenny Rogers pounced on the ball and elected to go to third for the possible force. But his throw was wild, and Gomez came around to score the winning run. Jon and I alternate extra innings and, luck of the draw, this was mine. I'm trying to think of how many Oriole game-ending victory calls I've had this season. Hmmmm. Counting tonight? . . . One.

Wednesday, August 14, Baltimore

If you ever come to Baltimore, I recommend the lunch cruise in the Inner Harbor. You see the city, Federal Hill, Fort McHenry (of National Anthem fame), and Matty's favorite—the Lehigh Cement Plant. (Where does my son get his warped sense of humor???) It was a great family outing . . . much better than yesterday, when we took boxes to UPS to be shipped back home.

Mark Williamson was indeed placed on the disabled list today, with a strained muscle. To take his place, we welcome back Mr. José Bautista. After being dumped by the O's following a horrendous April, Bautista has played for Miami (A level); was loaned out to Texas's Triple-A club, Oklahoma City (which tells you how much the Orioles covet this "prospect" that they're willing to loan him out to another organization); and recently was assigned to Rochester. From what we understand, he's improved, he's rested, and he's breathing.

Rookie Mike Mussina pitched a gem and recorded his first major league victory, 10–2, over the Rangers. After giving up a single and homer in the first inning, Mussina settled down and allowed only one other hit through seven innings while striking out ten. The Orioles may just have lightning in a bottle with Mike Mussina.

Another rookie who continues to impress is Chito Martinez. Tonight he belted two home runs. His .310 average is the highest of any rookie with over 100 at-bats. This seven-year minor leaguer is an overnight sensation. They talk about Ken Griffey, Jr., who has a candy bar named in his honor. I wouldn't be surprised to see Chito have a potato chip named after him.

8

Thursday, August 15, Baltimore/Milwaukee

Hell day. My family went back to Los Angeles. The sight of my children's sad eyes as they waved good-bye will haunt me for a good long while. Yes, they'll be back for a week in September, but they'll be three weeks older. I will not take my daughter to her first day of kindergarten next week; I will not be at her birthday party at the end of the month. Instead I will be in Texas and Minnesota, calling two very meaningful ball games, I'm sure.

Before they left, we had one final lunch together. I had a $200 crab cake. I know what you're thinking, but it did come with German potatoes. (The restaurant we stopped at had a gorgeous stained-glass window for sale. I wrote out a check from my "guilt account," and along with the meal, the window was ours. The owner tried to sell us the tables, chairs, and his back sink, but we were content with just the one item.)

The Orioles concluded their longest home stand of the year by sending José Mesa out to face Texas. Mesa had been in Rochester for the past month searching for his elusive breaking ball. Reports are he's found it. His mound opponent was Dennis "Oil Can" Boyd, the longtime, flamboyant Red Sox pitcher recently traded to Texas from Montreal. Boyd apparently was very happy in the National League, finding it a welcome haven from all the turbulence and "innuendoes" (his word) that swirled around him in Boston. Imagine his surprise and dismay when the Expos dealt him to Texas on July 21 and his first two starts were against the Red Sox, the second one being in Fenway Park. His comment at having to pitch again in Boston: "God must hate me." I hardly believe that's true, but I do submit He has a sly sense of humor. Since coming to the Rangers, Boyd is 0–3 with a 6.86 ERA. The Rangers may soon hate him.

The result tonight: Mesa's curve was back better than ever. He pitched the first complete-game victory for the Orioles since McDonald had one way back in May—9–2 was the final. Chito and Leo each hit big home runs en route to kicking the "Can." The Orioles have now won five straight—a season high.

Roster news: Billy Ripken was activated, José Bautista designated for assignment. Bautista was up for no more than a bean of coffee.

Rotisserie news: In order to attract fans to the Pit to watch our last-place club, we instituted "two-for-one" night last week, whereby fans could get two seats for the price of one. It resulted in yet another riot. Next time we do the promotion, we'll have to remember to give the fans their two seats *next* to one another, not one in right field and the other in left.

The late-night flight to Milwaukee was smooth, pleasant, and best of all—nonstop. Refueling in Madison was not necessary. I turned out the light in my room at the Pfister at three-thirty.

Final note: You'd think a five-game winning streak would garner John Oates some of the respect he deserves. Tonight he walked into the hotel, picked up his room key, entered the elevator, pushed 6—which was his floor—and when the elevator arrived at 6 said good-night to everyone and stepped out . . . into the parking garage. Even the announcers have better accommodations than that. (His room was actually in the other tower.)

Friday, August 16, Milwaukee

Longtime Brewer broadcaster and TV personality Bob Uecker is recovering from major abdominal surgery he underwent on July 19. Two potentially life-threatening aneurysms were removed. He is expected to recover fully, and today made his first appearance at County Stadium since the operation. He looked understandably tired and drawn—he's lost twenty pounds—but his eyes sparkled as bright as ever and his sense of humor was still razor sharp. He said that he learned of his serious health problem on July 16 but decided to work the game that night because he had an aneurysm clause in his contract. He got a bonus for doing it.

On the day of the surgery, the Brewers had dedicated that game to him. His reaction: "They won one for me, then lost seven in a row. I figured they must really hate me."

His most difficult moment in the hospital: "When that lady put a suppository in me. She did it with a peashooter from eight feet away."

Regarding the family support he received: "I'd like to thank my wife too. She did a great job by moving to another home."

Seriously, Uecker has been very moved by the tremendous public support and affection he's received, and hopes to be back in the radio booth doing a few home games in perhaps a couple of weeks.

Our rotisserie team has scheduled a "Bob Uecker Night" at the Pit. In honor of Bob and the commercial he's so famous for, all fans will be given bad seats.

With the four M's now in the starting rotation—McDonald, Milacki, Mussina, Mesa—that leaves only one vacant spot. For now Dave Johnson will fill it, but that is subject to change depending upon his performance and the Orioles' desire to preview some of their stars of the future. If tonight's outing was any indication, D.J.'s days in the rotation are numbered. He lasted only 2⅓, giving up five hits and four runs. Reliever Roy Smith was no better, yielding four runs on seven hits in 2⅔ innings. It was quite ugly, trust me. The Orioles lost to the Brewers, 8–5, in a game that will be quickly forgotten by all but reliever Todd Frohwirth.

Frohwirth was born and raised, and still lives in Milwaukee. Tonight, for the first time, he played a major league game in his own hometown. Forty friends and family members cheered wildly as he was introduced into the game in the fifth inning. The rest of the 18,000 cheered a moment later when his first pitch was launched into right field by Paul Molitor for a two-run double. (So much for the storybooks.) The next batter, Willie Randolph, walked, but then Frohwirth settled down and retired the next ten batters. All in all, a great performance if you were out getting a bratwurst and a beer during Fro's first two batters.

After the game I joined Jon, Greg Massoni (director for Channel 2's Orioles' telecasts), and Jim Palmer for a little Mexican food (when you think Milwaukee, you automatically think Mexican food). Palmer has always had a love/hate relationship with former Orioles' manager Earl Weaver, and invariably when you're with Jim, the topic turns to Earl. He's got some great stories. The one he told tonight is priceless. One night Weaver had a "little too much to drink" and plowed his car into a parking meter (that was not the funny part, I assure you). A cop happened by, and thus the following conversation:

COP: Do you know who you are?
WEAVER: No.
COP: Do you know where you are?
WEAVER: No.
COP: Do you have any physical impairments?
WEAVER: Yeah. Jim Palmer!

Saturday, August 17, Milwaukee

The first thing I did today was change my room. I had been placed on the twentieth floor, presumably in a choice location. But upon entering my room last night at twelve-thirty, I learned that the hotel had a discotheque on the roof—only three stories up. Try sleeping or even brushing your teeth in the inside of a bass drum. For an hour this pounding continued. How can a hotel put a nightclub directly above its best rooms? I am now on the sixteenth floor. (At least the phone is by the bed.)

The bellman moved me, handed me the key (actually a credit card with a coded strip that you insert into the door), snatched up his tip, and promptly left. I then went downstairs to have lunch with Bob Miller. When I returned a couple hours later, it occurred to me that I did not know exactly which room I was in. The card key was of no help. By design, it was blank. I had to try a few rooms first before finding mine. It's a good thing I did this at two P.M. and not A.M.

The Pfister is hosting some sort of "Irish Fest" this weekend. There're a lot of people walking around with funny green hats. So far, things have been relatively quiet. Last year I understand there was a fistfight in the lobby. What are the *second*-class hotels like in this town???

With two outs in the eighth inning tonight, the Oriole bats

came alive. In the next 1⅓ innings they scored six times (highlighted by another three-run homer by Chito). Final score: Milwaukee 7, Baltimore 6.

Jim Palmer and Brooks Robinson invited me to join them for an inning on Channel 2. That was a kick. Unfortunately, I had dressed for radio. People in Baltimore must've been wondering, Who was that bindle stiff in a golf shirt? As much as I adore radio, I'd love the opportunity to stretch my wings and do some more television. As media go, I've heard good things.

Sunday, August 18, Milwaukee/Arlington, Texas

Best lunch in Milwaukee: Szaz's near the Miller Brewery. Try the apple dumplin's. Discuss the new 1956 T-bird.

The Orioles lost to the Brewers, 2–1. Let's move on.

Did you know that "Old Milwaukee" beer is not brewed in Milwaukee? In reality it should be named "Old Detroit."

Glenn Davis has been activated and will join the club tomorrow in Texas. Who he will replace on the roster is not yet known. In a related move, the Orioles have purchased the Hagerstown contract of twenty-five-year-old pitching phenom Arthur Rhodes, who will make his major league debut Wednesday. Welcome back to the bullpen, Dave Johnson.

After the game the Orioles flew down to Dallas. One advantage of your own charter is that a much greater degree of informality exists. How often on commercial carriers are passengers invited to sit in the cockpit during flights (unless the plane is taking an unscheduled detour to Havana)? The offer was made on *Orioles One,* and I was the one who accepted. Great fun. Spectacular view. The ultimate Disneyland ride. I was a little disappointed that they wouldn't let me actually land the plane, but still, it was a once-in-a-lifetime experience (meaning they'll probably never ask me back).

Arrived at the Sheraton Centre Park at nine-fifteen and along with PR poet Bob Miller made a beeline for the Atchafalaya River Café, my favorite restaurant on the circuit. We étouféed and tchoupitoulased ourselves into oblivion. Tomorrow we're back at noon.

Returned to the hotel to learn of Gorbachev's ouster. The next few days figure to be very unsettling.

Monday, August 19, Arlington, Texas

The news from the Soviet Union is already hopeful. While reports are still sketchy, it appears the coup is not on very solid ground. It's rather difficult to concentrate on baseball and the pennant races when the world is being torn apart, but today's events are encouraging and we can only hope for more of the same tomorrow.

Matty began the fourth grade today, and Diana started kindergarten. My baby is now a big girl. I would've given anything to be there.

Mike Mussina was looking for his second major league victory tonight. His opponent was in quest of his 311th. Nolan Ryan would be the winner, 4–1.

Make no mistake—Nolan Ryan *is* the franchise in Texas. And deservedly so. Teams are built around stars, and even though the Rangers have some amazing young talent in Rafael Palmeiro (leading the league in hitting), Julio Franco (number three in average), Ruben Sierra (future MVP), and Juan Gonzalez (future Ruben Sierra), it is Nolan Ryan who packs 'em in at Arlington Stadium. The future Hall of Famer is good for about 15,000 additional butts in the seats per start. (Of course, seven no-hitters and records in practically every pitching category imaginable will do that for a player.) It also doesn't hurt that he's a local hero. Ryan doesn't just represent this team, he represents the state, and does so with the ultimate style and grace. "Mama, don't let your sons grow up to be cowboys. Let them grow up to be Nolan Ryans."

Glenn Davis returned to the lineup for the first time since April 24. Three months ago he believed his career was over, and medical experts from coast to coast agreed. His is a story of enormous perseverance, courage, and triumph. I asked him before the game to pause for a second when he went up to the plate for the first time and reflect upon how he felt at that instant. We both wondered what emotional response he would experience—joy? anxiety? relief? He said afterward that the immediate impression was one of comfort. Standing in the batter's box, taking a couple of practice hacks, zeroing in on just what that pitch would be and what he would do with it—it's as if "this was where he belonged." His soul was at rest.

Glenn Davis went one for three with a single and a walk.

To make room, the Orioles shipped out journeyman change-up specialist Roy Smith. For every Glenn Davis and Nolan Ryan there are a thousand Roy Smiths, maybe ten thousand. For a while he was Baltimore's winningest pitcher. On one sunny June day at fabled Fenway Park, he beat Roger Clemens. In Minnesota he was hailed with banners. But for now it's back to Rochester, where a road trip to Scranton–Wilkes-Barre means an eight-hour all-night bus ride. I hope Roy Smith makes it back up. If not with us in September, then next year with Houston, or Seattle, or Milwaukee, or Pittsburgh, or Montreal, or California, or Texas, or Philadelphia, or San Diego, or Tokyo.

Hooray! I'm not the only idiot to forget his room number! After the game tonight one of the players (a veteran you probably know and respect) had to go down to the front desk to find out which room he's in.

By the way, finding your room is only half the battle. In the middle of the night in a strange hotel, finding your bathroom is even tougher.

Tuesday, August 20, Arlington, Texas

The coup is crumbling and events are occurring almost hourly. My days are spent monitoring the news, which so far has been good. Among the newspapers I read today came this tidbit: A CBS correspondent in Moscow ordered a Domino's pizza and it still arrived in less than thirty minutes. I guess that means we're out of the water over there.

The weather is extremely hot here, with a dry, arid wind blowing steadily across the prairie. Game-time temperature was 99 degrees at 7:35. By eight it had climbed to 101.

One can only imagine what this season would have been like with a healthy Glenn Davis. Tonight we got a glimpse. Davis belted a double, a homer that is still rising as you read this, and drove in five. The Orioles won, 8–6. Dave Johnson had a fine outing in relief, which, after his most recent disaster in Milwaukee, was not just welcome, but needed. For now the bell tolls for Roy Smith, but tomorrow the Orioles will activate left-hander Arthur Rhodes, so there will be another bell. D.J. may just have saved his job tonight. At least until his next outing.

Wednesday, August 21, Arlington, Texas/Baltimore

What an incredible day!! The Communist coup has officially failed, and Debby got the okay to wear shoes. Gorbachev and Yeltsin are in, guys with long names and ill-fitting suits are out. Statues are being toppled, prerevolutionary flags are flying in Russia for the first time in over seventy years, and the Communist party is on the verge of complete and utter collapse. The significance of the events of the past sixty hours may well resonate for one hundred years. Did I mention that Debby can now wear shoes?

The mood at the ballpark was noticeably brighter today. It was permissible again to care who won. In fact, for the Orioles it was a night of excitement and anticipation. Another can't-miss prospect, Arthur Lee Rhodes from nearby Waco, Texas, made his major league debut. (Sidelight: To make room on the roster, Brady Anderson will spend the next ten days in Upstate Purgatory.) Rhodes, only twenty-one, has two qualities that make organizations drool. He's a left-hander, and he has a fastball in the nineties. Coaches will tell you, "You can't teach ninety-five miles per hour." Very few have that gift, and Rhodes is one. With the rotation of McDonald, Mesa, Mussina, Milacki, and now Rhodes in place, we may be seeing a preview of the Orioles' starting five of the nineties. (Milacki is the graybeard of the group at twenty-seven.)

Rhodes's debut was less than impressive. In four-plus innings he allowed three runs, four hits, and walked four. Two of the runs scored on wild pitches. Players say that just stepping onto the field for the first time in a major league game can be overwhelming; imagine being the starting pitcher. All in all, Oates was satisfied with Rhodes's maiden voyage (or at least professes to be) and expects to keep him in the rotation for the remainder of the year. He'll get about eight more starts.

Thanks to some timely hitting by Joe Orsulak, the Orioles won anyway, 4–3. A word on Orsulak: Without much notice or fanfare, Orsulak has now racked up a 19-game hitting streak. The Orioles' all-time record is 22, shared by Doug DeCinces and Eddie Murray. No question about it, Orsulak needs a press agent. He has been one of the Orioles' most consistent performers for years and yet is the team's best-kept secret. Jeff McKnight's baseball card probably goes for as much money as Orsulak's. The leading hitter on the club in '88 and '89 was not Cal Ripken or Randy Milligan or Mickey Tettleton. It was "Slack," as his teammates call him. Brett Butler of the Dodgers had a 23-game streak earlier this year that made news on a daily basis. Hopefully, with Orsulak's streak now approaching twenty, he too will grab some limelight.

Orioles One touched down in Baltimore at five-fifteen. You haven't lived until you've seen the sun rise over the Lehigh Cement Factory.

Thursday, August 22, Baltimore

An off-day. Zzzzzzzzzzzzzzzzzzzzzzzzzzzz.

While we were on the road, some baseball aficionado/vandal made off with the "405" portion of Memorial Stadium's padded outfield wall. Another, less aesthetic thief broke into Cal Senior's car, stealing his radio. Thank goodness we have twenty-four-hour security. Otherwise the DiamondVision board might be halfway to Tijuana by now.

Friday, August 23, Baltimore

John Oates: "Guys, don't get your wives pregnant. This is the year of the Twins."

This possible team of destiny roars into town with the best record in baseball, 74–49. Minnesota is currently leading Chicago by six games in the West. Preceding the All-Star break, they went on a 22–2 spurt highlighted by a fifteen-game winning streak (snapped, incidentally, by the powerful O's). They have the best hitting team in the A.L., and their pitching is near the top as well. They stand a good chance of being the first team in the league to go from worst to first in one year. Gosh, it's good to see them again!

The only way the Orioles can beat the Twins, it seems, is with two outs in the ninth. Their only other victory was via that route, and tonight an eleventh-hour (literally) single by David Segui gave the Birds a dramatic 5–4 win. Dwight Evans's three-run homer in the fourth helped too.

Ben McDonald managed to go eight innings, although he was in and out of trouble all night. There are two Ben McDonalds these days: One has great command and is unhittable, and the other is susceptible to lapses in concentration and mechanics. From start to start you never know whether you're going to get Jekyll or Hyde. The papers and talk shows are already questioning whether McDonald *is* the "Second Coming," as he has been heralded for three years, but there is one factor that should not be overlooked. He is only twenty-three. That's young even for baseball. Way back in the olden days of baseball, a young prospect would spend three or four years in the minor leagues honing his craft and learning to throw a fastball that wouldn't slip and hit the organist in the press box once per game. Today there is little time for nurturing. The Orioles, like *all* organizations, need to win NOW. There's too much money and too many luxury boxes depending on it. Ben McDonald could still well be the dominant pitcher of the nineties who will lead the Orioles to fame, glory, and an occasional appearance on the CBS primary *Game of the Week,* but like so many great ones who've gone before him, Ben will need a little time and patience. Hopefully, the fans will be willing to give him that. (Remember Sandy Koufax!)

Allen Anderson, a left-hander, started for the Twins, so Joe Orsulak got the night off. His hitting streak is in cruising position at nineteen.

Saturday, August 24, Baltimore

The apartment seems very quiet, too quiet, these days. There's usually a mild depression that accompanies a lonely home stand in Baltimore, but this one seems heightened following the last two with Debby and the kids here. As the season winds down, I'm beginning to think more and more about next year. There are a lot of factors to consider. This year's arrangement vis-à-vis the family has not worked out well at all. Debby's ankle mishap exacerbated things certainly, but still, with the L.A. school system now on an all-year schedule with classes beginning in August, the only way to improve matters significantly is to enroll the kids in school in Baltimore next spring. That means a big adjustment for them and a further adjustment in the fall when we move back to Los Angeles. Living in

Baltimore, one of the options originally under consideration, really makes no sense. My primary profession is still screen-writing, and my partner and the industry are in California. If there was some way to broadcast baseball on the West Coast, *that* would be ideal, but who knows?

Another factor in the equation is Chuck Thompson. One of my true delights this year has been working half the season with Chuck. His counsel, support, and companionship have been invaluable. Chuck just turned seventy. Does he want to do this again next year? I dunno. And if he does, what will his participation be? Should he not come back, who will be his replacement? Arranged marriages are tough per se, and worse when you don't know whose name will be on the license.

In any event, it's not a decision I have to make tonight, and besides, the Twins are in town.

What a shock! Even Mike Flanagan is human. For one of the very few times this year, "Ol' Reliable" had a bad outing. Even when Flanagan's not at the top of his game, he always battles and somehow manages to get a key out or two. (Flanagan and Toronto's Duane Ward are the league leaders in relief innings pitched.) Well, tonight was not Flanny's night. The Twins touched him for three runs, two hits, and a walk in only a third of an inning. And that inning was the ninth. Flanagan let a 2–1 lead get away, and the potential "team of destiny" won 5–2. It's getting harder and harder to find things to believe in.

Joe Orsulak grounded to second in the first inning, hit back to the box in the third, flied to right in the fifth . . . and ripped a single to right in the seventh. He's now hit in twenty straight. Will somebody please call the papers?

For the first time this year I caught a foul ball. Well . . . not exactly "caught," but I did fetch it from the rolled-up plastic curtain above our heads that serves as the booth's rain shield. After ricocheting around our booth like a pinball machine, the ball finally settled in that spot. When a spectator makes a nice catch at Memorial Stadium, P.A. announcer Rex Barney traditionally says, "Give that fan a contract!" I did not receive one, but then again, I work for the club; it would hardly be fair.

This was a CBS Radio *Game of the Week.* In the "Hometown Inning" I was again on the radio coast-to-coast. Twelve pitches, three outs. It was a two-minute portion of my life I will always treasure.

Cal Junior is thirty-one today. Just before the ninth inning a young lady bolted out of the stands, ran out to Cal at shortstop, gave him a big smooch, did a cartwheel, and bounded back to the seats, where ushers were waiting to escort her out of the park. This practice began years ago with Morganna, a young woman with breasts from here to Tuesday. Earlier this year a new girl burst upon the scene. "Topsy Curvy," as she calls herself (for good reason), recently invaded Yankee Stadium, kissing the Yankees' Scott Kamieniecki and the Twins' Kevin Tapani. Tonight's bimbo at Memorial Stadium does not have the figure of the other two (she's rather zoftig, in fact), and I suppose as a result was not as well received as the others. It's a sad truth, but looks are important, even in idiot behavior.

Farm report: Luis Mercedes is having a helluva year in Rochester. We saw him in spring training and he looked good there. Currently, he's batting .338 with a twenty-one-game hitting streak. Mercedes was a cinch to get a September call-up.

Until tonight.

The Red Wings were in my old alma mater, Syracuse, to play the Chiefs. As I understand the story, Mercedes became engaged in a heated argument with Chief third baseman Tom Quinlan during the course of the game. Mercedes apparently snapped and, at point-blank range, fired his helmet in Quinlan's face, chipping several teeth and bloodying his face. Needless to say, the mother of all bench-clearing brawls ensued. State troopers had to be dispatched to restore order.

Mercedes has had discipline problems in the past (already one suspension this year), but certainly nothing like this. We're talking a Sunday drive into Albert Belle/Rob Dibble country here. I suspect the league will suspend him for probably the remainder of the season (two whole weeks), but the bigger question remains: Will the Orioles still bring him up in September? I know John Oates wants to take a look at him, but in light of tonight's digression, will the Birds have second thoughts? We'll know in ten days.

Sunday, August 25, Baltimore

Rookie Mike Mussina pitched into the ninth inning against the best team in baseball and led the O's to a 7–3 victory over the Twins. With improved pitching and Glenn Davis back in the lineup, the Orioles could just make their move. Fifth place? One can dream.

Orsulak went two for four. He's now hit in twenty-one straight, one shy of the Orioles' all-time mark.

Michael Hill, the TV critic for the *Evening Sun*, invited me over to his house after the game to watch the Emmys with him and his family. It was truly a great night. *Cheers* won for Best Comedy Series, and among the other winners was no one that I hate.

Monday, August 26, Baltimore

My *People* magazine article is on the newsstands now. It's the Fall Preview issue, and just so you know, this fall will be an "entertainment harvest." My one-page story appears prominently on page 85.

I suppose it's good.

The top half of the page is taken up by the picture. It never fails that if a photographer takes a thousand flattering shots of you and one where you're goofy, the goofy pose is the one they'll use. Jon and I are in the booth. He's peering at me through binoculars from two feet away while holding a microphone, and I'm pointing at him as if to say, "Wow, you are one wacky, zany guy!" (When *Time* magazine does a profile on Justice Thurgood Marshall, I wonder if they ask him to take a couple of kooky shots??)

The text of the article is pretty straightforward. However, I might not have chosen the following words to describe my early practice sessions:

> A few years ago he began skipping out on wife Debby, son Matthew, now 8, and daughter Diana, 5, to sit in the upper deck of Dodger Stadium and practice his own play-by-play into a tape recorder.

SKIPPING OUT? My, isn't that flattering?

All in all, I'm glad the piece ran. I never in a million years thought I'd ever be a subject for *People* magazine, and I guess I'll know in a few days now whether or not, as the reporter predicted, she'll have made me famous. Even if not, it's fun—even for a week—to be a pop icon.

Back to baseball.

On July 15 the Toronto Blue Jays had a whopping eight-game lead over the second-place Detroit Tigers in the A.L. East. Today they're in a flatfooted tie. The Jays have had pitching woes and have swooned since the All-Star break, while Sparky Anderson's Tigers are shattering the tried-and-true baseball adage that you win with pitching and defense. They're winning strictly on walks and home runs by the truckloads.

Tonight the Blue Jays began a three-game series at Memorial Stadium. José Mesa was scheduled to start for the O's but developed a sore elbow over the weekend. He's now in DL land while another prospect, Anthony Telford, is on his way to Baltimore from Rochester. (I asked Oates why Telford was selected and not, say, off the top of my head, Jeff Ballard. The answer: Telford is a right-hander. They need a right-hander to replace Mesa. Can't argue with that.)

So instead of Mesa tonight, Dave Johnson was handed the ball. Johnson has been the yo-yo of the starting rotation all year. As a reliever he seems to do well, but as a starter—thud. This evening was no exception. By the sixth inning he was gone, having given up five runs on nine hits. The Jays kept the pressure on the Tigers by beating the O's 5–2.

Detroit is in California playing the Angels under their new manager, Buck Rodgers (dethroned earlier this year in Montreal). Doug Rader was fired today. Given that the Angels went from first to last in a month, this announcement was not totally unexpected. Many believe Buck Rodgers is one of the best managers in the game, and personally, if the Angels had to make a change, I think they made a good one (although it would've been nice to have been consulted on this matter *first*).

Despite the fact that the Orioles are a woeful 52–73, they have now drawn over two million people this year. That's an incredible number.

Luis Mercedes update: The International League made it official—Mercedes is fined $300 and suspended for the remainder of the I.L. season. The Orioles will respect the suspension and not bring him up before September 1. But afterward?? The jury is still out.

Tuesday, August 27, Baltimore

The syndicated *Cheers* package has moved here in Baltimore from WMAR to WBFF (Fox 45, if you're scoring). To celebrate its kickoff, WBFF has asked me to host a week of the "Best of Levine & Isaacs." Ten of our *Cheers* episodes will run next week (two each night at seven and seven-thirty), and I have been asked to tape introductions. Today was the day.

I wanted the intros to have that Alistair Cooke *Masterpiece Theatre* feel, so we recorded them in a large study with an imposing fireplace and the obligatory high-backed overstuffed leather chair. Verrrry pretentious. For the only time in my life I regret not owning a smoking jacket.

The intros were all done very tongue-in-cheek. So that my partner David could be included, I had an eight-by-ten picture of him sitting at my side—except the picture wasn't of David per se. Every intro it changed. During the course of the week Cal Senior, Arnold Schwarzenegger, Robert Conrad, Frank Robinson, Julio Iglesias, Michael Douglas, Jim Palmer, accordionist Myron Florin, John Davidson, and recently-arrested-for-indecent-exposure Pee-Wee Herman, were all identified as David Isaacs.

Arthur Rhodes made his second major league start tonight. Have you ever had that dream where it was the day of the final exam and you realize that you've never been to class even once and you know nothing at all about the course and your entire college career depends upon this grade? Or the dream where you're completely naked, forced to run through the streets of town? Well, for Rhodes tonight it was a living variation of both nightmares. Standing alone on the mound in a major league ballpark before 25,000 people and a national audience on ESPN, he could not—no matter how hard he tried or what he did—get the ball over the plate. In the second inning Rhodes walked the bases loaded with nobody out. You wanna talk about a slow, agonizing death! All three runners would score (of course), only one driven in by a hit. After four innings he was put out of his misery. His line: four hits, six runs, four walks, one strikeout, one home run (a two-run shot by Devon White).

At this point Rhodes is a very unpolished product, but again it must be pointed out—he's only twenty-one years old. I just hope this big-league preview doesn't shatter his confidence and perhaps impede his future development and progress.

Note: Levine's Law—the leadoff walk will always come around to score unless it doesn't. I challenge anyone to prove me wrong.

Toronto's starter was also a rookie, but by contrast is twenty-five and spent several years in the bushes honing his craft. Juan Guzman, after years of hard work, now has great command of his blazing fastball and sharp-dropping, split-finger fastball. The Orioles saw the result tonight. Guzman twirled a complete-game five-hitter as the Jays won, 6–1.

Guzman is another tribute to the Toronto farm system, which consistently cultivates superior talent year after year. Jimmy Key, Dave Stieb, Todd Stottlemyre, Mike Timlin, David Wells, Pat Borders, Greg Myers, Kelly Gruber, Manuel Lee, John Olerud, and Ed Sprague are all homegrown products; not to mention former Toronto farmhands who are faring well elsewhere, like Lloyd Moseby, George Bell, Fred McGriff, John Cerutti, Glenallen Hill, Mark Whiten, Mark Eichhorn, Tony Fernandez, and a guy named Cecil Fielder. There's little wonder why the Toronto Blue Jays, despite being an expansion club born as late as 1977, have been contenders for ten consecutive years.

Anthony Telford pitched in relief for the O's and hurled five strong shutout innings. Now a breaking-ball pitcher, Telford in his early days had a fastball compared to Dwight Gooden's, but shoulder surgery in '88 changed that. The human arm was not designed to throw a baseball 100 miles per hour, as Telford and so many others have sadly learned. Last year Telford got into eight games with the Orioles after a sensational season in Double-A ball. This year he's fared well in Rochester and is getting another look. No longer a super-hot prospect, but still someone the Orioles like, Telford has a good chance of sticking around if his breaking ball can find the plate.

The Joe Orsulak watch: In the eighth he came up to the plate still needing a hit to keep his streak alive. After working the count to 2–2 and fouling off a couple of pitches, he finally swung and missed a Guzman splitter to snap the string at twenty-three. That's still quite an accomplishment, one that most players you *have* heard of have never achieved.

From the "Oops! Department" comes this tonight from

yours truly: Recapping a play, I said, "In the third inning Devereaux was out trying to stretch a double into a single." I'm usually good for two or three of those a year. In the past I've been known to utter: "Final score tonight—Syracuse shuts out Maine two-one," "For Smith, that's his fifteenth stolen theft of the year," and, "Thornton stands at second with his hands on his fists." Considering I'm on the air for three hours a night, I'm surprised I don't have a thousand of these.

Wednesday, August 28, Baltimore

I was right about critic Phil Jackman. He hates me. Every week now there's another little shot in his "Radio/TV Repairman" column. Here's an example: He wrote recently that he was sick and tired of hearing about "my boyhood dream" to announce baseball and that I was a comedy writer. That would be valid if those were topics I talked about on the air, but they're not. I don't tell *People* magazine and *USA Today* what to write. If they find the story of suitable interest to print, that's their business. I'm sick and tired of *telling* the story. His jab at me had nothing to do with my performance or the broadcast. But then again, it *was* Phil Jackman.

The temperature topped 90 today for the fifty-sixth time this year, almost twice the annual average. Nights at the ballpark are steamy and sticky. It's as if we're all stuck in a Tennessee Williams play. Ben McDonald, who hails from bayou country and is no stranger to this weather, started tonight and lost nine and a half pounds. He also lost the game. But the defeat was not of his own causing or even the heat's. After giving up two quick runs in the first, McDonald settled down and pitched seven scoreless innings. His opponent, however, pitched a masterpiece. Tom Candiotti—recently traded from Cleveland—gave up a single to Orsulak and a walk to Davis in the first inning and then *nada*. The knuckleballer retired the next twenty-two Orioles. Leading 3–0 going to the ninth, acting manager Gene Tenace—Cito Gaston was hospitalized this week with severe back problems—elected to bring in his ace, Tom Henke, who closed it out with a perfect ninth. The Jays left immediately after the game, so I didn't get a chance to talk to Tenace, but I wonder why he would lift Candiotti, who was en route to a one-hitter? How often does a pitcher (save for

Nolan Ryan) get that opportunity? Candiotti pitched the best game I've seen all season . . . and I've seen two no-hitters.

John Oates believes the knuckleball should be outlawed. As he says: "The batter can't hit it, the catcher can't catch it, and the umpire can't call it."

In any event, Toronto came into town tied with Detroit for first, and left up by two.

You're welcome.

Thursday, August 29, Baltimore/Minneapolis

An off-day of sorts. No game, but a flight to Minnesota. I had lunch with TV critic Michael Hill at Sabatino's (the "bookmaker salad," of course) and swam all afternoon to beat the heat. At seven the team assembled at the ballpark for our evening's trek, and by ten-fifteen Minneapolis time we were all in our Marriott hotel rooms watching *Baseball Tonight* on ESPN. Major league travel—it's how God would get around if He had business out of town.

Friday, August 30, Minneapolis

Diana Bess Levine turned five years old today. Her daddy is in Minnesota. On Monday she'll have her party with cake and ice cream and games and a piñata and all her friends. Her daddy will be in Toronto.

I spoke to her first thing this morning and she was very excited. She got a new bed and many wonderful toys.

"When are you coming home so that you can see them, Daddy?" she asked.

"Soon, honey. Six more weeks," I replied.

"Six weeks? That's not too long," she said, "I'll still be five."

I had lunch with reliever Todd Frohwirth. After years of bouncing around in the minors, he appears to have found a home with the Orioles. But experience has taught him not to become too comfortable. Although things look good for a return in '92, he knows that he could be right back in limbo if in September he—to use his words—"gives up the groceries" (i.e., pitches poorly). Frohwirth can't really revel in the joys of being in the big leagues, because in the back of his mind he knows that on any given day it could all be taken away. While with the Phillies, he was demoted four times. He says he doesn't think about it when he's at the park, but during the day when he's alone, just strolling through one city or the other, he thinks about it a lot. Ah, the glamorous carefree life of a major league ballplayer!

The Twins' backup catcher Junior Ortiz has gone back to being "Junior." A few weeks ago he was "Joe." Ortiz, one of the true characters of the game, can usually be found in the clubhouse wearing nothing but his scruffy beard, underwear, cowboy boots, and a bandanna around his head. After a recent slump, he shaved the beard and declared that he was Junior's identical twin, Joe. Talking about his departed brother, Joe told reporters: "Junior could hit .400, .350, .300, or .200. He could do it all." Unfortunately, Joe went hitless for a week. The beard and Junior quickly returned. "Joe was terrible," he said. "He couldn't hit a foul ball. He's back in Puerto Rico. I sent him back to the minor leagues."

Ortiz is famous in Minnesota for his antics and quotes. Earlier this year he wanted to come off the disabled list as soon as possible, saying that "maybe they could have me play third base, because they have to have my brain in there someplace. Really, what catcher is better than me defensively? Johnny Bench maybe, but I think he's retired." (You *think* he's retired???) Ortiz did come off the DL during the Twins' celebrated fifteen-game winning streak, saying: "Today I consider myself the luckiest man on the face of the earth. If we had lost today, the guys would have beat the hell out of me. Now we're really going to get on a roll." The streak ended the next day.

Last year he had a modest hitting streak and boasted that he was only fifty-eight games short of breaking Gehrig's record. The fact that it was fifty-six games and DiMaggio's record didn't seem to faze him.

My favorite quote is his response to hecklers: "They can tell me that I stink and that I'm overpaid. That's okay. I already know that."

Junior Ortiz can play on my team any day! (But I agree with him about Joe.)

Another deadline is approaching. Players eligible for postseason play must be on a team's twenty-five-man roster by midnight September 1. This is the last chance for a club to obtain that elusive left-handed reliever or veteran slugger off the bench. Again the names of Mike Flanagan and Dwight Evans have been bandied about. We'll know very soon.

After being one-hit on Wednesday, the Oriole bats woke up tonight against the Twins. They pounded out seventeen hits and crushed "destiny's darlings," 11–5. Cal drove in four runs and had two doubles, Leo Gomez (who leads all rookies with twelve home runs) socked a 428-footer to left, Devereaux had three hits, Hoiles contributed four, and red-hot Smokin' Joe O had a career-high five.

Tonight our broadcast was heard around the world again via Armed Forces Radio. Four years ago in Syracuse I was on a station with such a weak signal that at night you could not hear it at the ballpark five miles from the transmitter. As a goof I began announcing that the station was merely the flagship for the much larger "World Wide Syracuse Chiefs Radio Network." Every night I welcomed another foreign country to the broadcast. ("Tonight I understand we're being heard in the imperial palace of Bhutan. With the Chiefs hosting the Indianapolis Indians, you could see why.") At the time, the Chiefs had a third baseman named Norm Tonucci; a big, sweet Italian kid who was completely overmatched by Triple-A pitching. One night as he came to the plate, I announced that the WWSCRN had added Borneo to its list of affiliates ostensibly because of him. I created this ridiculous story of how Tonucci's father was a hero during the Second World War and had single-handedly saved the people of Borneo from the Japanese. "Norm Tonucci is a folk hero in Borneo," I told the six or seven people who could pick up the station, "the currency is in 'tonucches,' ninety-eight percent of the male babies born in Borneo are named Norm; ninety-three percent of the girls," etc. This bit caught on and although night after night Norm went 0 for 4 or 0 for 3 on a good night, the good people of Borneo were hanging on to every at-bat. Norm himself liked the routine and even recorded some promos. ("Hi, this is Norm Tonucci of the Syracuse Chiefs, and I would like to say hi to all my many fans in Borneo.")

One night we were in Oklahoma City after having taken a five A.M. flight from Syracuse. To say I was punchy is putting it mildly. In Tonucci's first at-bat he tripled. I, of course, went nuts. "They're dancing in the streets in Borneo over what is happening here at All Sports Stadium!" I gleefully announced.

The next time he came to the plate he swung at the first pitch and hit one of the longest home runs I've ever seen. Caught up in the excitement, this was my home-run call: "Tonucci swings and it's belted to deep left field! Back goes Steve Kemp . . . to the wall . . . he looks up and . . . *No school tomorrow in Borneo!!!"*

I wonder if we were on the air in Borneo tonight??

Saturday, August 31, Minneapolis

I saw Dwight Evans in the lobby this morning. "Are you still here?" I asked. "As far as I know," he said. Dewey is on pins and needles. He'd love to finish the season with a winner (who can blame him?), and if he's not traded, it's a bit of a blow to his ego. After a twenty-year career filled with memorable playoff and World Series heroics, he's not wanted by a single contending team?? I've heard the Dodgers are interested. I know the Twins are interested. What I've also heard is that the Orioles' asking price is too dear. In any event, they've got till the witching hour to work something out. (If he does go to Minnesota today, I'm sure traveling secretary Phil Itzoe will have no trouble getting him there.)

Minneapolis, it has been said, is "the town that never oversleeps." With so many spectacular parks and lakes and recreational facilities available, you'd be a damn fool to waste half the day in bed (the way I've done my first two days). Today my cousin Marty and his family chauffeured me around the area, and again I fell in love with Minnesota. I don't want to live here per se, but I'd give anything to go to camp here.

Ballplayers are superstitious creatures—pitchers in particular. Some develop pregame rituals that they adhere to with the fervor of an Oscar Levant. On the Orioles, Ben McDonald eats a can of mustard sardines before every start. (He'd heard that fish was very healthy, but in college mustard sardines were all he could afford. Old habits die hard.) And Mike Mussina, tonight's starter, always goes to McDonald's the day he pitches. Mussina must live right, because no matter where he pitches, there always seems to be a McDonald's nearby. You talk about an incredible coincidence!

Unfortunately, tonight "Big Mack" ate him. Shane Mack had two key hits and drove in a run, lifting the Twins to a 5–2 win.

However, Mussina did not pitch that badly. He did deserve a break today.

I'm pretty good friends with the Twins' winning pitcher, Kevin Tapani. We were both in Tidewater together in '89. Kevin, who's currently emerging as one of the top right-handers in the game, just became a first-time father on Thursday. He and his wife, Sharon, had a beautiful baby girl. Kevin was on hand for the delivery, which lasted fourteen hours. I said on the air that Kevin had to stick it out for the entire time. Steve Bedrosian was not going to be brought in to relieve him.

Sunday, September 1, Minneapolis/Toronto

As we approach the last full month of play, here's a look at the standings.

A.L. East		G.B.	A.L. West		G.B.
Toronto	73–58	—	Minn.	78–53	—
Detroit	69–61	3½	Oak.	71–60	7
Boston	66–63	6	Chicago	69–61	8½
Milw.	62–67	10	Texas	67–61	9½
N.Y.	58–70	13½	K.C.	67–61	9½
BALT.	53–76	19	Seattle	67–63	10½
Cleve.	43–86	29	Cal.	63–66	14

In the National League West, Atlanta leads Los Angeles by one game, with Cincinnati in third by eight. The East finds Pittsburgh enjoying an eight-game cushion over second-place St. Louis. Meanwhile, back to our story . . .

Dwight Evans is still here.

Mike Flanagan is still here.

Brady Anderson is back, and Mark Williamson is too.

Major league rosters can expand to forty today, but the Orioles don't figure to add many more than they already have. In the words of John Oates, "Who else is there? All our prospects are here." The only notable exception is Luis Mercedes, and his status remains very much in doubt.

For the present, the Orioles are looking to the future. One glance at today's lineup confirms that. Six rookies were out on the field, including starter Arthur Rhodes. The result: As bullpen coach Elrod Hendricks said after the game, "We sent boys after men." Minnesota 14, Baltimore 3. (With this being Week

One of the NFL, I reported the score as the Vikings 14, Colts 3.)

We flew on to Toronto, arriving at the Harbour Castle Westin at ten P.M. My partner, meanwhile, is in San Diego for ESPN. Just another jet-set weekend for Jon Miller. Thursday night he flew with us to Minnesota, took off yesterday morn' for San Diego, will fly to San Francisco for a Labor Day ESPN game tomorrow, then will wing to Vancouver tomorrow night, where he'll clear Canadian customs (hopefully) and hop the red-eye for Toronto. He'll be here early Tuesday morning for our game that night. Next week will be much easier. He'll merely commute back and forth from Baltimore to Anaheim.

Monday, September 2, Toronto

It's Labor Day, my least-favorite holiday of the year. I see no reason to celebrate the conclusion of summer, the approaching end of baseball, and the beginning of the school year (some anxieties are deep-rooted). Canada observes this occasion as well. (The Canadians also share America's three big sacred holidays—Easter, Christmas, and Oscarcast Monday.)

My little girl's birthday was a smashing success, I understand. Everyone who is anyone (but one) was there. Despite the fact that Debby is still hobbling around, she somehow managed to organize the entire affair, complete with games, arts and crafts activities, songs, and a homemade cake. Do I feel guilty for not being there? Hell, even *divorced* fathers get to their daughters' birthday parties.

There is only one real tradition of Labor Day that I can see, and that is monumental evening traffic jams as people return home Monday night. To ensure that their fans could be in their cars at night, the Blue Jays held their game with us in the afternoon. I had nothing better to do, so I hopped an early cab and arrived at the Skydome four hours before game time. Throughout this second swing around the league I've been taking pictures. (After all, how many of my friends actually know what Yankee Stadium or Fenway Park look like?) Usually, half a roll will suffice for a venue, but the Skydome will probably require two. For an hour I explored her nooks 'n' crannies, snapping shot after shot, angle after angle. The roof-retracting sequence alone should be worth the price of developing.

The combination of a holiday, spectacular weather, and the Baltimore Orioles was enough to draw one of the largest crowds in the history of the Skydome (and remember, they sell out every night). The paid attendance was only two hundred less than the all-time mark. Ballplayers, as a rule, love playing before big crowds. Dave Johnson, today's starter (yes, he's in the rotation for now), was saying that any time you go out on the field, you have a job to do, but when there's a huge audience, then you really have something to prove. "And that's what it's all about," to use his cliché.

Jim Henneman of the *Evening Sun* has coined the phrase "reverse lock." A "reverse lock" is when the odds are stacked so greatly in favor of one team that the other team has to win. (Remember Roy Smith beating Roger Clemens at Fenway, or the Orioles snapping Minnesota's fifteen-game winning streak?) Well, today's game looked like a "reverse lock" for the Orioles. They were coming off a humiliating defeat against the Twins, playing a divisional leader that is murder at home, facing Tom Candiotti, who last week allowed them one hit and retired twenty-two in a row, and that one player who got the hit (Joe Orsulak) jammed his shoulder yesterday and cannot play.

By the second inning it was 4–0, Orioles.

But by the end of twelve it was 5–4 Blue Jays. A few bad AstroTurf hops, some shoddy defensive play, and an unearned run combined to do in the O's. "Reverse locks" are not always sure things.

The strain of the long losing season is beginning to take its toll on Oates. Even the "world's nicest guy" has his limits. Still affable and accessible, Oates is displaying a much greater intolerance with the play of his ball club. (Can you blame him???) No, he's not at the Lou Piniella/Tasmanian devil stage yet, but at times he can get a little, let's just say, cranky. Additionally, the Orioles still have not signed him to a contract for next year, and that must be weighing heavy. He is guiding a team he inherited, not formed, yet still is responsible for their performance. And when they lose games like today's, which they should've won, it can only reflect badly on him, although it's not really his fault. I think Oates deserves the chance to manage a team from Day One in spring training and take it all the way through. Anything else is not a true test. My guess is the Orioles will give him that chance, but for whatever their reasons, mum is still the word.

In other news: Bo Jackson was in the White Sox lineup for the very first time today, just eight months after his "career ending" hip-pointer injury. He went 0 for 3 with a sacrifice fly, but who cares? He made it back. Bo may know baseball and football and hockey and track, but he also knows determination and extremely hard work. It would be worth twenty dollars to shake his hand on this day.

A night off in Toronto meant dinner at Bigliardi's with Chuck, Dr. Paul, and Phil Itzoe. As Chuck would say, "We told lies for hours."

Tuesday, September 3, Toronto

Here's how the *Toronto Star* daily newspaper is sold downtown. Stacks of the morning edition are placed on various street corners accompanied by cups and signs that read: PLEASE LEAVE 40 CENTS. The papers remain untouched except by those who deposit the required change. Can you see the honor system working in New York? Within fifteen seconds everything would be gone, including the sign.

If you ask me, Frank Sinatra sings about the wrong towns.

Dining tip: The best lunch spot in the American League is Mövenpick in downtown Toronto. It features a large, eclectic menu, imaginative Swiss dishes, and a dessert menu second to none. To remember the name, just think of the NBA—Move-'n'-pick.

I've seen outdoor games and indoor games, but never one that was both. Tonight, for only the fourth time this year, the Skydome roof was closed during the game. (An unexpected thunderstorm pattern appeared on the radar, I'm told.) For the twenty minutes that it took to close the roof, no one watched the game; 50,000 people were all staring straight up. A Blue Jay would get a base hit and receive only mild applause. (At least I think a Blue Jay got a hit. I was on the air at the time, but really, how often can you watch an eleven-thousand-ton roof move?)

The Orioles crushed the Jays, 8–4, thanks in great measure to Glenn Davis and Dwight Evans, who both came to bat in the ninth needing triples to complete hitting for the cycle. (Neither got it.) Dwight was my guest on the postgame show, and all he could talk about was not *his* accomplishments, but the team's. This was a big win for the *team*. After yesterday's defeat the *team* really needed this one. So much is made of pitching and defense (except in homer-happy Detroit), but baseball lifers will tell you the single key ingredient to a winning club is teamwork. The ability to play together and jell as a unit is what ultimately makes for champions, and the good ones know it. Yes, it's selfish on my part, but I'm sure glad that the *team* Dwight Evans is currently playing for is the Baltimore Orioles.

Wednesday, September 4, Toronto/Baltimore

Bob Milacki pitched his best game of the year, all things considered. He hurled a complete game, struck out a career-high ten, and allowed Toronto only three runs. The Orioles lost, 3–1. But as Oates said after the game, "If Milacki can give us twenty starts like that next year, I'll take our chances in seventeen of them."

At least if the O's were to lose, they did so quickly. This was getaway night, and God bless 'em, the Birds were polished off in 2:01, our shortest game of the year. Still, by the time I walked through my front door in Baltimore, it was three A.M. The hourlong bus trip to Hamilton, Ontario, and clearing customs back in the United States ate up much of the night. I don't envy the Blue Jays their travel schedule. Every time they enter or leave Canada, they have to go through the same rigmarole. There's no such thing as a quick pop. Anywhere from an hour and a half to two hours must be added to every journey involving a border crossing. (But then again, they do play half their games in the Skydome, so too bad for them.)

Jon was telling me that when he went through customs early Tuesday morning in Vancouver, he was asked to produce a work permit. Not having one, he was ushered into an immigration official's office. A very sweet woman with a thick French accent asked why he was in Canada. Jon told her that he was a radio announcer working for the Baltimore Orioles and was on his way to Toronto to broadcast back to the United States a couple of Baltimore Oriole/Toronto Blue Jay baseball games. She nodded, then turned to the customs officer next to her and said, "Do you have the slightest idea what he's talking about?"

Thursday, September 5, Baltimore

In fashion news: The latest rage among the Oriole players these days are Zubaz pants. Zubaz must be a foreign word for "clown." You can't believe these clothes. They are loud, baggy sweatpants-type numbers with shocking multicolored zebra-stripe designs. Now I know why the league insists that ballplayers wear uniforms.

Another off-day, another movie. Lately I've seen quite a few winners. *Dead Again* and *The Commitments* top the list. The film I really want to see is *Barton Fink,* the latest from the wildly inventive Coen brothers, but alas it's not yet playing in fair Baltimore. Maybe if I come back next year.

Fox 45 is showing the "Levine & Isaacs" film festival all this week, and I was able to catch a couple of episodes tonight. My intros looked totally ridiculous. I was quite pleased. Only one thing was missing, however. I should've worn a pair of Zubaz pants.

Friday, September 6, Baltimore

Poor Sam Horn has been the odd man out. Ever since Glenn Davis came off the DL on August 18, Sam has had no place to play. (Davis and Milligan have been alternating between first base and DH.) He's maintained a very positive stoic attitude, and who knows, next year Glenn and/or Randy might not be back and Sam could be in the lineup every day, but still it's been very hard on the big man. Horn's last start was August 18. In the last fifteen games, he's made four pinch-hit appearances. Understandably, he's had only one hit in ten trips. Well, tonight, with two-time Cy Young Award winner Bret Saberhagen on the mound for Kansas City (the Royals kick off our home stand with a three-game series; plenty of good seats still available), Sam was in there. As tough as "Sabes" is (just two weeks ago he hurled a no-hitter against Chicago), he has never had good luck with Horn. Going into tonight's game, Sam was seven for fifteen with three home runs against Saberhagen—astonishing numbers.

Tonight, in the first, Horn struck out with the bases loaded.

He struck out again in the fourth, then grounded out in the sixth. Horn came up again in the eighth with two on and the Orioles leading by one. You're the manager. Do you pull "Sabes"? Horn has hit Saberhagen well, but certainly not tonight. A right-hander's warming up.

Well??????

Hal McRae elected to keep him in. Horn lofted an opposite field, three-run homer just inside the left-field foul pole. (I know. You would've pulled him.)

The Orioles won, 6–2. Glenn Davis also had a big night, hitting a homer, a single, and a freaky double that hit the third-base bag and kangarooed over the third baseman's head. With the score tied 2–2 in the top of the eighth, the Royals got runners on first and third to chase starter Mike Mussina, but lefty Jim Poole came on to strike out formidable Kirk Gibson and get future Cooperstowner George Brett to fly out. Good bit of pitching, no? Jim Poole picked up his first major league victory.

Before the game, the Orioles added two more September call-ups. Jeff Ballard is back after a 3–3 record with Rochester. He'll be used out of the bullpen. (Does the expression "mop up" mean anything to you??) And young catcher Jeff Tackett (who has a rocket launcher for an arm) also got the nod. Luis Mercedes (the man who has to register his batting helmet as a lethal weapon) is here working out with the team and will be activated Sunday. Remember the only thing important in major league baseball?—W I N N I N G.

The California Angels made a major move today. Whitey Herzog has been named their VP in charge of player development and operations. The deal he struck is apparently the richest ever for that position. "The White Rat" (as he is known) is uniformly regarded in baseball circles as one of the best if not *the* best. There had been much speculation that he would oversee one of the two new franchise clubs, but today the Angels beat 'em to the punch.

The Angels are an interesting ball club this year. Currently, they have three 15-game winners (Langston, Finley, and Abbott), one of the game's best closers (Harvey), an excellent setup man (Eichhorn), and any number of hitters having good years (Joyner, Polonia, Winfield). And yet they are in the cellar. The Angels may well be the best last-place team in history.

9

Saturday, September 7, Baltimore

Deb and the kids are back! They returned this evening and will fly back to L.A. after the Jewish New Year on Tuesday. They arrived just before the game, which lifted my spirits considerably. Meanwhile, the Zubaz kids lost to K.C., 7–4. Highlights: Sam Horn hit another home run. Danny Tartabull didn't.

After the game we took the kids to P.J.'s Pub (run by H, remember?) for a late bite. The game plan is to keep Matty and Diana on California time. So consequently their bedtime is later than mine.

Earlier today, I toured the new stadium with Bob Miller. As unfinished ballparks go, this one was very impressive. I'm continually amazed, however, that they can employ the latest, most innovative architectural and engineering designs, stay on time and on budget, and still be unable to find a name for the place. The contract states that the governor and the Orioles each have an equal say in the name. The "Guv" favors "Camden Yards" while Mr. Jacobs is sweet on "Orioles Park." Neither will budge. Ridiculous, wouldn't you say? I say just call the damn thing "Dr. Paul Eicholtz Field" and be done with it!

Sunday, September 8, Baltimore

Debby and Diana stayed home to cook for the holidays—we're having people we've met over for lunch on Tuesday—and the boys headed out to the yard. Matty met another future immortal, George Brett. Matty's classmates are having a hard time believing he actually *knows* Bo Jackson, Ken Griffey, Jr., Jim Abbott, etc. (Of course, at that age kids are boasting that they've flown in spaceships and broken up armed robberies, so the skepticism is understandable.) I'm sure the autographed Nolan Ryan baseball will do wonders for his credibility.

Luis Mercedes made his major league debut today, and right from the start he was electric. There's an upside to his extremely aggressive manner of play (if properly controlled), and this afternoon we were treated to several examples. Aboard on an error to lead off the first, he took two bases on a groundout to third. With the third baseman charging the ball, Mercedes saw the bag unoccupied and seized it. The crowd went nuts. A moment later he scored on a groundout by Cal, and the O's had manufactured a run. The second time up, Mercedes drilled a base hit up the alley in right, and although the center fielder cut it off, Mercedes was still able to blaze into second with a hustle double. A sacrifice and a single later (by you know who), and the O's had two manufactured runs. Jerry Narron, his manager in Double A last year, says, "Mercedes runs the bases until one of two things happens. He's either thrown out or he scores."

Mercedes has always been an excellent hitter. He finished second in the I.L. with a .334 average, and won batting crowns the previous two seasons in the Eastern and Carolina leagues. The Orioles see him as a potential leadoff hitter (taking advantage of his lightning speed), and this year asked him to improve his on-base percentage. Mercedes responded by drawing many more walks while still maintaining a very high average. Luis Mercedes could well become one of the most exciting young players of the game.

As for his demons . . .

They're not all his fault.

Imagine being a teenager asked to leave home for a foreign country in which you have zero knowledge of the language or the customs. Completely isolated and alienated, you then are asked to compete with people who are from that country in a sport that nobody really has mastered. The compensation you receive is minimal, and even at that you may be asked to support your family back home on it.

Such is the case for Luis Mercedes and a growing number of other Latinos who are playing pro ball in the States. Organizations are quick to utilize the talents of these young men but not so quick to provide guidance and education. The Texas Rangers have gone the furthest in this regard, but all clubs need to improve their relations with their foreign players.

Luis Mercedes, it seems, asked the Orioles for a loan at the end of the last season to cover certain family debts. The club obliged. But then in spring training when it began deducting salary to repay the loan, Mercedes could not understand why his paychecks were so small. The lack of communication due to Mercedes's inability to express his confusion and anger, and the Orioles' unawareness of any problem, led to his moody behavior and eventual early-season suspension. A problem that could've been avoided? *Sí!*

Mercedes had one real friend in Rochester, one teammate whom he could talk to and share his feelings with—David Segui. In late May, Segui was called up to Baltimore. So much for the support system.

None of this is to justify Mercedes's recent episode in Syracuse; it was clearly inexcusable behavior. But there were circumstances, and they need to be addressed. I will say this: The chief proponent for education and special training for foreign ballplayers is Frank Robinson, assistant general manager of the Baltimore Orioles.

And now back to the game: Birds vs. Royals. The Orioles had a golden opportunity in the ninth to tie or win. With one out, Mercedes walked on four pitches (he always seems to be on base), and Sam Horn pinch-hit for Brady Anderson. K.C. closer Jeff Montgomery was laboring and fell behind, 3–0. Cal Ripken was on deck. Oates, however, gave Horn the green light, so of course he swung at the next pitch and grounded into a game-ending double play. Final: Royals 3, Orioles 2. Pin that loss on Johnny Oates.

After the game I suspect the Orioles drove Danny Tartabull to the airport to make sure he got out of town. Against the O's this year, Tartabull finished with a .523 average, five home runs and fourteen RBIs. If he did as well against the rest of the league, he'd finish with 65 home runs and 182 RBIs. Instead, he's only batting .329 with 28 homers and 90 driven in. "The Bull" has picked the perfect year to have a career year. He's eligible for free agency after this season. I suggested on the air he have his driveway paved so that when the Brink's trucks roll up to his house, the guards won't be tearing up his front lawn lugging the heavy moneybags into the house.

The 50-millionth fan entered Memorial Stadium today. He received a whole bunch of great gifts, including a trip to anywhere in the USA (and even back). For two days I've been saying that Debby has been trying desperately to position herself to win that prize. The winner, a season-ticket holder, sent me a nice note apologizing for shoving her out of the way.

After the game, we had a lovely family Rosh Hashanah dinner at a place called Harvey's. Debby discovered it, of course. I've been living here five months; I know how to get to the Sizzler and Pizza Hut (but only coming from one direction).

Monday, September 9, Baltimore

Timingwise I caught a break. Rosh Hashanah began Sunday at sundown and lasts until sundown Tuesday. However, most people (myself included) only observe the first day. Since the Orioles didn't have a night game Sunday and don't play an afternoon affair today, I don't have to miss any broadcasts this week. Next Tuesday night is Yom Kippur and I will take that game off. (Sandy Koufax refused to pitch a World Series game in the sixties because it fell on the High Holiday. I can skip the Orioles game that might seal their elimination this year.)

As a family we observed the day, then Matty and I headed to the ballpark while Debby and Diana went to Bonnie Levitt's for a holiday dinner.

The always-fun-to-hate-despite-their-record New York Yankees are in town. Memories of their three-game sweep here in May still linger. Matty was very excited to meet Don Mattingly and Steve Sax. One thing about my son, when he's not inadvertently insulting these ballplayers, he is extremely courteous. To Alvaro Espinoza: "Hello, Mr. Espinoza. I've enjoyed your work."

The Yankees (as usual) have been a team in turmoil lately. After flirting with .500 at the All-Star break, they have taken a nosedive in the second half, manager Stump Merrill is not long for his job ("Stick a fork in him. He's done," as Leo Durocher used to say), and in a recent blunder that recalls the heydays of the Steinbrenner era, the team suspended their captain and most popular player, Don Mattingly, for one game because he wouldn't get a haircut. (Club rules are club rules, you know.)

This edict, sent down by the normally very levelheaded GM Gene Michael, caused a major brouhaha in Gotham. One of the New York rags ran a huge headline, PLAY BALD! and doctored a photo of Mattingly to make him appear bald. Then, throughout the sports section, all the columnists' photos were similarly altered. It was a riot. After one day and a trim, the one current Yankee who at times has been compared to DiMaggio and Gehrig was "graciously" allowed to play.

Mattingly has been a cranky Yankee this year. The Yanks are doggedly sticking to their youth movement and displaying patience for the first time in ages, but that means several years could pass before they are contenders again. That's fine for the organization but not so fine for the thirty-year-old Mattingly, who'd like to be on a winner right now. (Of course, no one put a gun to his back and made him sign that long-range mega-million-dollar contract a couple of years ago.) In any event, he asked to be traded several weeks before the grooming suspension, and there is some speculation that the two incidents are not unrelated. Do I feel the Yankees will adhere to Mattingly's wishes and trade him? Not if it means ending world hunger.

On the pregame show I asked John Oates (a former Yankee) why he gave Horn the green light yesterday in the ninth with a 3–0 count, the tying run at first, and Cal on deck. Oates responded that he screwed up. He was greedy. He was looking for a home run and felt he cost the team the game. For a manager to completely and publicly accept full blame is rare. He might not know what it means, but John Oates is a "mensch."

Bob Milacki was super tonight—a complete-game, five-hit shutout, if you please. The Orioles won, 8–0. Chito Martinez and Sam Horn went deep (Horn hitting his third home run of this home stand. Let's hear more from this young fellow).

Meanwhile, the Cleveland Indians continue to pack 'em in. Tonight they hosted Boston in a makeup game and drew a grand total of 1,695 people. Remember that Cleveland Stadium seats 74,483. It was their lowest single-game attendance in seventeen sizzling seasons. We go in there next weekend. I can just imagine what *we'll* draw. I hope they have "Free Car to Every Fan Weekend," because I'd love to see at least three or four thousand in the house for each of our games.

Tuesday, September 10, Baltimore

"Talk to you tonight, honey. Good-bye, Matty. Good-bye, Diana. I'll see you in a few weeks. I love you."

The limo to the airport left at three-thirty.

Christ, this is getting old!

The Orioles made it two in a row over the Yankees; 6–3 was the final, with Arthur Rhodes unable to go five innings again due to wildness.

Cal hit his first home run in nearly a month. Not to worry about Cal; he is still batting .322 and among the league leaders in most offensive and defensive categories.

I returned home and couldn't sleep. Maybe if I could've read somebody a story . . .

Wednesday, September 11, Baltimore

The Orioles swept the Yankees! Sam Horn was Joe Hardy and hit yet *another* home run, as did Joe Orsulak. Mike Mussina pitched well, and Gregg Olson got the save, Glorious Orioles 4, Damn Yankees 2.

After the victory, Oates was asked if this was the kind of game—the starter going into the seventh, Olson getting a save, and timely hitting—the Orioles expected when the season began?

"Yes," he said, "if . . .

"If Jeff Ballard and Bob Milacki pitched like they did in 'eighty-nine . . .

"If Jeff Robinson pitched like he did three years ago . . .

"If José Mesa pitched like he did the last month of last season . . .

"If Ben McDonald could step in as expected . . .

"If Craig Worthington played like he did as a rookie . . .

"If Glenn Davis hit thirty-five home runs . . ."

After a pause he concluded, "None of those 'ifs' happened."

As the old saying goes: "If 'if' and 'buts' were candy and nuts, we'd all have a wonderful Christmas."

Thursday, September 12, Baltimore

The Cleveland Indians stagger into town for a four-game set. At 45–93, they have the worst record in baseball and have already been eliminated. They've had fifty-three different players on their active roster—five more than their club record, set in 1912 and again in 1946—and have six key players on the disabled list, five on the sixty-day. A mid-season managerial change (Mike Hargrove for John McNamara) has helped little. Since Hargrove took over, the Tribe is 21–41 (not that it's his fault, certainly). They're near the bottom in team hitting and pitching, and are dead last in team fielding. I think it's safe to say that nothing has gone right for the Indians in 1991.

Tonight they almost blew a four-run lead in the ninth.

Leading 6–2, they gave up three runs and allowed the O's to load the bases with one out with Mike Devereaux coming to the plate. But Devo grounded into a double play, and that was that (1991 has not been a charmed year for the Orioles either, as I recall).

Notable achievements: Joe Orsulak threw out three Indians from left field. (You'd think they'd learn after two.) Orsulak now has seventeen outfield assists, two more than anyone else in the majors. And it's not because he has such a cannon of an arm. If anything, he's gotten these assists because teams feel they *can* run on him. Let's see how many assists he ends up with next year.

Cal hit home run number 28, tying his career high established in his rookie season, '82. He should finish the year topping his personal best in just about every category. Wouldn't you love to be the agent negotiating *his* next contract? Oh, by the way, Cal Ripken also leads the league in fielding percentage.

Dubious achievement: José Mesa had another calamitous start. He walked six, and of the six, five came around to score. How big a factor was that?

Again, the final: 6–5, Cleveland.

Lack of achievement: The new stadium still does not have a name.

Friday, September 13, Baltimore

Things are still going better for the Cleveland Indians than they are for the Montreal Expos. They're dead last in the N.L. East and their stadium is falling apart. A fifty-five-ton block of concrete crashed from the structure to the ground at Olympic Stadium yesterday. Fortunately, no one was hurt. The Expos will be playing their home games next week in New York and Philadelphia. This white-elephant stadium has cost taxpayers almost $1.5 billion since 1976. And there's more. Their parachute-type retractable roof suffered a 110-yard hole in the Kevlar fabric during a windstorm in June and they've been playing open-air ever since. (Rick Griffin, the very witty PR man of the Expos, reported that the retractable roof was the first roof to go on the DL since Gene Roof in 1983.)

Olympic Stadium is major league baseball's answer to the Pit.

I did a station promotion today for WBAL. From time to time we're asked to make public appearances on behalf of 'BAL and the Orioles, and I really don't mind doing them. They're a good way to meet people and get involved in the community. This afternoon my assignment was to go down to the main branch of a major local savings and loan (a sponsor) and conduct a drawing for two pairs of tickets for Closing Day. Why did I think anyone would show up? Why did I even think anyone would be invited? There was no one there but the ad-agency guy and the branch manager. I pulled out two names, posed for a picture with the branch manager, was thanked, and left. My status as a celebrity was once again put into proper perspective.

Maryland governor William Donald Schaefer was in attendance this evening at the stadium that *does* have a name and sat with Orioles' owner Eli Jacobs. No agreement was apparently reached. How hard can it be, guys???

Ben McDonald, who has been experiencing nagging shoulder problems, felt stiffness warming up and could not answer the bell. He'll be examined mañana. Anthony Telford was the emergency starter and lasted all of 4⅓. Trailing 4–1 in the eighth, Mike Devereaux hit a three-run homer to tie the game, and a flurry of singles in the ninth (capped off by David Segui) gave the O's an exciting 4–3 victory over them Injuns.

Tonight was a night to stay out of Jon's way. The constant travel is very understandably starting to wear him down emotionally and physically. When I see him slamming down headphones and getting seriously pissed when the Orioles make an error or miss a cutoff man in a late-season game with the Indians—a game that truly means less than nothing—I know it's time for Jon to take a little "Miller Time." It has to be the stress, because no one in his right mind would risk an ulcer or a heart attack over *this*.

Also, Jon began the night with a scratchy throat, which set into motion a series of unfortunate events. To soothe his pipes, he had a Styrofoam cup of hot water by his side. Already simmering at the play of the O's, he accidentally spilled a full cup onto his score book while calling the fifth inning. An entire season's worth of score sheets were instantly transformed into one large, soggy brick. Being the consummate pro, Jon continued his broadcast as if nothing had happened, and quite frankly was brilliant. But the effort required to do the inning took its toll, and by the seventh he had completely lost his voice. I had to call the rest of the game.

It is doubtful whether he'll be okay for tomorrow. Of course the biggie is Sunday, when he does his nationally televised ESPN game, but fortunately it's in New York this week and not Anaheim or Oakland, so he's spared the red eyes and coast-to-coast flights. Considering the grueling schedule he keeps, I think the season is ending three weeks too late.

Saturday, September 14, Baltimore

Toronto beat Oakland today 6–0.

So??????

So with that win the 1991 Baltimore Orioles were officially eliminated from postseason play. Twenty-one games remain on the Orioles' schedule.

Play ball!

Our rotisserie team has also been eliminated. As a result, all remaining promotions at the Pit have been canceled.

Jon wisely took the night off so WBAL morning sports anchor Jim West (who substituted for me when Debby mistook her ankle for a wishbone) pinch-hit in his stead. Bob Milacki, who has been the O's most consistent pitcher in the second half, was lit up for five runs and eight hits in 2⅔ innings. We're playing the lowly Cleveland Indians here. Without going into the grisly details, the O's lost 6–5 in eleven innings.

The new stadium still does not have a name.

Sunday, September 15, Baltimore

"How's Bayou?" Department: Here's the word on Cajun Ben McDonald. He has an abnormality of the right posterior labrun (membrane in the right shoulder). Recommended treatment: rest. The Birds' number-one starter is out for the remainder of the year.

The Baltimore Orioles paid tribute to the Baltimore Colts today in pregame ceremonies honoring one of pro football's legendary franchises. A little more than seven years has passed since Colts' owner/carpetbagger Robert Irsay did the unconscionable and moved the team to Indianapolis by packing up moving vans in the middle of the night and fleeing under the cover of darkness. It was a jolt that the undeserving city of Baltimore has yet to recover from. Well, the Orioles, in conjunction with the Maryland Stadium Authority and Greater Baltimore Committee, relived some of the color and pageantry of the "Blue & White" in ceremonies that were really quite moving. Emceed by Chuck Thompson, the longtime voice of the Colts, the "Colts Band" made an appearance, serenading the "World's Largest Insane Asylum" (as Memorial Stadium used to be known on those glorious fall Sundays) with the stirring Colts' Fight Song one final time (well . . . fifteen final times). The team mascot "Dixie" (a white colt) cantered around the warning track as in heydays of old while the Diamond-Vision board replayed classic Colt highlights of what now seems the distant past. "The Big Wheel" (Len Burrier), who was the original in-the-stands cheerleader, spelled out C-O-L-T-S, and the big crowd responded thunderously.

Finally came the introduction of twenty-two former great Baltimore Colts, among them Jim Parker, Lenny Moore, Artie Donovan, and Johnny U. Many limped out onto the field, suffering from arthritis and injuries that never healed.

These heroes of yesteryear played for a team that no longer exists in a stadium that may soon be torn down. At the entrance to Memorial Stadium are the following words: THE DEEDS OF THESE MEN WILL NEVER BE FORGOTTEN. Assuming the sign itself survives, I hope its message is true.

Watching from the booth, I found myself very moved by the tribute. And I hated the Colts as a kid. I was a Rams fan.

I did, however, worship Johnny Unitas, and thanks to Chuck, Johnny joined us for an inning of the broadcast. I would not have been more impressed had it been the queen of England (who, by the way, had her chance).

The period at the end of the story: The Indianapolis Colts lost to the Raiders today, 16–0. (Not that the Raiders have a shred of loyalty to the community that supported them for over twenty years.)

Turning to the summer game: The Orioles gained a split with Cleveland, shading the Indians, 4–3. Unbeknownst to practically everyone in the ballpark, the hero was catcher Chris Hoiles. He didn't homer; he didn't throw out a key base runner or block the plate to choke off a critical run. All he did was go out to the mound in the second inning and have a little chat with wobbly rookie Arthur Rhodes. Rhodes had gotten off to his usual poor start, serving up a three-run homer to slugger Albert Belle before two outs in the game had been recorded. It looked as though Rhodes would be gone by the second, but Hoiles noticed a possible flaw in his mechanics. He was gripping the ball too tightly when throwing the curve. Chris pointed this out to his battery mate, and suddenly Rhodes became a different pitcher. He wound up going a major league high 6⅔ innings, not allowing another run, and during one stretch retiring eleven in a row. The great Sandy Koufax's career was similarly steered on course by catcher Norm Sherry, who detected almost the same flaw. These are the kinds of intangibles that never show up in arbitration hearings but do separate the good ballplayers from the potentially great. The Orioles may have a real find in Chris Hoiles. (The jury's still out on Rhodes.)

What a home-run stand this has been for Sam Horn. He went deep again today, to give him five for the week along with eleven RBIs. Some players, when relegated to bench warmers, sulk, cry to the media, or rearrange their manager's office furniture. Those with class (and a respect for decorating) state their cases on the field. Sam Horn was slated to start maybe twice in this ten-game home stand. Now, when the Orioles face a right-hander, he's one of the first names penciled in. (Are you listening, Jack Armstrong in Cincinnati?)

Show Must Go On Dept.: Sounding more like Brenda Vaccaro than Jon Miller, my partner was a trouper and did the broadcast tonight on ESPN.

Bullshit Must Go On Dept.: The new stadium is still without a name.

Monday, September 16, Baltimore/Boston

The O's play the next thirteen of sixteen games on the road. These are the real tough days. Going through the motions. Garbage time. The suitcase seems heavier, the road seems longer.

Fortunately, our first stop is Boston. I have no problem whatsoever, no how, getting up for games at Fenway. Let's see how I feel this weekend in Cleveland.

Of course, with Boston comes the Boston Sheraton. Ugggh! This time I'm in the South Tower. Twenty-nine floors with four elevators . . . but only two of them operational. It takes fifteen minutes to get either up or down from my room. We arrived at twelve-thirty. Finally, at three, I went down to the lobby myself to get my bag (which had been sitting there for an hour). At least my card key to get into the room works. Chuck Thompson needed four different ones. John Oates is in a suite near a stairwell that is under reconstruction. The hotel must assume he doesn't mind the sound of incessant hammering and power drilling.

Please understand, this is not a knock at all Sheratons. Most are first-rate. But for some reason *this* hotel is a lemon (which, by the way, is the smell emanating from my air-conditioning vent).

Question: Who's the only man to play for the Red Sox, Celtics, Patriots, and Bruins?

Answer: Organist John Kiley.

Well, Kiley has given way to Kilroy, but his organ stylings are just one more reason why there is no greater place to "experience" a major league baseball game than Fenway Park. The atmosphere is so thick you can cut it with the knife used to spread mustard on your savory Fenway Frank. I've seen 'em all now in the American League, and this is the best!

There is, however, one myth I must dispel about Fenway Park. Four former Red Sox have their numbers retired—Ted Williams (#9), Joe Cronin (#4), Bobby Doerr (#1), and Carl Yastrzemski (#8). Their numbers are displayed on the facade of the roof shielding the lower level down the right-field line in the following order: 9 4 1 8. Legend has it that on that date, 9–4–18, the Red Sox clinched their last world championship. Great story, huh? It's not true. On 9–11–18 Boston beat the Cubs 2–1 to win their last World Series. What the Red Sox have to do in all good conscience is unretire Joe Cronin and retire Bobby Doerr three times.

Since we're on a trip to the Northeast in the middle of September, I naturally packed sweaters and a jacket. Game-time temperature tonight was a steamy 86 (the daytime high was 90). I brought the jacket anyway. Chuck has had nothing to rib me about lately.

For the next three days the Orioles are back in the pennant race . . . sort of. Boston currently trails first-place Toronto by only two and a half, so the Orioles can at least be spoilers. Do teams like to be cast in the role of spoilers? Management usually says no. Its agenda is building momentum and shaping for the future. No one game or opponent is placed above another. But the players will tell you that's pure bullshit. It's a pisser to wreak havoc with the standings. As Randy Milligan put it: "What else do we got to play for?"

Well, the O's were magnificent spoilers tonight. They shelled Boston 9–2. Mike Devereaux and Chris Hoiles both homered over the Green Monster, and Randy Milligan authored two. The Birds are really on a power surge. Here in September they've hit 25 and have homered in seven straight. (Just like the Tigers, except that they seem to win a lot more games.) The pitching was standout tonight as well. Rookie Mike Mussina, hurling his first major league complete game, was not at all intimidated by the mystique of Fenway Park.

Luckily for Boston, Toronto lost in Seattle in the eleventh inning, so the Sox didn't lose any ground. The Red Sox rise has been remarkable. As late as August 8 they were eleven games back. Since then they've won 27 of 37, overtaken Sparky's Tigers, and now have a real shot at the divisional title. Toronto is the swing team this year, finishing up against the much tougher Western Division and logging jumbo frequent-flyer miles, while Boston stays much closer to home, primarily entertaining spoiler-wannabes.

I'll tell you who's rooting for Boston, rooting hard—CBS, which paid an outrageous $1.1 BILLION for exclusive over-the-air TV rights, and very likely could be covering play-offs featuring Minnesota-Toronto and Pittsburgh-Atlanta (fine cities all, but not what the networks would call their "A" cities in terms of population or nationwide interest). Yes, $1.1 billion. For that tidy sum, you could make a lot of *Murphy Brown* episodes (or Levine-Isaacs pilots).

"Fear of Flying" starting course: The Chicago White Sox were winging back from California last night when the left engine on their 737 went out . . . 35,000 feet above the ground. Apparently Bo Jackson was sitting up in the cockpit at the time, observing, and when the engine blew, he ran into the cabin with an expression of absolute stark terror. The combination of the engine loss and the sight of the normally unflappable Bo was enough to completely freak out most of the passengers. The pilot managed to land them safely at the Des Moines airport, and there were no injuries. Gee, I remember when flying was considered one of the *perks* of this gig.

Tuesday, September 17, Boston

A day well spent strolling through Beantown. Among my travels was the Bull & Finch, the bar that *Cheers* was patterned after. Talk about a license to print money! More people, I'm told, visit the Bull & Finch than walk the Freedom Trail. Tom Kirshaw owns the entire building, has for years, and now lives quite comfortably in a penthouse apartment on the roof (complete with swimming pool). At one time the Bull & Finch was a quaint neighborhood bar "where everyone knew your name," and now it's a spot where tourists from Louisville to Portugal can stand in line together and compare sweatshirts and coffee mugs at the gift shop.

Tonight marks the beginning of Yom Kippur, the holiest day of the Jewish year. Not being from this area and not knowing where to observe, I had to fast and atone for my sins alone in "Beth Sheraton." (But like I said to Debby on the phone this evening, "It's great being on the East Coast. You get to eat three hours sooner.")

Wednesday, September 18, Boston/Cleveland

What better way to break a daylong fast than with a Fenway Frank? I'm sure I'll be paying for that for weeks.

The Orioles lost 4–3 last night. José Mesa couldn't hold a three-run lead. Tonight they dropped a 7–5 decision.

Game notes: Cal Ripken belted his thirtieth home run, placing him among a select group of only four shortstops who had thirty or more a season. (Can you name the other three? Ernie Banks, Rico Petrocelli, and, of course, Vern Stephens.) Also, Joe Orsulak became the O's all-time assist leader when he threw out two Red Sox tonight. He now owns a major league–leading nineteen. And one final note: Wayne Housie of Boston got his first major league at-bat this evening and sacrificed.

The Sox remain two and a half games back of Toronto. Okay, so the Orioles are too nice a bunch of guys to *really* be spoilers.

Both engines worked on our postgame flight to Cleveland, I'm happy to say, and by two o'clock I was in my suite at the Radisson. That's right, a suite.

Thursday, September 19, Cleveland

All rooms in the Cleveland Radisson are suites. Next to the Ritz-Carlton in Dearborn, this is far and away the best hotel on the circuit. Complimentary continental breakfasts and hors d'oeuvres are also provided, along with microwave popcorn in the rooms. In a word: MAJORLEAGUEALLTHEWAY. (The traveling secretary of one of the other teams won't stay here because he's afraid his players will get spoiled.) The last time we were here, the Radisson was booked and we had to stay at (of all places) a Sheraton. Everyone's fervent hope is that next year *this* becomes our permanent haven in Cleveland.

The weather has changed dramatically. An arctic front from Canada has swept into the United States, bringing record lows where only two days ago there had been record highs. Boy, am I glad I packed those sweaters now. The high in Cleveland was in the fifties and the low is expected to dip into the forties. My sinuses have completely given up.

Since this is an off-night (our second in Cleveland), I took the opportunity to watch the season premieres of *Cheers* and *Wings,* the two shows David Isaacs and I are associated with as writers and creative consultants. They both looked real good. I don't know if they were funny, because I couldn't hear a word of them. Who can hear anything in a crowded yuppie sports bar? But our names were spelled correctly on the screen, so I'm going to have to say both shows were a rousing success.

Friday, September 20, Cleveland

My taxi driver on the way over to the park was grumbling that he was no longer going to take up station at the Radisson. I was his fifth quick fare over to Cleveland Stadium. Jokingly, I said, "Well, at least you get to meet some great major league ballplayers." "Yeah," he said, "like the last one. As we came up on the ballpark"—which is right along the shores of Lake Erie—"he asked me, 'What ocean is that?' " (The answer, of course, is the Indian Ocean. Why do you think they're called the Cleveland Indians???) I agreed the driver might be better served shuttling people to and from the airport.

I was concerned that the near-freezing conditions at the ballpark would hold down the crowd tonight, but I worried for naught: 5,057 flocked to Cleveland Stadium to see the Birds shade the Tribe 2–1. As for highlights: The game lasted only 2:26, and no one was treated for frostbite.

The poor Indians. Even when they achieved a bit of notoriety from the very popular movie based on them (*Major League*), most of the scenes you see that are supposed to be in Cleveland Stadium were actually filmed in County Stadium, Milwaukee.

The Montreal Expos learned today that they will have to play their remaining home games on the road this year, because of the fifty-five-ton slab of concrete that fell from the structure several weeks ago. I guess the Krazy Glue isn't holding sufficiently. I feel sorry for the players, but more so for the Expo season ticket holders. They're going to have to do a lot of traveling for the next month.

Back in Baltimore, our new stadium is still without a name.

Saturday, September 21, Cleveland

Well, Arthur Rhodes must've been gripping his curveball too tightly again because for the sixth time in six starts he was wild and was hammered; 10–1 was the final. (The Indians! We're playing the Indians!) The only Oriole run came on Cal's thirty-first homer and RBI number 100. (Why don't they just name the new stadium "Cal Ripken, Jr., Field," for God's sake?) Albert-formerly-Joey Belle was the Indians' big star, hitting a double and a homer and driving in a career-high five.

Okay, last night the Indians only drew 5,057, but the weather *was* truly horrid. Today (the first day of fall) we had brilliant sunshine and temps in the high sixties. Ideal! And as I expected, the improved conditions meant a big improvement at the gate. Almost 2,000 more people streamed in this afternoon.

Cal Ripken P.S.: In the first inning he hit a foul ball that accidentally struck a fan in the stands. Nothing serious, but the man was taken to the hospital for a few hours of observation before being released. Cal sent over a bat and several autographed balls and called the gentleman at home later in the evening to see if he was all right. Believe me when I say that not *every* big leaguer would've done that. (Hell, why don't they just rename Baltimore "Cal Ripken Juniorville"?)

After the game Rick Vaughn, beat reporter Peter Schmuck, and I ventured out to suburban Cleveland Heights to the Cedar Lee theater where Cannes Film Festival winner *Barton Fink* was showing exclusively. I've been wanting to see it for a month. My reaction: I'm not sure. Parts of it I adored, but other parts, well . . . I'm just going to have to see it again with Debby so she can explain it to me.

Sunday, September 22, Cleveland/Baltimore

Mike Mussina let a 1–0 lead get away in the ninth, and the O's lost to the Indians 2–1. Should Oates have pulled him when he got in trouble in the last frame? I don't think so. Every time closer Gregg Olson is summoned you have to hold your breath. Yes, he has 29 saves, but he is no longer (at least not now) the thoroughly dominating pitcher he was a couple of years ago. In '89 if Olson came in, the game was over. Set it and forget it. This year it's a different and more suspenseful story. He's been giving up a lot of base hits and a number of walks, and is one of the worst pitchers in the league in holding runners. A leadoff hit or free pass to, say, the tying run, often results in the man quickly taking second. Now a bloop single can blow the save. This is not the classic makeup of a closer. For my money (which isn't much even with the per diem), Oates was right to stick with Mussina. He had thrown a minimum of pitches, still had great stuff, and is a bulldog. Today he lost, but there will be a lot more tomorrows.

You watch. The Orioles' number-one starter next year might not be Ben McDonald. It could be the kid from Stanford with the knuckle curve, who is so confident these days that he no longer has to eat at McDonald's before every start.

The game lasted only 2:06 (I hope the 6000 attendees didn't feel cheated), and the O's winged back home. A yearlong question was answered. Three years in the minor leagues taught me one truth: Team buses break down. Ours always did; so did the other teams'. But here in the majors, even though we travel with two buses, which should double the odds, not one has konked out. Are the Laws of Nature not constant? Well, this evening I learned that they are. The players' bus broke down (right near the still-unnamed new ballpark, by the way). Sure it meant a delay, as we had to double back and pick the boys up, but that's a small price to pay for restored order in the universe.

National League news: The Pirates clinched the N.L. East title today while the Dodgers took the rubber game of their crucial three-game series with Atlanta in Los Angeles. L.A. leads by one and a half with two weeks to go. I'm not in the majority anywhere in the United States east of Figueroa Boulevard, but I hope Los Angeles wins. I'd love to go to a play-off game. (I can't believe that after seeing 185 of these things, I'm really rooting hard so I can go to another baseball game.)

Monday, September 23, Baltimore

The pennant race has come to Memorial Stadium! Even more important—1992 Orioles' schedule magnets will be given away!

The Red Sox invade town trailing Toronto by only one and a half. This is a crucial series for them; and for me, at least for three days, it's a refreshing change to be calling games that actually *mean* something.

The Spoilin' O's came from behind twice to post a 4–3 victory. With the win, they've now clinched the season series, 7–4 (if for some ridiculous reason you're keeping track).

I suppose it was a bad omen for Boston when a black cat interrupted play by streaking across the warning track past their dugout to the backstop. A moment later surehanded shortstop Luis Rivera kicked a grounder, allowing a key Oriole run to score. (There are fifty such cats that live under the Memorial Stadium grandstands. Their purpose is to hold down the "rodent" population. Many stadiums have this problem. Some employ cats, others—like Montreal—drop fifty-five-ton concrete slabs on them.)

Tuesday, September 24, Baltimore

Rained out! Doubleheader scheduled tomorrow. Length of *Orioles Talk:* 1:15. Best question: "Do you think the Orioles should trade Randy Milligan to get Frank Viola?"

Wednesday, September 25, Baltimore

Although I haven't seen it, I understand that *Emmy* magazine (put out by the Television Academy) has an article about me in this month's issue. It apparently talks in glowing terms about my supportive wife . . . Linda.

Toronto beat California this afternoon to up its lead to two and a half. The pressure is really on the Sweat Sox now. This was my first question on the "Johnny Oates Report" today (and bear in mind it didn't come out "exactly" as I had intended) : "Well, John, the Red Sox are really in a spot. It's gotta be much tougher to win two games in one day than one game in two days." I meant to say, "It's gotta be much tougher to win two games in one day than *two* games in two days" (which still is not, perhaps, the best way to phrase that thought, but at least it makes sense). John's answer was "Huh????" On take-two it was "Yes."

"Foot-in-Mouth Disease" strikes all announcers. It's embarrassing and could attack at any time. We're on the air *live* for three hours a day, every day, for practically seven months, and slips of the tongue are bound to occur. No one is immune. Jon recently had Leo Gomez hitting a home run just over the reach of the leaping Leo Gomez. Earlier this year he reported that Andre Dawson hit a grand slam for Chicago to tie the score with Pittsburgh, 4–3. Ralph Kiner, the longtime voice of the Mets, is famous for these spoonerisms, and recently a Detroit paper printed some of his gems from this year. Again, as I share them, it is not with an ounce of smugness or superiority, for remember, I'm the nimrod who had Mike Devereaux out trying to stretch a double into a single.

Anyway, enjoy the following:

- "Tony Gwynn was named Player of the Year for April."
- "Scott Sanderson was traded from Montreal on Pearl Harbor Day, June seventh, 1983."
- "And Ricky Jordan takes a ball for a strike."
- From Cincinnati's Riverfront Stadium, which opened in 1970—"Baseball began right here in this very stadium back in 1869."
- "If Casey Stengel were alive today, he'd be spinning in his grave."

. . . and finally . . .

- "The [Hall of Fame] ceremonies are on the thirty-first and thirty-second [of July]."

About an hour before our 5:05 start it began raining again.

There was a good possibility it would not let up. Tomorrow is an off-day for both clubs, and the forecast is much improved, *but* . . .

What if, and I'm not saying it's gonna happen, but what if the doubleheader is rained out tonight and tomorrow?

And what if the Red Sox need those games to decide the divisional title?

When would they play them?

Monday, October 7. No problem. The play-offs don't start till Tuesday.

Yes, problem.

Sunday, October 6, is the scheduled final game at Memorial Stadium *ever*. This entire season has been pointed toward that date. Tickets have been sold out for months. This is supposed to be the day to end all days, the greatest day in Baltimore Oriole history. Hell, I'm even flying my father and son out here to see it.

I don't have to tell you how the front office is squirming. Can you imagine a worse worst-case scenario? Needless to say, the umpires were prepared to wait a goooood lonnnnnnngggg tiiimmmme tonight.

And that, of course, meant: *Orioles Talk!!!*

We stayed on the air for four hours until the games were called. They're now scheduled for twelve-fifteen tomorrow. The Red Sox had already checked out of their hotel, so they had to make new arrangements for the night. (I can just imagine their traveling secretary on the phone: "Hello? Downtown Marriott? . . . Yes, would you happen to have thirty-five rooms available tonight? . . . Nonsmoking . . . You do? Fantastic! . . . Well, before you confirm those I should tell you that there's a chance we won't be coming. . . . When can we let you know? A half hour before we get there . . . Wow, that's quite a deposit.)

Thursday, September 26, Baltimore/Detroit

I had planned on using this scheduled off-day to tie up all my loose ends here in Baltimore. Boxes needed to be packed for UPS, bank accounts had to be closed out, leftover lasagna from April had to be thrown out of the fridge. Unfortunately, with the doubleheader beginning at twelve-fifteen, I barely had time for any of it. I did manage to get the UPS stuff ready (packing until two-thirty A.M.) and at least shipped that off before zooming out to the park at nine. (The lasagna I'd prefer to keep another week anyway. I'm on the verge of creating a new form of bacteria and I'm very excited about it.)

The weather improved *dramatically.* Clear skies, bright sunshine, and 71 degrees. To paraphrase Ernie Banks: "Let's make up two!"

For the Red Sox, trailing idle Toronto by two and a half, nothing less than a sweep would do, and that's a tall order even with seventeen-game winner Roger Clemens and surprise sensation Joe Hesketh going to the hill. Even a split with the Orioles could be a killer.

Roger Clemens was Roger Clemens in Game One, and the Sox took it, 2–1. The sweep was definitely within their grasp as the Orioles trailed 5–4 coming to bat in the ninth of the finale. But then the Birds made it interesting.

Greg Harris got the first out, then gave up a single to Hoiles. Mercedes struck out, but Devereaux kept the game alive with a single to center, sending Hoiles to third. Guess who was comin' up? You got it. Franchise Ripken, Jr. By now Harris was in his third inning and the tank was nearing "E". Time to bring in the closer, Jeff Reardon, right?

Nope.

Jeff Reardon has been experiencing back pain and was unavailable.

So bring in someone else?

I thought the same thing.

Skipper Joe Morgan, however, elected to stay with Harris. And I guess that's fair. If the BoSox are going to challenge for the pennant, they have to play like champions, and that means being able to retire one tough hitter to win a crucial game.

Cal singled to left. Hoiles scored. The game was tied at five.

Next up, Randy Milligan. In the seventh Harris had induced him to ground into an inning-ending double play with the bases loaded.

Milligan walked on four pitches. They weren't even close. The bases were loaded. Bring in somebody *now,* you say???

Right-hander Dennis Lamp and lefty Tony Fossas were warming. Neither was summoned. Morgan was sticking with Harris. Ohhhhh-kayyyyyy.

Now who would you like to see come to the plate? Bear in mind the divisional title just might be decided right here with this at-bat and the team in question is the Boston Red Sox.

Dwight Evans stepped into the box.

The crowd, as one, rose to its feet. Ten thousand people creating the noise of fifty, hoping that by the sheer magnitude of their volume they might will a base hit.

"Dewww-Eeee! Dewwww-Eeee! Dewww-Eeee!"

The first pitch—way outside. Ball one.

The next pitch—inside, almost hit him. Two balls, no strikes.

"Dewwww-Eeee! Dewwww-Eeee! Dewww-Eeee!"

Lamp and Fossas both ready in the bullpen.

But Harris was still the pitcher, and pitch he did. Outside. Ball three.

Every Oriole was on the top step of the dugout.

Their first-year announcer had a death grip on the counter.

Harris got his sign . . . went into his move . . . and delivered.

Very high. Ball four. Evans walked in the winning run.

If the Toronto Blue Jays go on to win the title, I think they should send over a bottle of champagne to Thirty-third Street in Baltimore.

God, it was great to be in a pennant race. Even for ten precious minutes.

10

Friday, September 27, Detroit

We arrived at the Ritz-Carlton in Dearborn just before midnight last night—the first stop on our last trip.

The program director of 95-Q, one of the top stations in Detroit ("More commercials, less music" . . . or is it the other way around?), is a friend of mine from UCLA. We wasted a great deal of our collegiate years together at the campus radio station. After graduation he set off for a career in radio and over the last twenty years has been first a DJ and now a PD in —among other places—Tulsa, Kansas City, New York, L.A., St. Louis, San Antonio, Seattle, and Detroit. He's quite successful and happy, but the thought did occur to me that if I were to continue being a baseball announcer, that's what my life would likely become—a few years in Baltimore, a move to Chicago, maybe the number-one job in Houston. Is that what I really want? Is that what my family really wants? And what about "Linda"? It's a major major major life decision, and one I'm going to have to make within the next few weeks.

The overachieving Detroit Tigers are one of the great surprises in baseball this year. With no real pitching and the league's lowest batting average, they have somehow managed to be a contender until as recently as last week (Boston's surge coupled with their being swept by the Indians in Cleveland pretty much polished them off). But while it lasted, it was quite a ride. How did they do it? Let's see.

They are the worst hitting team in the A.L. and lead the universe in strikeouts. BUT . . . they are number two in the league in runs scored, number one in home runs, and number two in walks received. They don't need ten hits a game to score six runs. They need only two or three. And they've been getting them. One other statistic stands out—the Tigers have hit into fewer double plays than any team in the majors. When Earl Weaver was skipper of the O's and one of his players would ground into an inning-ending double play with two or three men on, he would take that player aside and say, "Hey, haven't you ever heard of a thing called a strikeout?!" Double plays are rally killers, the "pitcher's best friend," etc. Detroit stays out of them. So if Cecil Fielder strikes out, Mickey Tettleton has a chance for a "big fly," or if he whiffs, there's Rob Deer, and Travis Fryman, and Pete Incaviglia, and on and on. Sparky Anderson has said this is the most enjoyable team he's ever managed—not the best, necessarily, but the most fun. From a fan's standpoint, they have to be the most fun to watch as well.

Cecil Fielder, who shocked the baseball world last year by coming back from Japan to hit 51 home runs, is having, in many ways, an even better year this year. He currently has 43 homers, tying him with José Canseco for the league lead, and has driven in a major league high 128 runs. In '90 he was the runner-up for MVP to Rickey Henderson. This year he's got Cal Ripken to contend with. This may be one of the few races that goes right down to the wire. (Watch. Juan Bell will win it.)

Final note—Fielder: Two weeks ago in Milwaukee he hit a home run that cleared the left-field bleachers and landed in the parking lot 520 feet away. It was one of the longest home runs *ever* hit. His bat must've been corked with "secret sauce."

The weather here is even colder and more raw than it was last week in Cleveland. The low tonight is expected to challenge the record set in 1899. It was 34 degrees on that date. Aw, the "Summer Game." The good news is—I have a big heavy parka and long underwear. The bad news—I shipped them both back to L.A. last month. (Am I a rookie, or what?) I went to the park tonight wearing two sweaters and a jacket. I looked like the Michelin Man. Fortunately, the booth at Tiger Stadium is heated to a degree (actually 2 or 3 degrees, maybe even 5), so I was at least able to hold a pencil.

How do the players fare in this frigid weather? They don't love it you'll be surprised to learn. Pitchers have the decided advantage, though. They're always on the move and therefore can stay warmer. Also, they can work the inside and outside parts of the plate with greater ease because batters don't wish to swing at pitches in those locations. A ball hit off the end of the stick or in on the fists will really cause the bees to sting. It's only when the weather gets REALLLL cold that pitchers are up the frozen creek. At a certain point the ball will perspire, get slick, and thus be hard to grip. But this is an extreme condition that rarely occurs. You may see it once or twice at the very beginning or end of the season in the extreme Northeast, and in August at Candlestick Park in San Francisco.

So now that I've explained how pitchers have the advantage in chilly conditions, which means that the games will usually be low-scoring affairs, I can tell you that the Orioles beat the Tigers, 9–7. Cal drove in four, and Sam Horn and Glenn Davis hit back-to-back home runs, Horn's hitting the facing of the roof in right field. Arthur Rhodes looked to get his first major league victory (in seven tries), but couldn't get anybody out in the fifth. Mark Williamson picked up the W instead. Between Rhodes and José Mesa, the Orioles have two starters who *combined* have won a grand total of one game in two months. However, help is on the way! Jeff Ballard returns to the rotation next week.

After the game, Jon and I decided to take a taxi back to Dearborn instead of waiting endlessly for the team bus. We're cruising along, talking and having a very pleasant time, when Jon notices that we're nowhere near the hotel. The driver was lost. We arrived at the Ritz-Carlton ten minutes after the team bus and had to pay twenty dollars for the privilege.

Diana told me over the phone tonight that she hated baseball. "Why?" I asked. (Could it be that baseball has taken her daddy away for seven months??) "You just sit and watch baseball players standing around," she said. "Where's the fun in that?"

Saturday, September 28, Detroit

As you step out of the Ritz-Carlton the doormen say, "Have a productive day." The Orioles did not.

Under clear skies and 56 degrees—perfect weather for college football—the O's took a 4–2 lead over the Tigers into the tenth inning. And then John Oates brought in Gregg Olson. Gulp!

He worked the count to 3–1 on leadoff hitter Dave Bergman but induced a groundout. Then he walked Travis Fryman and gave up singles to Milt Cuyler and Skeeter Barnes to load the bases.

What followed next was one of the weirdest plays I had ever seen.

Tony Phillips singled. Nobody scored.

How can that be? Phillips ripped the ball between first and second, seemingly driving in the tying runs, but the ball hit runner Skeeter Barnes going down to second. Barnes was out. The ball was dead. And Phillips was at first, credited with a base hit.

How often do you see a runner hit with a batted ball? You could easily go one or two seasons without it occurring once. This was the second time I've seen it this year. The other was when a line drive winged Milt Cuyler . . . *last night.* And the Tiger who hit it? Tony Phillips.

So now the Orioles received a huge break and needed but one more out. Lou Whittaker stepped in. Olson got two quick strikes. Sweet Lou let a ball go by, then jumped on a hanging curve and blooped a double to left-center. This time runners would score—three of them—and the Tigers pulled it out, 5–4. Blown save number eight for Olson.

Is it time for the season to end? You bet it is.

Everyone is starting to make off-season plans. Some will play winter ball, others will stay home and catch up with their families and business managers, a few will suffer the obligatory grizzly-hunting or garden-tool accidents that always seem to befall major league ballplayers, and still others like Mike Devereaux, Leo Gomez, and Arthur Rhodes will be heading down to the Instructional League in Florida after next week. Devereaux will look to improve his base-running skills, Gomez will try to sharpen his defensive play (notably his lateral range), and Arthur Rhodes will try to get acquainted with the strike zone.

Sunday, September 29, Detroit

"Ernie Harwell Day." Today's the day Hall-of-Fame broadcaster Ernie Harwell (fired after thirty-two seasons) and his partner of nineteen years, Paul Carey (who voluntarily resigned), are to be honored in pregame ceremonies at Tiger Stadium. The public outcry since Ernie announced his ouster last December has been loud and constant. Last Thursday the *Detroit Free Press* devoted an entire section to Ernie and Paul. There was page after page of letters to the editor. On and on they went, lavish in their praise, poignant and eloquent, expressing their appreciation to Ernie and Paul for their many contributions and lasting companionship. People in Michigan had grown up with these two men. They aren't just baseball announcers, they're a part of their lives.

The ceremony itself was very understated—*too* understated. Not one senior official from the Tigers was present. Al Kaline spoke briefly, a few proclamations were read (one by Commissioner Vincent), each honoree was presented a framed lithograph of Tiger Stadium, and then Ernie and Paul each said a few words. By contrast, when the Braves honored retiring broadcaster Ernie Johnson, he was showered with gifts, such as annual accommodations in Florida during spring training, a satellite dish, a new car, a trip, and golf clubs. Now the Tigers were certainly under no obligation to match this largesse, but still! A lithograph?

Fans in the center-field bleachers displayed huge banners. One read FAREWELL ERNIE, another said, BO FIRED ERNIE. BO MUST GO! The latter was removed, but not before the entire section broke out into a defiant chorus of "Bo must go! Bo must go!"

Both men stood at home plate and spoke briefly to the thousands of cheering fans. Ernie's booming voice echoed throughout the ancient stadium. "I had the greatest job in the world—a job I loved to do," he said. "But most of all, I appreciate you fans. I appreciate your loyalty, your support, and your love that you've shown me, especially the love."

And then, to further prove what a consummate gentleman he is, he hoped the fans would treat his successor with the same kindness they had shown him.

Ernie Harwell has left a lasting impression on millions of Tigers fans. A strikeout won't be a strikeout without Ernie saying the batter "stood there like the house by the side of the road," and foul balls will never be the same without Ernie telling his listeners they were caught by residents of Birmingham, or Oak Park, or Hamtramck.

His partner, Paul Carey, is planning to retire in Florida. Ernie hopes to be behind a microphone next year, possibly even in Baltimore. Nothing would please me more.

WBAL and the Orioles Radio Network carried the pregame ceremonies in their entirety.

The Orioles won, 7–4. Cal collected his 200th hit, then his 201st, 202nd, and 203rd. Among the hits were two home runs good for four RBIs.

Poetic justice: Today's loss officially eliminated the Tigers . . . on Ernie Harwell Day.

Meanwhile, the Minnesota Twins clinched their division as Seattle knocked off second-place Chicago. The Twins thus become the first team since divisional play began to go from last place to first in one year. From what I understand, they got the good news while busing from Toronto to the Hamilton, Ontario, airport. Oh well, anything to break up the monotony of another hourlong bus trip.

Meanwhile Part II: The Mets fired manager Buddy Harrelson today (the eighth skipper to be offed this year). Why they felt this change was necessary with one week left to go in the season, I do not know. Third-base coach Mike Cubbage has been named the interim replacement. Cubby was our manager in Tidewater in '89 and I have a great deal of respect for him and his abilities. Like John Oates, he's a good baseball man—knowledgeable, experienced, handles players well. I have every confidence that Mike Cubbage will be able to turn the Mets' program right around. After all, he does have seven days.

Monday, September 30, Detroit/New York City

Foul balls continue to be a problem at Tiger Stadium. From our vantage point in the broadcast booth, we're as close to the hitter as the pitcher is, and you've seen how fast "the little white sports car" (as ballplayers call it) can zip back to the mound. A foul ball missed me today by about a foot. In 1984 Larry Oesterman, one of the Tigers' TV announcers, was drilled in the forehead. The ball struck the monitor and ricocheted back so quickly and forcefully that the blow knocked him over backward. It all happened so fast that this was his call: "Here's a swing and a f———." His partner, Jim Northrup, was stunned, but was told by the director to keep talking. In a few seconds a hand reached up and grabbed the edge of the counter. Another soon followed. Finally, Oesterman—somewhat dazed—slowly hoisted himself erect. He had a huge welt on his forehead but was otherwise fine. Northrup took one look at him and busted up laughing. Ernie and Paul are no fools. They have a net shielding their booth. I said on the air after my near demise that I would like a net in here to protect me as well—Annette Bening. (Rimshot!)

The weather has changed yet again. Friday night it was 40. This evening it's 80. I guess it's true—the seasons do change quickly when you reach middle age.

The Orioles begin the night tied with New York in *fifth place*! That's right, *fifth place*! This is the first time since April 24 that they've been that high in the standings, and I guess it was too much for them. They quickly went out and lost to Detroit, 8–3.

Tonight was the Tigers' final home game of the season, meaning the final time for Ernie and Paul behind their net. More banners were festooned in the outfield (e.g., GOOD-BYE, ERNIE. GOOD-BYE, PAUL. GOOD-BYE, TIGERS. GOOD RIDDANCE, BO!), and most spectators brought radios to the game. During the seventh-inning stretch they both received a two-minute standing ovation, and after the game many fans remained in the park, gravitating to the box seats directly under their booth to say good-bye one last time.

GOOD-BYE, ERNIE. GOOD-BYE, PAUL. GOOD RIDDANCE, BO!

The president of the company that owns our plane was on our flight to New York tonight. He was there to "meet us all" and "answer any questions." (Hmmmm? Could it be that the Orioles have not renewed yet for next season???) I thought the best question was Billy Ripken's: "When the fuck are we taking off?" We had been sitting on the ground for close to an hour waiting for the aircraft to be loaded.

At two-thirty (more than four hours after the last out), we pulled up to the Grand Hyatt in Gotham.

Tuesday, October 1, New York City

Nice hotel but very thin walls. Jim Henneman of the *Evening Sun* is in the next room, and last night I could hear him typing his game notes . . . on his computer.

Perfect bopping-around-Manhattan weather today—mostly sunny and 80 degrees. The local papers are filled with speculation on who will be the new Met manager. Personally, I hope interim skipper Mike Cubbage gets the job, but I have a feeling the Mets are seeking an experienced heavyweight. Among the names bandied about is Frank Robinson. He's here for the Yankee series and apparently arrived a day early, leading to speculation that he might've interviewed for the position. Frank denies that he's been contacted, but every time I see him I ask questions like, "Where are you going to play Jeffries next year?" and "Any plans to trade Viola?" He always laughs and says he's taking me with him.

Cal Ripken was named the American League Player of the Month for September. During the past thirty days he batted .349 with eight homers and 29 RBIs. An even greater honor was bestowed upon him today when I selected him the Loyola Federal Peak Performer of the month. Whatever happens now for the man in his major league career is just gravy.

I went out early to Yankee Stadium (after finally finding a cabbie who would agree to take me there) and spent a good half hour moseying around the monument garden beyond center field. For a baseball fan this is sacred ground. There is a history and a tradition to baseball that is unmatched in any other sport, and nowhere is that tradition more evident than at that big ballpark in the Bronx. If only it wasn't situated in the DMZ.

The paid attendance tonight was announced at 12,991, but most of those people must've come dressed as seats. The park was empty.

The game was awful. New York won 3–2 in eleven interminable innings. Two runs were scored on ground balls, the winning run came home on a sac fly. It's been two hours since the game ended and I've already forgotten the losing pitcher.

Wednesday, October 2, New York City

At the beginning of the season I was pulling for the Orioles to win the pennant. By the second month I was just hoping they'd be contenders. By the third month I had my fingers crossed that they could just reach .500. As late as Monday I was rooting hard for them to finish in fifth. And now? No extra innings and no rain delays.

The Orioles lost, 4–3, on a home run by dangerous slugger Steve Sax (his career high tenth). Arthur Rhodes failed in his eighth and final chance to win his first major league game in '91. It did not rain. The game was played in regulation.

The Toronto Blue Jays clinched the A.L. East division title tonight with a ninth-inning victory over the Angels at the Skydome. The Red Sox (as predicted by this humble reporter) went right into the porcelain canyon after losing Game Two of that doubleheader to the Orioles last week. So now the ALCS is set —Minnesota vs. Toronto. (In the N.L. West, the Dodgers and Braves are tied with three games to go.)

One final note, Toronto: The Jays reached the four million mark in attendance this evening to set a new big-league record. Play-off tickets should be *real* easy to get.

In a strange quirk of scheduling, the Jays will now finish the year in Minnesota, then take a day off and begin the play-offs there. Three dress rehearsals. Three "friendlies," as the ballplayers say.

Thursday, October 3, New York City/Baltimore

I can almost see the barn from here. Only four days left in the season. I am reeeaaaalllly looking forward to . . .

. . . an evening with my family . . .

. . . a home-cooked meal . . .

. . . not getting on an airplane every Sunday night . . .

. . . not giving a shit about the weather. A forecast of rain means I turn on my windshield wipers . . .

. . . prime-time television . . .

. . . prime-time access television . . .

. . . a weekend in Santa Barbara with my wife . . .

. . . Los Angeles, and even parts of the Valley . . .

. . . going to sporting events and arriving only ten minutes before game time . . .

. . . going to sporting events and leaving early . . .

. . . seein' all my "buds" . . .

. . . Tetris (an addictive Nintendo game) . . .

. . . lunch at the Daily Grill . . .

. . . breakfast at Café 50's . . .

. . . playing hoops with Matty on the driveway . . .

. . . playing Barbies with Diana on the deck . . .

. . . getting together with my partner, David, and secretary, Sherry, and writing FADE IN. ACT ONE . . .

. . . getting my hair cut by someone who shouldn't be trimming hedges . . .

. . . rewrite night at *Wings* (unless the script is in trouble) . . .

. . . Diana's ballet recital . . .

. . . Matty's ninth birthday . . .

. . . and finally, QUIET. I never realized it, but after spending three hours a day every day for six frenetic months in big-league ballparks, I could really use a few days of serenity and silence. And it's not because of the large, noisy crowds (especially in Cleveland). Them I love. They're intoxicating. No, it's because of the ear-shattering P.A. systems, and "We will we will rock you," and dot races with obnoxious chase music, and the *Addams Family* theme between every batter, and that sound effect of glass shattering or a grenade being tossed after every foul ball, and "New York, New York" in New York, New York, the cavalry "Charge!!!," bugle horns, flügelhorns, "Hava Nagila," "Na Na Hey Hey, Kiss Him Good-bye," "Another One Bites the Dust," "Thank God I'm a Country Boy!" and the ultimate Chinese torture—the "Mexican Hat Dance."

ON THE OTHER HAND . . .

I know I am going to miss (probably by next Tuesday) . . .

. . . marveling at the exploits of the phenomenal Cal Ripken . . .

. . . Cajun food in Texas . . .

. . . movies on the road with the beat writers . . .

. . . introducing Matty to players I'm excited knowing myself . . .

. . . pausing for station identification . . .

. . . just showing my A.L. Working Press Pass and getting into any stadium in the league . . .

. . . Bigliardi's in Toronto . . .

. . . Mövenpick in Toronto . . .

. . . the Skydome in Toronto . . .

. . . Toronto . . .

. . . just being in Chuck Thompson's presence . . .

. . . hourlong chats in the office of the Orioles' assistant general manager Frank Robinson . . .

. . . Stan the Fan, H, Greg of Greg's Bagels, and all the other real-life characters from *Diner* . . .

. . . calling a Sam Horn home run . . .

. . . calling a Dwight Evans grand slam . . .

. . . tuning in to WBAL the next day and hearing my call of a Sam Horn home run or a Dwight Evans grand slam . . .

. . . my best pal on the Orioles, Bob Miller . . .

. . . ducking foul balls in Tiger Stadium . . .

. . . going to the airport and bypassing the terminal . . .

. . . the bratwursts at County Stadium, Milwaukee . . .

. . . the ghosts at Fenway . . .

. . . the daily "John Oates Report" . . .

. . . did I mention the Cajun food in Texas? . . .

. . . the serenity of batting practice at Fenway. Just the sound of bat hitting ball and "Satin Doll" over the stadium organ . . .

. . . Nancy Faust and her rendition of "Runaround Sue" . . .

. . . late-night games on the West Coast on ESPN . . .

. . . discussing pitching with Jim Palmer . . .

. . . being mistaken for Leo Gomez . . .

. . . the Esskay Out-of-Town Scoreboard . . .

. . . Ernie & Paul in Detroit, John & Joe in New York, Herb & Tom in Cleveland, Al & Bob in Anaheim, Bob & Joe & Sean in Boston, Ueck & Pat in Milwaukee, Dwayne & Tony in New York, Wayne & John in Chicago, the Scooter, Tom & Jerry in Toronto, Tommy H in Toronto, Bill & Lon in Oakland, the "Veteran Spieler" & Rick in Seattle, Denny & Fred in K.C., Herb & John in Minnesota, Tom & Jim in Minnesota, the "Hawk" & "Wimpy" in Chicago, Ken & Ken in Anaheim, and Eric & Mark in Texas (along with the Cajun food).

With only four days left, my mood swings almost hourly. At times I want the season to go on forever, at others I can't wait for it to end. How do I feel at this particular moment? Well, I'm about to get on a bus for a forty-minute drive through traffic and squalor to get to a meaningless game with the forecast of rain (cloudy with occasional *Orioles Talk*), and another red-eye flight back to my empty town house in Baltimore. Guess.

We caught a break. The rain didn't come until we were already on the plane. The Orioles lost, 9–6, thus completing the Yankees' three-game sweep. It's bad enough to lose to the Yankees, but especially in New York. For ten minutes after the game, over and over and over, they play Sinatra's "New York, New York." I guarantee you, if they did that *before* games, they would go 0–81 at home.

Well, FINALLY!!!!!! The Orioles' new park at Camden Yards has a name—"Oriole Park at Camden Yards." I'll pause for a moment while you finish laughing. This took two years. "Oriole Park at Camden Yards." This was the rumored choice six months ago. The honorable governor, William Donald Schaefer, made the announcement earlier today on WBAL. He and the equally honorable Eli S. Jacobs hammered out this compromise to both/neither of their satisfaction. "Oriole Park at Camden Yards." Okay. Now we can get on with our lives.

The final flight on *Orioles One* landed us safely in Baltimore at one-thirty A.M. A word of thanks here to the crew. They were terrific. And you have to bear in mind their passengers were not exactly a tour group on a fun junket to Hawaii. Usually, we'd straggle onto the plane in the middle of the night following a loss or series of losses, and we would not be in the "best" of moods. Still, they were always cheerful, helpful, and only lost one sports jacket (which they later found). Kudos for a job well done!

11

Friday, October 4, Baltimore

There is an electricity in the air. With great anticipation and sadness we have come to the final weekend of Memorial Stadium. It's all you hear about in these parts. It's all you see. Yes, the new stadium will be magnificent (Ken Rosenthal of the *Evening Sun* called it the "Fenway of the 21st Century"), and yes, it will generate more jobs and revenue for the city, but Memorial Stadium is where most of these people saw their first game, or took their children to see their first game, or saw the Colts beat the Packers, or Jim Palmer outduel Sandy Koufax in the '66 Series, or Rick Dempsey go into the stands to catch a foul ball and take a bite out of a woman's tuna fish sandwich. I've only been here one year, but I must admit that I too am finding myself caught up in the nostalgia and sentiment. This promises to be a very emotional weekend.

Especially since I have decided not to come back next year.

For several weeks I have been leaning in that direction, and today I decided to make it official to WBAL (although it will not be announced to the press until after the season). My relationship with WBAL has always been one of mutual respect and trust, and I feel I owe the 'BAL people as much time as possible to find my replacement. (Personally speaking, I hope they hire Ernie!!!)

So why am I leaving?

As much as I've loved this year (and I have truly loved it), to continue in Baltimore would mean moving to Baltimore. It would mean for the kids, transferring to new schools; for my wife, trying to establish herself as a social worker in a new community; and for me, it would mean completely restructuring my career and lifestyle. One year in Baltimore, fine. My wife, my partner, the folks at *Cheers* and *Wings*, have all been amazingly supportive and tolerant. This was a once-in-a-lifetime adventure, a chance to live out my dream, etc. But two or three years? That's a different story. Is doing three innings a night of Oriole baseball really worth uprooting my family, possibly jeopardizing my career, and altering my entire lifestyle?

The answer—the honest answer—is NO.

Not that I'm getting out of broadcasting, because if I can find a play-by-play opportunity that keeps me based on the West Coast convenient to family and partner, I'll grab it, but if not, there's more to life than what's inside the white lines.

In 1983, after coproducing the first year of *Cheers*, David and I left the show to produce the spin-off of *M*A*S*H*. There were many reasons (both personal and financial) to recommend it, but still—what a colossal career blunder! (*Cheers* for *AfterM*A*S*H*. What the hell were we thinking???) Things worked out anyway, and a year later we were back with *Cheers*, but even at the moment we made the decision to leave, I just knew in my heart that I was making a mistake. As a result, I was miserable for the next year agonizing over that decision. My one fear about leaving the Orioles was: Would I regret this the same way I did leaving *Cheers*, knowing full well that, as opposed to *Cheers*, there was no going back to the O's?

Happily, again, the honest answer was NO.

I walked out of WBAL feeling not remorse, but peace of mind. Ever since the bad experience producing the Mary Tyler Moore comeback debacle in '86 (and reaching my mid-thirties), I have been questioning certain aspects of my life. (I know. "Welcome to the club.") These questions have taken me from the upper deck of Dodger and Anaheim stadiums to Syracuse and Tidewater and fourteen other Triple-A garden spots ending up in Baltimore, with stops at most major cities and Cleveland. Well, finally, I'm beginning to see some answers. I'm starting to get a sense of who I am. And more important, I'm beginning to feel comfortable with that person.

Will I miss doing the games next year? No question. I'll miss everything about 'em (except *Orioles Talk*). Broadcasting Oriole baseball has been an honor and a true privilege. But do I regret the decision? Don't tell anyone, but this is the best I've felt in weeks.

Weather for the historic weekend: clear and balmy tonight,

turning cooler tomorrow with a gooood chance of rain tomorrow night. Sunday looks iffy at best. This is not the kind of suspense the Orioles were hoping for for Closing Day.

I'll tell you what I'm most looking forward to this weekend. It's not the salute to former Oriole broadcasters, or the gala fireworks show tonight, or the introduction of the all-time Orioles tomorrow, or even the last good-bye on Sunday with "secret" postgame ceremonies guaranteed to pack an emotional wallop. It's that I get to share it all with father and son.

They arrived in Baltimore at three and taxied right to the ballpark. There were a lot of hugs in Bob Miller's office. Even though Dad and Matty didn't have press passes or field passes or even field glasses, I was able to get them anywhere I wanted. That's when you know you're really a big shot—when you can walk onto the field and not be thrown out by some eighty-year-old thug in an orange blazer and straw hat.

The big crowd began gathering early. They were almost all in place by the start of the pregame ceremonies. First on the agenda was the introduction of a number of International League Orioles from pre-'54. Professional baseball on some level has been played in Baltimore since before the turn of the century.

The National Anthem then followed, sung by Baltimore native Joan Jett. Okay, she lip-synched, but credit where credit is due—she mouthed the lyrics perfectly, forgetting not a word.

Next was the salute to four longtime Orioles' broadcasters. Jon Miller, Chuck Thompson, Ernie Harwell (the O's first voice in '54), and Tom Marr assembled near home plate. Jon was the emcee. He strode up to the mike, said hello, and the mike went dead. For the next three minutes the DiamondVision board was filled with a gigantic close-up of Jon, seething, but with a big frozen grin on his face. Finally, they got the mike to work. Jon made a joke about the screwup, saying it resembled his nightly radio broadcast. 47,000 people, not a single laugh. He then introduced the other gentlemen, highlights of their work were shown on DiamondVision, and they each spoke a few words. When it was Jon's turn, this was the highlight: "Here's the two-two pitch—" At that point the tape cut out. Nothing further was heard. Does somebody in Master Control have something against Jon??

The ceremony did provide one great moment, however. One

exceptional moment. When Chuck Thompson was introduced, the capacity crowd spontaneously rose to its feet and gave him a thunderous three-minute standing ovation. Clearly, he was visibly touched. For once in his life words were hard to come by. In a voice choked with emotion, Chuck thanked the crowd and saluted his late partner of sixteen years, Bill O'Donnell. Another standing ovation.

Chuck Thompson is in a class by himself. There is an ingenuousness and humanity to this man that is rare and enormously appealing. He has a sincere respect for the game, the gifted men who play it, and the fans who appreciate it. Chuck Thompson belongs in the Hall of Fame, and if someday he is elected, I will travel halfway around the world if necessary to be in Cooperstown to see him inducted.

Me and my BIGGGG MOUTHHH! In the fourth inning with the Orioles and Tigers tied 1–1 I made the offhand comment that "Gee, this is the final night game ever at Memorial Stadium. It's a beautiful Indian summer night. This would be a great evening for 'bonus panels' (extra innings)."

Mickey Tettleton's two-run home run won the game for Detroit . . . in the fourteenth inning. Time of game: 4:28. For the next two days I'm givin' balls and strikes, and the score, and *that's it*!

The postgame fireworks show was spectacular. However, it wasn't nifty background ambience for our postgame show. I said on the air, "Welcome to *Orioles Clubhouse* with all the scores and highlights. Tonight we're coming to you from Baghdad, where, as you can hear, the bombing continues."

The night ended on a very somber note. Rex Barney, the longtime P.A. announcer of Memorial Stadium (and member of the Brooklyn Dodgers Hall of Fame, who, among his many accomplishments, pitched a no-hitter against the Giants at the Polo Grounds forty years ago) collapsed in the elevator going home. He was rushed to Sinai Hospital.

Saturday, October 5, Baltimore

The report on Rex Barney is thumbs up. He is suffering from nothing more serious than anemia. These last few weeks leading up to this weekend have drained him physically and emotionally, and although more tests will be administered, the doctors have recommended rest, rest, and more rest. I know it's a major disappointment for Rex not to be at Memorial Stadium for the last two games, but there is the opening of Oriole Park at Camden Yards only six short months away.

So far, the weatherman's right. It's getting cloudy and cold. Tomorrow is still a question mark, a *big* question mark.

The pregame scene in the Orioles' locker room looked more like homeroom in high school on the final day before summer. Instead of annuals, however, team balls were being exchanged and signed. I got one for Matty.

For only the second time this year the Orioles were involved in a bench-clearing incident. And like most bench-clearing incidents, this one was weenie. Tiger starter Mark Leiter grazed Sam Horn with a pitch in the first inning, and the big man started out to the mound. Everyone came running out onto the field, but no punches were thrown, no shoving took place, not even a love tap. The players milled around for ten minutes (probably exchanging phone numbers and wishing each other good luck during the off-season) and went back to their respective dugouts and bullpens. Ho-hum. (I once saw a bench-clearing brawl at Dodger Stadium that was a doozy. It involved the Dodgers and the Reds during the seventies, when they were quite the rivals. Cincinnati pitcher Pedro Borbon was so angry and out of control that he started swinging at his own teammates.)

There were 49,289 in the park today, and you'd think they were witnessing a play-off game. It was unbelievable. They screamed and yelled on every play. I can't imagine what it would be like if the Orioles were, say, a fourth-place team or even a third-place club. Ambulances would have to cart these people away. Baltimore has the best fans in baseball! Every time Cal came to the plate they would chant in unison loud enough to be heard in Pennsylvania: "MVP! MVP!" When local boy Dave Johnson was lifted in the sixth after walking the first two batters, he received a huge ovation as he crossed disconsolately to the dugout. (By contrast, I remember an incident at Yankee Stadium in the early sixties when Roger Maris crashed into the outfield wall and lay dazed on the ground. Kids from the bleachers ran over to spit on him.)

Jon surprised me by asking me to do the ninth inning. Since

this is the last game we would be working together (he's doing Channel 2 tomorrow), Jon wanted me to do it. It was a nice gesture much appreciated. Other than misidentifying the first baseman on a play, I did a helluva job.

The word came over the wire during the postgame show. I was on the air at the time. The Braves had just beaten Houston, and now the Giants defeated the Dodgers. The Atlanta Braves are the N.L. West champs. This has not been a good year for my teams. First the Orioles, and now the Lasordas. Oh, and my rotisserie team (shared by my partner David) is in last place. Imagine, a major league baseball announcer in a league of lawyers and comedy writers and I finish dead last. You think I'll be taking a little shit from the guys during the off-season???

Ralphie's Diner was our destination for dinner. I wanted my dad to sample a *real* Maryland crab cake and he was not disappointed. Matty enjoyed the hot dog. (I, by the way, will not be able to look at another hot dog for at least three years, hopefully ten.)

The rains came at nine and continued throughout the night.

Sunday, October 6, Baltimore

"And then there was one."

Jon's pregame opening said it all.

Only in the movies and Memorial Stadium does the rain cease, the clouds part, and the sun come out . . . one hour before game time. It was a sign of things to come.

The parking lot opened at seven-thirty. The Levines arrived at eleven. The lot was already teeming with Orioles faithful . . . and opportunistic vendors ready to fleece the lambs. Souvenir T-shirts, jackets, sweatshirts, mugs, jugs, pennants, pencils, caps, key chains, wooden moving vans depicting the old stadium as well as the new, postcards, painted baseballs encased in plastic, an elaborate $240 embroidered portrait of the stadium—you name it, someone was selling it and someone else was buying it. The 35,000 final-game programs were offered at four dollars a pop and sold out in a matter of hours. One enterprising young man snatched a handful of evergreen shrubbery that decorates the stadium and held it over his head, proclaiming: "Five dollars! A real bargain!"

Today the security was tight, in part due to all the extra media attention, and also because Vice President Quayle had decided to make a return appearance. The joint was crawling with Secret Service agents (why they're called "Secret" Service, I don't know. Who else wears ill-fitting suits and earplugs everywhere they go?), so getting around was cumbersome. I dropped Matty and Dad off at the WBAL bullpen party (the picnic area behind the O's pen) at noon and sought out Johnny Oates for our final pregame show. There are a few people I am telling about my decision not to return next season. Johnny is one of them (Jon, Chuck, Dr. Paul, and Oriole president Larry Lucchino are the others). I've learned a lot about baseball from Johnny and I'm very grateful for his support and friendship. This was a very tough good-bye—I'm sure the first of many today.

It's always easy to tell when a lot of celebrities are in the ballpark; George Will is in attendance. I never seem to see George on just a lazy Tuesday night when the O's are hosting, say, the Indians or the Mariners, but when Dick Cheney or Pat Sajak is in the owner's box, there he usually is. Today's guest list includes: (in addition to the veep), Dick Cheney, White House chief-of-staff John H. Sununu, baseball commissioner Fay Vincent, Baltimore mayor Kurt Schmoke, numerous congressmen and senators, and author Tom Clancy. Mr. Will must've had a busy afternoon.

The first-ball ceremony alone was worth the price of admission. Talk about a nice touch, two first balls were tossed—a baseball by Brooks Robinson and a football by Johnny Unitas. Arguably the greatest third baseman and quarterback ever to play professional sports returned for one last hurrah. And they didn't have far to return. Both men make their homes in Baltimore.

The 2:05 game began promptly at 2:24. Within ten minutes the Orioles were trailing Detroit 4–0. So much for the game.

Knowing this was my last broadcast for the Orioles made the day even tougher. I can't imagine what it's like for Ernie Harwell two booths over ending a thirty-two-year relationship with the Tigers.

In the fifth inning we invited Ernie over to chat with Chuck. The man who broadcast the very first Oriole game at Memorial Stadium also got to broadcast the last.

My approach for the day was to play against the sentiment. If I gave in to it, I felt, it would engulf me. Consequently, my focus was not on the nostalgia of the day but on the current team. Every year on Closing Day I have a tradition whereby I throw away the statistics and game notes and concentrate solely on the personalities of the players. I talked about Todd Frohwirth playing in his hometown Milwaukee for the first time in his career, recalled standing on the prairie in Sioux Falls, South Dakota, listening to Dwight Evans talk about playing baseball for the pure love of the game. I reprised the Glenn Davis injury, the four-man no-hitter, and Leo Gomez getting lost driving to Rochester. I spoke of the players no longer on this year's squad—Ernie Whitt, Craig Worthington, Jeff McKnight, Roy Smith, Shane Turner, J. J. Bautista, Stacy Jones, Paul Kilgus, Kevin Hickey, and the infamous Jeff Robinson. I riffed on the queen attending a game, Kevin Costner taking BP, Johnny Oates predicting Juan Bell's first major league dinger, the Dirty Half Dozen, and Cal Ripken hitting a home run on Cal Ripken Night. And in four innings I could barely scratch the surface.

Bill Ripken made the last out in my last inning. He rolled out to shortstop. "So the Orioles go up and down in order in the eighth," I said casually as if it were the end of any inning on any day, "and the score at the end of eight—the Tigers seven, the Orioles one."

Chuck Thompson had the well-deserved honor of calling the final inning ever at Memorial Stadium, and true to the spirit of the day, it was a wondrous inning. With one out in the Tiger ninth the crowd began to chant, "We want Flanny! We want Flanny!" John Oates popped out of the dugout and headed to the mound. Thunderous applause. Oates signaled to the pen that he wanted the lefty, and Mike Flanagan stepped out onto the field. The crowd rose to its feet. The ovation was now deafening. And as the fourteen-year Oriole veteran slowly made his way across the late afternoon shadows into the sunlight that washed the mound, the following message appeared on the DiamondVision board: LADIES AND GENTLEMEN, THE ORIOLES ANNOUNCE THAT THEY HAVE REACHED AGREEMENT WITH MIKE FLANAGAN ON A CONTRACT FOR 1992 WITH AN OPTION FOR 1993. "The Asylum on Thirty-third Street" was reborn. (Do Rick Vaughn and the Orioles' PR staff have a flair for the dramatic, or what???) For what seemed like an eternity, the cheering continued, and Chuck, with his usual elegance and grace, described the scene in such a way as to elicit chills.

Dave Bergman finally stepped in for Detroit. And struck out.

The Asylum erupted yet again.

Travis Fryman was next. The count was 3–2, the pitch a sidearm breaking ball. The swing was a mighty rip, and the result—strike three.

Flanagan has a pretty good flair for the dramatic himself.

Few will remember that the Orioles still had to bat in the ninth, and fewer will remember that it was Cal Ripken who grounded into the double play that ended major league baseball forever at Memorial Stadium in Baltimore, Maryland, at 5:07 on October 6, 1991. Absolutely no one will remember that the O's lost to the Detroit Tigers 7–1, but everyone will remember that top of the ninth. It is one of those so very rare innings that will cross into legend; 50,700 were lucky enough to witness it. Hundreds of thousands more were even luckier. They had the privilege of hearing Chuck Thompson describe it.

After the game we were joined by Jon, who anchored our postgame coverage. For the first time since the first game of spring training, all three of us were on the air together.

A gleaming-white sixty-six-foot stretch limo emerged from the bullpen and cruised around the cinder track from the left-field corner, along the center-field wall, on down the right-field foul line to an area just in front of home plate. Paul Zwaska, the head grounds keeper, and several of his assistants stepped out of the limo. They were clad in all-white tuxedos with orange bow ties (not their normal attire, by the way). They looked like the Temptations. A receiving line was formed from the car to home plate. Shovels and pickaxes were sent down the line, handed from one to the other to the other. Finally, all was in readiness and they went to work . . . digging home plate out of the ground. Five minutes later their prize (attached to a fifty-pound anchor) was raised from the earth as if it were a coffin. Ever so gingerly, it was placed into the trunk, the Temps got back into the car, and it sped out of the stadium led by police escort, sirens blazing, blue lights flashing. Its destination: the new downtown ballpark, where its arrival would be documented on the Memorial Stadium DiamondVision board with Baltimore native Jim McKay hosting arrival ceremonies.

By now my dad and son had made it down to the booth. Although I was on the air, I chose to say little, preferring instead to let Chuck and Jon describe the scene. Matty sat on my lap. My father stood over my left shoulder.

And now for the finale. Here's the concept. The final game is over, you're sitting in the stands reflecting on all the memories and glories that have taken place on this field over the last thirty-four years. How many times had you seen Jim Palmer trot out to the mound or Frank hustle into right field or Brooks Robinson stroll out to third base? Ten times? A hundred times? Who kept count? No need to. They were always going to be there. And now, today, it was over. The memories were all that was left.

And then, suddenly, as if in a dream, Brooks Robinson, in full uniform, trots out to third base. No introduction, no fanfare. Just Brooks just like before. It's as if *Field of Dreams* had come to life. Imagine your surprise and delight.

Thanks to the brainchild of O's media director Dr. Charles Steinberg, DDS, that's what the Orioles had in store for the last hurrah.

The P.A. blared James Earl Jones's classic speech on the meaning of baseball from *Field of Dreams*. His booming voice reverberated around the "yard," as did his message. And then came the music from the film: lush, haunting, bittersweet.

And then . . .

There he was. Brooks Robinson, toting a ball and a mitt, did step out of the Oriole dugout and trotted out to his position. He stood there for maybe thirty seconds, kicking at the dirt and staring in from third. It was as moving a moment in sports as I've ever seen.

Frank Robinson joined him on the field. Retired number 20 jogged out to right. You could not hear the music over the cheering.

"Booooooooogggggg" Powell then followed. First base was waiting for him, as it had been on this site for so many years.

And then Jim Palmer. He had made his comeback after all.

Don Baylor to left, Rick Dempsey to the plate. They were coming faster now. Bobby Grich to second, Lee May, Jim Gentile, Davey Johnson, Luis Aparicio, all filing out to their positions. I looked at my eight-year-old son. Suddenly, I was his age again. Was my father my age?

They appeared in groups now. Dave McNally, Pat Dobson,

and Mike Cuellar joined fellow twenty-game winner Jim Palmer on the hill. So did those Martinez boys, Tippy and Dennis.

Don Stanhouse, the only former player wearing road grays and an orange warm-up jersey, made his conspicuous appearance. You'd never know he was a flake, would you?

John Lowenstein and Gary Roenicke used to platoon in left, but today they both got into the game.

Robin Roberts was back. So was Al Bumbry. "Orioles Magic" began with a Doug DeCinces home run, and he was here. Check the water bottle in the visiting bullpen for goldfish—Moe Drabowsky has returned. Likewise Pete Richert, Dave Skaggs, Gene Woodling, Eddie Watt, Steve Barber, Scott McGregor, Lenn Sakata, Kenny Singleton, Russ Snyder, Milt Pappas, Billy O'Dell, Rich Dauer, Hal "Skinny" Brown, Mark Belanger, Paul Blair, and on and on and on.

MEMORIAL STADIUM, THIS IS YOUR LIFE!

In all, seventy-eight took their bows. Thirteen times in the space of only fifteen years (1966–1980) the Baltimore Orioles had won championships—six divisional titles, five pennants, and two World Series. Five times they had won over 100 games per regular season. Six Cy Young Award winners wore Oriole uniforms, seven Hall of Famers. The men on the field were not just former players, they were among the finest who ever played the game.

And then it was time to return to the present. The 1991 Orioles took their place among their esteemed predecessors. Fresh memories sprinkled in with past glories. Dwight Evans's dramatic grand slam against Oakland, Gregg Olson completing a no-hitter, Randy Milligan's thrilling two-out double in the ninth to snap Minnesota's fifteen-game winning streak. These were *my* heroes . . . despite the fact that they lost 95 games this year—the Moose, Otter, Dewey, Slack, Flanny, BoMo, Big Bird, D.J., Fro, Chito, and Tito.

And Junior.

The Orioles had saved the best of the best for the last of the last. Even I set down the microphone, stood, and applauded as Cal Ripken emerged from the dugout.

There was still someone missing, and the day would not be complete without him. The skipper, Earl Weaver, made his way to home plate and, just for old times' sake, kicked the dirt.

There was not a dry eye in the state.

A 360-degree camera was set up on the mound, and the O's formed a circle in the infield. Pictures were taken and more tears were shed.

Rick Dempsey stepped forward and led the emotionally drained crowd in one more rousing O-R-I-O-L-E-S cheer, and for well-needed comic relief, he stuffed a pillow in his jersey and reprised his famous impression of Babe Ruth hitting a homer and running the bases.

By now the motorcade had arrived at the new park and we watched the ceremony on DiamondVision.

It was time to cry again. The players lobbed baseballs into the crowd as "Auld Lang Syne" came over the loudspeaker.

And finally, at 5:41, Rex Barney (in a taped message from his hospital bed) appeared on DiamondVision. He said just two words, his twenty-year signature:

"Thankkkk yoooooooooooooo."

The crowd let out one final roar, and that was that. Most began filing out, but many just remained, allowing the memories to linger.

It was time for us broadcasters to leave as well. We exchanged good-byes and saluted the sponsors and production staff. I thanked any number of people, including my family and father, and then, for the last time, signed off the broadcast. "Once again, the final score: the Tigers seven, the Orioles one."

At that moment I asked myself a question. In light of all I've seen today and how moved I was by it, had I made a monumental mistake by walking away from this job?

N-O.

This was a magnificent adventure that had reached its natural conclusion. Sure, I'm a little sad that it's over, but primarily I'm just grateful for the ride. In the words of Rex Barney:

"Thankk yoooooooooooooooo."

That night the club held a private banquet (or "wrap party" as we say in my other life) at the Inner Harbor Omni Hotel. It was the perfect way to say good-bye to so many people.

The Levines hit the buffet, then wandered through the big banquet hall looking for a table where we'd fit in. The Hall of Famers were sitting with Hall of Famers, the current O's were sitting with current O's, even the current-but-probably-not-for-long Orioles were bunched as a group. We spotted an empty table and sat down. A few minutes later a hand tapped my shoulder and a voice asked if he could join us. We had our final dinner in Baltimore with Brooks Robinson.

Monday, October 7, Baltimore/Los Angeles

Our USAir flight left Baltimore at nine-ten A.M. After seven months, 190 ball games, two no-hitters, three blown home run calls, 40,000 miles, a loss of fifteen pounds, and 6,754,392 memories, it was time to go home.

"So long, everybody!"

The Postgame Show

Final Standings:

A.L. East		G.B.	A.L. West		G.B.
Toronto	91–71	—	Minn.	95–67	—
Boston	84–78	7	Chicago	87–75	8
Detroit	84–78	7	Texas	85–77	10
Milw.	83–79	8	Oak.	84–78	11
N.Y.	71–91	20	Seattle	83–79	12
BALT.	67–95	24	K.C.	82–80	13
Cleve.	57–105	34	Cal.	81–81	14

Some Notes:

- Cal Ripken was named the American League MVP.
- Cal became only the third player in baseball history to earn the award while playing for a losing team (Ernie Banks and Andre Dawson being the other two).
- A furious Cecil Fielder finished second.
- Cal finished the year batting .323, 34 home runs, 114 RBIs, 210 hits, 46 doubles, and 368 total bases.
- Cal finished fifth in hitting, third in home runs, fourth in RBIs, second in hits, second in doubles, second in slugging percentage, first in total bases.
- Cal has now played in 1,572 consecutive games.
- Gehrig's record is 2,130.
- Julio Franco won the A.L. batting crown with a .340 average.
- Fielder and Canseco tied for the home run lead with 44 apiece.
- Paul Molitor was healthy this year. He led the league in hits with 216.
- There were two 20-game winners in the American League: Scott Erickson and Bill Gullickson.
- Roger Clemens was the ERA champ with 2.54.

- Roger Clemens captured his third Cy Young Award.
- Bryan Harvey led the league in saves with 45 for the last-place Angels.
- No Oriole pitcher was anywhere near the top in any pitching category they would be proud of.
- Chuck Knoblauch of Minnesota was named the Rookie of the Year.
- The Angels were the best last-place club in history.
- Three Angel pitchers finished with 18 victories (Jim Abbott, Mark Langston, Chuck Finley).
- The Mariners did finish above .500 for the first time in franchise history.
- The Orioles broke their all-time attendance figure.
- Cleveland announced that it would move in the fences next year.
- The Minnesota Twins defeated the Atlanta Braves in seven games to win the 1991 World Series.
- Two days after the World Series, and before the confetti had been removed from the streets of Minnesota, Game Seven winner Jack Morris announced his free agency.

SOME MORE NOTES:

- On October 7 Johnny Oates was given a two-year contract to manage the Baltimore Orioles.
- Pitching coach Al Jackson was fired. First-base coach Curt Motton was "reassigned."
- The Mets hired Oriole hitting coach Tom McCraw in the same capacity.
- The Mets also hired Al Jackson as a roving instructor.
- Curt Motton will be an advance scout at the major league level for the Orioles next year.
- Ernie Harwell did not get my job. The returning Joe Angel did.
- Ernie Harwell did get a job with CBS Radio calling the Saturday *Game of the Week* broadcast nationally.
- Ernie Harwell also signed with the California Angels to fill in on fourteen radio broadcasts in '92.
- His first assignment for the Angels was to be on Monday, May 4 . . . at Tiger Stadium in Detroit.
- Glenn Davis signed a two-year $6.6 million contract to stay in Baltimore.

- Pitcher Jeff Robinson was released. He signed with the Texas Rangers.
- Craig Worthington was traded to San Diego, then released by the Padres during spring training. He latched on with Cleveland and was assigned to Colorado Springs.
- Stump Merrill was fired as manager of the New York Yankees.
- Bucky Showalter was fired as third-base coach of the New York Yankees.
- Three weeks later, Bucky Showalter was hired as the manager of the New York Yankees.
- Joe Morgan was fired as manager of the Boston Red Sox. Butch Hobson, skipper of Pawtucket, was named to replace him. Don Zimmer will be the new third-base coach.
- Jim Lefebvre was fired as manager of the Seattle Mariners. Third-base coach Bill Plummer replaced him.
- Tom Treblehorn was fired as manager of the Milwaukee Brewers. Phil Garner gets to move into his office.
- There has been bad blood for several years between Milwaukee and Seattle, caused, many believe, by the dislike between ousted managers Tom Treblehorn and Jim Lefebvre.
- Jim Lefebvre has named Tom Treblehorn as one of his new coaches in Chicago.
- Jeff Torborg resigned as manager of the Chicago White Sox to take the same position with the New York Mets.
- Gene Lamont, coach of Pittsburgh, has been handed the reins of the White Sox.
- The Orioles signed free-agent pitcher Rick Sutcliffe.
- The Orioles released free-agent hitter Dwight Evans during spring training.
- Michael Kay, an excellent newspaper reporter, got Joe Angel's job with the Yankees. He had done some play-by-play in college. Over one hundred broadcasters applied.
- Rick Rizzs, the second man in the Seattle booth, got the number-one job in Detroit.
- Bob Rathbun, my partner in Tidewater in 1990, got Paul Carey's spot. Bob had been in the minor leagues for well over ten years.
- Larry Mintz won our rotisserie league.
- The number-two position in Seattle was filled by Ken Levine.

ABOUT THE AUTHOR

KEN LEVINE has been a screenwriter for eighteen years. He and his partner, David Isaacs, are the recipients of one Emmy and two Writers Guild awards. They have written over 100 episodes of prime-time television, including numerous scripts for *Cheers, M*A*S*H, Wings, The Simpsons, The Tracey Ullman Show,* and *The Jeffersons.* Ken and David were the head writers of *M*A*S*H* (1977–78) and coproduced *Cheers* (1982–83). They were the creators and executive producers of *Mary* (1985–86). An evening of their one-act plays, *City of Angles,* was performed in Los Angeles in 1980 and 1982. Their feature work includes the screenplay for *Volunteers,* starring Tom Hanks and John Candy. Currently, they serve as creative consultants for *Cheers* and *Wings,* and have several screenplays in development.

Ken lives with his wife, Debby, and his children, Matthew and Diana, in Los Angeles. This is his first nonfiction effort.